BECOMING
JOHNNY
VEGAS

BECOMING
JOHNNY
VEGAS

HarperCollins*Publishers*

HarperCollins*Publishers*
77–85 Fulham Palace Road,
Hammersmith, London W6 8JB

www.harpercollins.co.uk

First published by HarperCollins*Publishers* 2013

1 3 5 7 9 10 8 6 4 2

A catalogue record of this book is
available from the British Library

HB ISBN 978-0-00-738272-9
TPB ISBN 978-0-00-738273-6
EB ISBN 978-0-00-744545-5

Printed and bound in Great Britain by
Clays Ltd, St Ives plc

MIX
Paper from
responsible sources
FSC C007454

FSC™ is a non-profit international organisation established to
promote the responsible management of the world's forests.
Products carrying the FSC label are independently certified to
assure consumers that they come from forests that are managed
to meet the social, economic and ecological needs of present
and future generations, and other controlled sources.

Find out more about HarperCollins and the environment at
www.harpercollins.co.uk/green

CONTENTS

PART I

THAT THERE MIKE PENNINGTON

I.

THATTO HEATH RHAPSODY

When I go back to the very beginning, I can't help but smile. Like a Ken Loach film, there was a joy to be mined from everything life threw my way. It was who we were and how we lived. It was the perfect comic breeding ground, where self-deprecation shielded us from the indulgent evils of self-analysis, and we loved it that way. If I start my search hoping to find out where I got the feeling that I alone was not enough, then I know I'll draw a blank from my early years in St Helens.

I was loved as a kid; I was raised with more love and emotional support than most folks could wish for. Now, if you have siblings, you'll already know that there's no guarantee how each individual brother or sister might turn out. But nothing about my family background suggested I'd end up aspiring to anything other than what I already had.

Did I say aspiring? You see? I didn't even aspire. That better world was meant for folk who needed more, as far as I could see. I daydreamed, as all kids do, but never feared those innocent flights of fancy not coming true. My emotional cup overfloweth-ed with positivity, and financial hardship was hidden behind a wisecrack or a definite no to any unrealistic pleas for whatever was the latest rage.

Instead we counted days, weeks, months even, for birthdays and Christmas to come around. That's the difference between the working and middle classes: our gifts weren't token gestures. A birthday or Christmas wasn't a time for sitting back and feeling grateful for what we had. We had fuck all, in the material sense, so it was a time for getting things your selfish little heart had convinced itself you really, really needed. To this day you'd be strung up in our house for trying to pass a Boots three-for-one 'gift' option off as a main present: 'I can shower with bloody Fairy Liquid ... I need a BlackBerry!'

The Fords, the Barnets, the Fenneys, the Croppers, the Rodens, the Leylands, the McGanns, the Dennings, the Carrs and the Kings – these were the whole street of supporting characters who made up the *Truman Show*-esque microcosm of my world. I was happy with my lot. I wasn't fat at that point, I was fairly bright at school, and I had some great mates. Bryan Davies, my best friend to this day, was built like a brick shithouse from the age of five. From the first day at school, I decided I would befriend the grumpy-looking git.

He had this intently furrowed brow when he was pissed off that would earn him the nickname Dan Aykroyd. My cousin, Dimon, was the same age, but appointed himself as my bodyguard. He was 'nowty' – no nonsense – and had a brilliant, mischievous look to him just before he'd belt a lad. All the Holker brothers have it, and it always helped lend a comic-book violence to any schoolyard scrap.

I had a huge crush on my first teacher, Mrs Powell. At break time the girls would link arms with her and stroll around the playground whilst a gang of us followed on behind, egging each other on to touch the back of her long, black leather coat. She was my first inkling of sexy, before I knew what sexy was. She didn't dress like any other grown-up I knew at that age. She was my Cagney (Sharon Gless) to all the mums and fellow teaching Laceys (Tyne Daly). When she handed out my class

photo and told me that I looked like 'a little film star', I accidentally squeezed out a little bit of wee.

But I digress. I do that a lot. I think it's my attempt to cam-
ouflage the short-term memory blips and attention deficits
resulting from JoHNNy's diet of Guinness, vodka, gravy and
Gaviscon. Still, back in the day, Mrs Powell, along with St Austin's Infant and Junior School, my family, my friends, that
death-trap called Hankey's Well at the end of our street (where
we used to build dens, light fires and basically go full-on *Lord of
the Flies*, minus the conch) – all these people and places were,
in retrospect, a beautifully coherent, well-integrated influence
on my happy-go-lucky young life.

But when I try to sift through and conjure up the atmosphere of my early childhood, it hits me like a giddy ton of bricks:
I don't know where to start. My memories aged nought to ten
don't sort themselves out individually – they're all bound up
together in a mesh of innocence and fun. And for someone with
definite OCD tendencies, I'm strangely content to have them
misfiled in no particular alphabetical order or coherent timeline. That's not to say every picture that flashes into my mind is a
happy one, but, like any strong relationship, or reality-snuffing
episode of *The Darling Buds of May*, there was always enough
good stuff stored up to cope with the bad.

While there's nothing there to satisfy HiS appetite for torture,
I already feel browbeaten by the paranoid suspicion that you
don't feel me capable of sharing the good things I associate with
Michael Pennington, or that perhaps these are the personal
insights you crave since you think you know all you need to
know about JoHNNy VegaS? So I will purge myself of all the good
things that held my hand from hitting The Priory speed-dial
button after one of HiS 'incidents' – and the only way I can do so
is to take a whole load of those images and throw them all out
there together.

I realise that the English teachers among you might hanker
after a few more full stops over the coming few pages, but please
don't worry: the joining words will be back in full effect in the

next chapter. I won't be giving it the full James Joyce any more, once I've done justice to the breathless childhood rush of:

Taking my birthday money into town under my cousin Gillian's supervision and buying 'Action Man: Helicopter Pilot' –
'Are you sure that's the one you want?'
'Yeah, deffo'
'Have you got the helicopter?'
'No, but it's all right, you see he's not just a helicopter pilot, he's been trained to kill just like the others'

Taking all my Action Men including 'Talking Commander' – as well as my motorbike and side-car, jeep with trailer, lorry with opening hatch and mounted machine-gun, and free Asian-looking enemy characters – into school on 'What did you get for Christmas?' play-day –
'This one's got no undies on!'
'That's how you know he's a baddie – that, and the eyes'

Watching *Star Wars* for the first time with the Holkers on one of Uncle Mike's access nights and leaving the cinema with a million questions whilst believing that there really was a galaxy somewhere far, far away … And not knowing how to ask why their dad didn't live at home

Climbing on the roof at Martin Hurley's and trying to summon Spiderman with a torch pointed at the moon through the plastic web rotor of his die-cast Corgi helicopter

Writing a short, farewell note on the back of an empty Cook's Matches box as we planned to run away to *Star Wars'* Mos Eisley and join the rebellion –
'We will have laser blasters or light-sabres so we will be safe'

My daft childhood crush on both Martin's sisters, especially Jane after she gave me an Ian Dury single with 'There Ain't Half

Been Some Clever Bastards' on the B-side –
  'Does he actually say the 'B' word?'
  'He does, 'cos he's a rebel'
  'I wanna be a rebel when I'm older'
  'Then this is perfect'

Exotic day-trips in the Hurleys' working car to Blackpool, Southport and the pre-bombed-out Arndale shopping centre, Manchester

Taking Martin to Morrison's on our weekly shop in a bid to return the day-trip gestures and shaming Mum into blowing her budget by buying us Yo-Yos at the checkout, then suffering a week of extra veg piled high at dinner as part of her quiet revenge

Martin's parents taking us into country pubs with them instead of leaving us in the car and then buying us our own drinks, *in our own glasses* –
  'Look at this straw … it bends!'
  'Michael, will you be having a starter?'
  'A what?'

Mum filling up a pop bottle with cordial and taking it with us to share when we walked to Taylor Park, or went wild and caught a bus to Victoria Park –
  'Mum, *floater!*'
  'Michael, what have I told you? Swallow your butty first, nobody wants to be drinking your leftovers'

Begging my dad relentlessly to be allowed to camp out on the big field with Ian Cropper –
  'But everyone else is going'
  'Well, good for them'
  'We'll be dead safe, honest. Ian's got a knife and matches and a proper paraffin lamp'

'Has he really?'

'Yeah!'

'Well, that's three good reasons why you're definitely not going'

Tying fishing-line to a purse and lying in wait in the bushes to yank it away when someone tried to grab it, knowing that the victims who got narky had intended on keeping it –

'Whoever you are, I know your dads – just you wait till I see 'em!'

Making breakfast in bed for my dad on Father's Day but accidentally putting salt on the cornflakes instead of sugar –

'And as soon as you've finished, you can open your card'

'There's no rush, you know I like to take my time with my food'

Going round Danny Rawlinson's house believing that the future had truly arrived as I sat and watched with awe and envy, waiting for my turn on Atari's Space Invaders –

'Are you rich?'

'No, why?'

'Dun't matter'

Saying my prayers in the firm belief that if technology such as Space Invaders was within our reach, then surely *Star Wars* was a realistic possibility –

'Please, please get me to outer space. I know it might mean killing people, Lord, but you saw what they did to Alderaan, I mean, that was a whole planet ...'

Making movies on Danny's Super 8 film camera and feeling magical the first time our film came back from the processors' and we watched it projected onto a sheet tacked to his front room wall –

'Look, look, there's me!'

Playing snooker on Danny's five-foot snooker table and dreaming of the day when Hurricane Higgins acknowledged the arrival of Michael 'The Storm' Pennington as the sport's new name to watch out for –

'... and as he lines himself up for a difficult angle on the blue into the right side pocket ...'

'Do you always talk to yourself when you play?'

'It makes it more like the telly'

'Weirdo!'

Fishing with Danny's spare tackle for four years –

'Can Danny come fishing, Mrs Rawlinson?'

'He's out with his dad, Michael'

'Oh ...'

'The tackle's in the garage – help yourself'

'Thanks!'

My mum finally accepting it wasn't a phase and buying me my own rod and reel from Makro for my birthday: a Shakespeare carbon-fibre ledger pro that you could bend right back on itself, although I never dared try –

'Bend it ...'

'No!'

'They're designed so you can bend 'em, to take the weight of a fish'

'So?'

'So bend it!'

'No!'

Trying to breed my own maggots for bait by hiding pork trimmings on top of the cistern in the outside toilet. My dad doing a bloody good impression of Michael Caine in that movie *The Swarm* after taking the racing page in there for his Saturday 'my time' constitutional –

'What the hell's wrong with just using a bit of bread?'

Going hell for leather playing Murderball at Grange Park Youth Club until volunteer Phil blew his whistle –

'Find a ball and you can carry on, otherwise the scrapping stops *now*!'

The first time we tried to play American football after watching *The Longest Yard* with Burt Reynolds, and my brother Mark kicked our Rob so hard that Mum and Dad had to take him and his baking apple-sized swollen balls to A&E, where the doctor suggested pressing charges before being made fully aware of the circumstances –

'His own brother did this?'

(Taking Mum and Dad to one side.) 'Is he adopted?'

Rob's glee at the stitches Mark had to have in his bum when Gaz Leyland stopped mid aeroplane-swing and dropped him on a broken bottle –

'Your arse looks like a *Sky At Night* chart'

'Shut up!'

'Give us a pen and I could draw the Plough on it'

'*MUM!*'

That huge terrifying swing off the flat shed roof and over the sharp, iron-tipped boundary fence of Hankey's Well that everyone had to pog onto – a forty-foot arc of white-knuckle terror for the nine or ten kids clinging on for dear life –

'Whoever's holding on there, *don't* – aim for the rope!'

The games of Skillie, or Manhunt, that covered the whole of Thatto Heath, Taylor Park, Portico, Red Rocks, Broadway and Eccleston Mere, despite always getting caught early and never, ever launching a successful escape bid for my team –

'Same bush, same spot, every bloody time! Look, I can see you from here, Mike, and if you make me go over there and tag you, you're getting a dead arm ... a proper one'

'I surrender!'

'And you wonder why you're always picked last?'

Our Dimon blowing his birthday money on sweets for every-one and ten packs of *Star Wars* cards for me down at the corner shop near Thatto Heath Park, and the bollocking we all got from Aunty Kath for filling up on Blackjacks, Sherbert Dips, Cola Cubes, Fruit Salads and Drumstick lollies before his birth-day tea –

'I'm cooking nothing this week till all that's gone, do you hear me?'

'Yes'

'Pat, get the clingfilm back on'

'What about my cake?'

'Don't push it!'

Me getting Astro Wars for Christmas after pleading with Steve Butler for a full term of playtimes for a go of his, then praying with all my might that his batteries would have an acid leak and he'd have to make do with a game of Bulldog like everyone else –

'I only ask Lord because you've seen him – he's a proper tight git'

All the patients from Rainhill Hospital wandering around Thatto Heath Lane, some shouting random swearwords, but most just dazed and confused from the institutionalisation –

'Bloody buggers ... bloody'

'Mum, that man just—'

'Shush and finish your pie'

The pig that used to escape from Piggy Fletcher's and run riot down the lane, stopping traffic and drawing out all the drunken wannabe rodeo cowboys from The Vine pub

My nan, Mary, taking us to Blackpool and telling us we could stay in the Funhouse for as long as we wanted, even if it meant missing our coach and catching a train home

My dad building us a sledge and dragging it – with me sitting on it – all the way to Taylor Park's big hill, just so we could crash it into a tree –

'You're not concussed, you'd be vomiting if … here, use my hankie, and not a word to your mum, all right?'

Sitting in the garden with my mum if I went home from school for lunch, watching *The Sullivans* courtesy of a long extension lead and eating my Blackburn's steak pie with cream cake to follow –

'Well, will you marry me?'

'Yes, yes, I will!'

'I think Kitty's gonna be all right, Mum. Mum, are you crying?'

'Shush and finish your cake'

Not sleeping for weeks after watching *Salem's Lot* but being grateful that Dad had a crucifix hanging in every single room in the house. And wishing our Mark wouldn't keep whispering –

'Michael, open the window, Michael'

Actually worrying that Mum might be part vampire as she applied her prescription sun-block after being diagnosed with a rare allergy to sunlight. Wondering if I could bring myself to stake her if the blood-lust ever overwhelmed her mothering instincts –

'That's not your mother, she belongs to the Master now'

'Forgive me, Mum!'

Realising that vampires don't tend to wear crosses around their neck as Mum did, and therefore deciding all was probably well

Dad taking the day off and taking me out of school to visit the Liverpool Maritime Museum –

'Shut? Ah, well, do you want to see the huge police station I built?'

'All by yourself, Dad?'

'I did the stairs. I remember telling the foreman that those drawings the architect sent were wrong ...'

All of Dad's stories and how adversity never seemed to get him down. Never even hearing him shout like some of the other dads on our street

All the front doors left open on our street and all the verbal snippets of family life –

'Mum, Muuuuum, come and wipe me bum!'

That camping holiday in Wales when Dad's old army tent ripped in half following a force twelve gale, and the sleepless night that followed as the rain blew in –

'Dad, I'm cold'

'Go to sleep'

'Dad, my sleeping bag's wet'

'Go to sleep'

'Dad, can I go and get a shower?'

'No, go to sleep'

'Dad, when can I get a shower?'

'When you wake up, now go to sleep'

'Dad, can I mind the torch?'

'No, go to sleep'

Mum having her drink spiked with Pernod at The Catholic Men's Society New Year's Eve party and her coming home singing 'Some Enchanted Evening' before getting poorly –

'No, the bucket! Under the stairs, next to the bleach!'

Butlin's! Us and the Holkers paying for two families of three in the self-catering chalets but smuggling the rest in. Simon getting the short straw and having to go in the boot of the car –

'Well, just take little breaths and for God's sake don't make a sound till we're well past reception!'

Rumbles with the Protestant school, St Matthew's, but making up by home-time as half the kids in our street went there –

'You don't get Communion because Jesus dun't even believe in you!'

Almost wetting myself laughing at watching a truck drive backwards at high speed thanks to rewind on Martin Hurley's brand new video recorder –

'Can I do it?'

'No, you might break it. You should tell your mum and dad to get one'

'Maybe ...'

'That's what you always say'

Wimpy's opening in St Helens and my dad acting genuinely bemused as to why I'd want to opt for that over a pig's trotter from Kwik Save's in-store butcher's department –

'But it's what Action Man would eat in a real war'

The Morris 1800 that my dad refused to scrap despite living under it with a tool-kit every spare Saturday afternoon. Putting it in our backyard after demolishing the wall to get it in. All the make-believe day trips we went on in it, although even then my brother made me sit in the back with my seat-belt on –

'Do you wanna go to Disney World or not?'

'Yes, but ...'

'Because any more out of you and I'll turn this car around right now and we'll go straight home, got that?'

The fights my brothers had with other kids in the street – the Rodens, Gaz and some of the Fords – all over nothing and for-gotten the minute a football appeared on the scene

Offering Lee a go on my bike the awful day I found him sitting looking lost on the kerb outside his house after hearing his dad had died falling from a ladder on a building site –

'Are you sure?'

'Yeah, just no going off kerbs, and don't let me mam see you'

Dunking cold toast in a flask lid of hot tea for breakfast in school because we'd attended early mass during Lent –

'Chocolate'

'Sweets'

'*Newsround*'

'*Newsround* dun't count – it's educational. You have to give up something you'd miss, like *Tiswas* or *Hong Kong Phooey*'

'He's right. You'll end up in purgatory for *Newsround*'

'*Blue Peter*?'

'Same difference'

That moody bloke who'd had the first ever double-glazing fitted in our street –

'Your dad doesn't earn in a month what one of these would cost to replace, now bugger off and play outside yer own house!'

Playing football in the grounds of St Matthew's Church and my dad not bollocking us when the vicar called round to grass us up because he never forgave them for not giving up their cast-iron gates during the war effort.

Flashing Julie McDonald and doing 'The Penguin' around the back of Rainhill cricket club in a giddy, nine-year-old fit of wild romantic abandon

'What you doing that for?'

'Dunno'

'You're not funny'

'Right'

Struggling to explain the flashing incident in Confession that week and being grateful I'd got funny Father Joyce instead of stern Father Turner –

'I accidentally showed myself to a girl from school'

'Accidentally what?'

'My pants were loose, they fell down'

'And what did she do?'

'Told all her mates in class. They kept calling me "The Flasher"'

'That's not good'

'No'

'And are you sorry?'

'Yes, Father'

'Well, say two Hail Marys, just in case'

'Okay'

'And tell your mum to get you a belt'

Missing out on Halloween because my dad reckoned it was a blasphemous celebration of the occult, but getting the money to go to the pictures instead –

'There's enough evil in the world without throwing a party for it'

Our Mark belting that posh lad sitting behind us during *The Spy Who Loved Me* because he'd already seen the film and told his mate, really loudly, that the car was about to turn into a submarine –

'Have you seen the bit where this happens?'

'I beg your pardon ...? Ow!'

Watching our Mark play rugby – he was a blinding scrum-half

Watching our Rob score that amazing goal from a corner

Offering to put out the corner flags for future footy matches after failing to get selected for the school team because I wouldn't quit goal-hanging and couldn't grasp the concept of off-side –

'You're a parasite, Pennington. Do you hear me? A parasite!'

Learning to swim courtesy of our headmaster, Mr McManus, after numerous lessons with my brother Mark had failed –

'Put your hands on the sides again and I'll stomp on 'em. Now move your arms, kick your legs and bloody swim!'

Paul Barnet sticking blades of grass up frogs' arses and inflating them a bit before gently squeezing to make them fart –
Phhhhht
'Can you make 'em burp?'
'Nah, they'd be sick. That'd be cruel'

Believing Paul Barnet when he told me he was born on a meteor that crash-landed in Taylor Park and therefore he was half werewolf –
'I don't turn into a full wolf, I just get a craving for sausages and chops or owt else meaty when it's a full moon'

Our Robert and Mark getting Paul to chase me down the street just so they could test their latest man-trap by lifting up a piece of fishing line at the last moment and nearly bloody decapitating me –
'It'd work if you weren't so bloody slow at running!'

Trying sterilised milk for the first time at Martin Hurley's house and throwing up for three days straight at home afterwards

Eating snails at their house and throwing up at home afterwards

Eating a Goblin meat pudding at their house and throwing up at home afterwards –
'Mum, can I go and play at Martin's house after school?'
'Yes, but best come home for your tea afterwards'

Martin's mum taking us to see *Grease* even though we were under age and then to a curry house where she let us have a real beer shandy, then my throwing up on Martin's hand after drinking it, which made him throw up in the restaurant fish tank –

'Just the bill, please'

Hearing that my nan had died on the first evening of our car-avan holiday in Rhyl and packing the car to go back home. There was no conversation to cover the sound of Mum weeping in the bedroom

Me and our Dimon pounding on a lad the afternoon after Nan's funeral for shouting –
'Ey-up, it's *Rentaghost!*'

Leaving Mum in church on Sundays as she knelt and cried her heart out week after week after week

Playing Kamikaze golf in the Holkers' bedroom and our Mark knocking the ball through their window and leaving a clean, golf ball-sized hole in it –
'Catch a bird, kill it, say it flew straight through'
'You're an idiot!'

Watching *Superman* with Christopher Reeve and actually believing a man could fly!

Watching *Superman II* with Martin Hurley and his dad and seeing families get up and leave during the scene where Super-man was in bed with Lois Lane –
'But Dad, why?'
'Never mind why, just get your coats. And bring that popcorn with you!'

Having nightmares about the bedroom filling with water and a shark getting in after our Robert told me all about *Jaws* chomp by chomp –
'DUUUH DUH. DUUUH DUH'
'Mum!'

I was crap at climbing. This tree had actually blown over in a storm.

The tree outside our bedroom window that looked like a witch

The parent alarm our Robert built with a Subbuteo floodlight and the switch contacts that he hid under the carpet outside our bedroom so we could play cards after lights out, not knowing that Dad used to stand outside tapping it for his own amusement –
'Right, your turn ... shush!'
'Twist ... shush!'
'Twist agai—shush!'
'Twi—shush!'

Watching the BBC Television Centre on telly and thinking it was almost as far away as the *Star Wars* galaxy, then committing the postcode to memory: 'W128QT, W128QT, W128QT'

Vowing never again to waste a Saturday morning trying to call *Swap Shop*.

The look on eagle-eyed Action Man Talking Commander's face when I brought home my first *Star Wars* figure –

'Who's this?'

'Just a friend. Nobody special, why?'

'No reason. I'll be in my jeep if anybody needs me'

Playing round Alan Hale's house with his massive collection of *Star Wars* figures and vehicles –

'I want your life'

'What?'

'I don't care if you have got Boba Fett, that is not enough troops to bring down an AT-AT!'

My sister Catharine's fear of moths and the weeks it took gathering twenty dead ones to hide under her duvet –

'I'm not going back in there, I'm sleeping round Janet's'

Getting told off by the dentist's receptionist for ripping a photo of Jimmy Connors from a magazine for my sister to apologise for the moths incident –

'I just saw you tear it out and put it in your pocket! Magazines cost money, you know. Did you stop to think about the next person who might want to look at Jimmy Connors before an extraction? No, you didn't, did you? Through there, second door on the right'

Thinking I was drunk after drinking Canada Dry at Father Chris's ordination party because I'd seen ginger 'ale' on the can –

'The bucket, Dad, in the cupboard, next to the bleach'

'Michael, bed, now!'

Keeping nicks for Father Turner whilst our Simon helped himself to altar wine –

'It's borrowing, and it's not a real sin 'cos it's not actually Jesus's blood yet'

'Well, give us a bit then'

Martin Hurley getting the holy mother of all rollockings for sticking his tongue out at me with the practice Communion host still stuck to it –

'This being a rehearsal does not change the fact that by your actions you have pulled a face at God and rejected Jesus Christ Our Lord!'

Losing a chunk of my front tooth when Bryan threw me over his back whilst playing 'Mad Bryan on the Loose'

Telling Bryan it would be okay after his mam dressed him in short trousers on the first day of junior school

Bryan beating me at maths and spelling in that big test

My mum buying me a comic when I cried my eyes out after losing the egg and spoon race at St Austin's sports day

Dad making 'a moral point of order' at Butlin's about the amount of rented costumes as opposed to the ingenuity of those put together from items found on site –

'It has nothing to do with the spirit of fun!'

My mum threatening to call the Queen on me for not wanting to go as Noddy in the fancy dress at the Silver Jubilee street party –

'Never you mind how I got her number'

'I told you I wanted to be a Womble'

'Well, Noddy can pick up litter'

'It's not the same!'

'Well, tough! Your Auntie Marjorie was up half the night sewing secret bells into those shoes ...'

The unmistakable weight and balance of a birthday envelope from Auntie Marjorie containing a classic car, golf trophy, gentleman fly fishing, or grouse shooting with a Labrador-themed card with money sellotaped to the inside of it –

'Don't just take the money! Read the card, properly, out loud!'

Uncle Joe's insistence on filling in every fifth word with 'doings' when explaining something technical –
'So I've stripped all the doings right back, cantilevered the cross doing with a strip of two by four doings and carried that through the same all the way along the doings. Do you see?'

My mum rocking and patting me as only she knew how whenever I was ill. There was rhythm to her mothering as beautiful and comforting as any Beatles ballad

My dad giving me a big slug of brandy when I was full of a cold, not knowing Mum had just given me a big dose of adult cough medicine. I fainted just like they do in the movies –
'He's going, Lol, he's going – catch him!'

My dad bringing crisps home from the club and using them to explain the nature of different faiths –
'So, imagine we're all stood around this giant, 40-foot bag of crisps. We're all looking at the same thing, but just from different angles. And people have to be willing to walk around and look at God from other folk's perspective, rather than stand their ground and dismiss other points of view'
'Including the Protestants'
'Aye'
'Even though they kept their gates'
'Even though they kept their gates'

My mum bringing back leftover sausage rolls, bits of things on cocktail sticks, and triangular sandwiches, a bit stale around the edge where the bread had been cut. All wrapped in little napkins from a buffet at somebody's party –
'What's this, Mum?'
'Erm ... pineapple'
'I don't like it'

'Well, leave it on the tissue and I'll clear it in a bit. Don't put it in the wicker bin, it'll smell'

Us moaning because Dad would nab the chicken drumsticks and stick them in his family-sized Stork margarine tub make-shift butty box for work –
'You have the butties, we'll have the chicken'
'When you go to work and I get to go back to school, it's a deal!'

Getting Dad to sing or recite a poem so we could stay up just that little bit longer, or just hear him talk about his youth, and his family doing singalongs and putting on turns in their Thackery Row parlour. His twinkle when he talked about the nan and granddad we never got to meet. Even Mum getting weary and worrying what the neighbours might think –
'So I'll meet 'im later on,
In the place where 'e is gone,
Where it's always double drill and no canteen;
E'll be squattin' on the coals,
Giving drink to poor damned souls,
And I'll get a swig in Hell from Gunga Din!'
'Lol, LOL! Get to bed … you're drunk'
'Goodbyeee, goodbyeee,
Save a tear, baby dear,
From your eyeeeee!'

The dream of turning fourteen so I could play on the snooker-tables at St Austin's Catholic Men's Society Club

Dad getting slapped when forced to point out to a drunken lady guest that the club's snooker tables were for men only –
'You're more than welcome to partake as a spectator'
'Sexist pig!'

The mini ploughman's lunches – two crackers, two onions, one mini slab of Red Leicester – that Jackie Henshall would buy me after his third Saturday afternoon pint before trying to teach me the basics of crown green bowling –

'Toe's not broke, just bruised, it'll be right. Now, next time, yon mon, hold the bowl with two hands, yeah?'

Our Mark's first Mod jacket, confirming his status as official family rebel. My contemplating cutting fishtails into the back of my kagool.

Hearing *Quadrophenia* for the first time –
'You say she's a virgin, well I'm gonna be the first in!
Her fella's gonna kill me, wooooooaaaaaaoooh fu—'
'Michael Pennington, get in here right now and explain to me what you think you just said!'

My mum always being there for us and maintaining a home, sometimes on a pittance, every day that God sent, always managing somehow to fill in the practical gaps that prayers so often seemed to slip through

My dad working every day God sent till Tory policy dictated otherwise, always willing to debate rather than simply dictate, and constantly trying to instill in me the need for patience and tolerance, who loved me even when I went out of my way to be thoroughly detestable –
'Can I go camping, please?'
'Nope'
'Urgh … I hate you!'
'I beg your pardon?'
'I said I hate yer!'
'Well, guess what? I love you. I've loved you since the moment you were born, and I'll never stop loving you, and what's more, you're stuck with that fact no matter what'
'So?'
'So … hate is a very powerful word, an awful word, and it's responsible for a lot of the evil and wrongdoing that goes on in

this world. And, one day, maybe not tomorrow, maybe not next week, or next month, maybe not for years to come, but one day, you'll remember saying that to me and it'll make you so, so sad that you did, and regret's an awful thing to carry on yer back'

'I didn't mean it ... not proper'

'Then try not saying it unless you do, all right?'

Our Mark trying to mend the inflatable beach-ball I'd won after a school trip to Southport fair with a fork heated over the stove and then trying to get rid of the smell by burning toast and spraying me in Pledge –

'Why does it have to be me what burnt the toast?'

'Because you're little'

'I said try a plaster first!'

Not that bloke who offered me a drink of real beer if I'd have a wee in front of him –

'I don't feel like a wee'

'You will if ya sups a bit of this?'

'I'm not supposed have beer'

'I won't say nowt'

My mum rushing me home after I started crying because Sharon Carr had kicked me really hard in the shins, and I instinctively knew I couldn't kick her back, partly because she was a girl, but mainly because she scared me –

'Are you gonna tell the teachers what she did?'

'I might have a word with her mam but, trust me Michael, you don't want it going any further than me, you and the front door'

My fear of fish night when Dad would bring home stinky 'Finney Haddey' from the docks, gagging at the sound of him coming through the front door –

'Why can't we have a normal chippy night like everyone else?'

'Action Man wouldn't ...'

'Action Man's gone, Dad. Just answer the question!'

My mum's baking. Her cherry pies and homemade quiche. Sitting peeling the skins off mushrooms while watching *The Waltons* with the smell of frying bacon drifting in from the kitchen

SAINTS!! Paying when Dad had the money, or climbing in to see a match when he didn't. Seeing windows around the town decorated in red and white like a second Christmas whenever they made it to a Challenge Cup final and knowing my town was best at rugby league. And making glass

Setting light to plastic beer-crates to watch the hot gloop spit and drip but having to hide the burn from Mum because she'd go ballistic if she found out we were playing with fire

The Sunday bonfire club and setting light to anything that would burn over Hankey's Well

Refusing to jump off the roof of St Austin's Infant School and starting to cry when our Robert tried to motivate me by lying about the police coming –
'You'll go to jail and never see me Mam or Dad again'
'They can come and visit'
'They'd be too ashamed. Now jump!'
'I'll write to them, every day'
'Suit yourself, ya tart!'

Watching our Mark pour meths on a car and light it then run down the street shouting, 'Get back! It's gonna blow!'

Throwing blackberries at car windscreens from the railway wall and hoping some angry bloke would stop the car and give chase

Throwing stuff onto the train tracks on the other side of the railway wall and watching the train demolish it when it left Thatto Heath, despite knowing we'd never be allowed beyond hand's grasp of our mum's apron strings again if we were caught playing near there

Climbing down the huge water-meter rule that ran up the side of an empty Hankey's Well and hating the peer pressure that had prompted me to do so, yet thinking it was like a picture I'd seen of the Colosseum in school once we were down there

A gang of us watching a kid whose name I won't use for legal reasons wipe his arse on the corner brickwork of our street, then examining the results for worms –
'Oh my God, that is sick!'
'What would you know? Girls, eh? Pah!'
'I think they've got a point'
'Ya girl!'

My dad pulling my pants down and smacking my bum in front of everybody for climbing on the electricity sub-station

Finding a Tom O'Connor cassette over the woods that still worked and listening to it with my dad, both of us laughing even though I wasn't always sure why –
'It's funny 'cos it was true, proper storytelling and with no effing and blinding like most of 'em nowadays!'

Crashing Paul Barnett's birthday party by pretending to return a bag of sweets our Mark had misplaced at home, just so I could see his Evel Kneivel

Stealing the car from Lee Leyland's *Starsky and Hutch* board-game and burying it in our rabbit hutch when guilt got the better of me

Volunteering my pet Blacky when I thought Dad was joking about whose rabbit was going in the pot, until I came home and found him skinned and strung up –

'I saved you these'
'What are they?'
'His ears, tail and feet. They're meant to bring good luck'

Waiting for Mark to get out of our shared bath so I could pour water on my willy with an empty shampoo bottle because I liked the tingle

Swapping a butty for a sip of the gravy from Chris Ramsdale's Pot Noodle packed lunch –
'It must be like this out in space!'

Teaching the whole year how to dance proper to 'Prince Charming' by Adam and the Ants –
'No, it's right arm up, step, then left arm up and cross, step, right arm down on hip, step, left arm down on hip, step. Sort of swagger when you do it and keep in time or else we'll all look stupid'

The first time I ever got caned for fighting with Phil Morgan for jumping the queue at break time –
'And you know why you're here?'
'Yes, sir'
'Yes, sir'
'And the punishment, as a result?'
'Yes, sir'
'Yes, sir'
'And have you anything to say for yourselves?'
'No, sir'
'Yes, sir'
'What's that, Pennington?'
'Did you know that I'm an altar boy, sir?'
'I do, yes'
'Okay'
'Okay. Right, well, altar boys first, then. Hands out, Pennington'
'Yes, sir'

Thursdays being velvet corduroy trousers day and hating how velvet corduroy felt against my skin, but still feeling guilty when I purposely took the knees out of them

Finding a pound note in the snow and believing my dad when he took it off me and said he was going to take it down to the lost property department at the local police station –
'But it's mine if nobody claims it?'
'Oh, aye'
'How long does it take before they decide?'
'About a year, give or take'
'Will they call as soon as they know?'
'I should imagine so. Either way, at least you know you did the right thing, eh?'
'Yeah'

My dad offering me five pence for every book I read and my tear-arsing it down to Thatto Heath library as a result –
'*Noggin the Nog* counts as a book!'
'Don't try kidding a kidder. There's too many pictures in that for a lad of your age and intelligence'
'I can't wait to get a paper round!'
'Well, at least you'll not be short of ow't to read while you're doing it'

Believing our Mark when he told me that Beecham's Clock Tower in St Helens' town centre was Big Ben

Believing our Mark when he told me that cars drove over the top hump of Runcorn Bridge

Marching through town to protest about a sex shop opening and feeling guilty because it used to be called Pennington's the Tailor's –
'First Benny Hill, now this. What's the world coming to?'

Busting our stereo by dropping a half-penny down between the cassette buttons and the casing and nearly electrocuting my mum when she needed some time alone with Johnny Mathis

Saying family bidding prayers in front of Archbishop Worlock in the Liverpool Wigwam and thinking –
'Don't think it, don't think it, don't think it, don't think it … but if you shaved the bits of hair off the sides of Derek Worlock and stuck 'em on his face … he would make a great Ming The Merciless. Sorry, God!'

Gasping on the tarmac while waiting for Pope John Paul to land at Speke Airport with people going mad because some blokes with trolleys were trying to charge 70p for cans of Coke and Fanta –
'Just one can between us?'
'No, here, have some of this'
'It's warm!'
'And it's full of floaters!'
'Michael …'

Watching my mum belt our Robert for necking with a random girl whilst Pope John Paul addressed the crowd –
'You're a ruddy disgrace. Well, I hope you're happy with yourself because his blessing did not include you!'

Feeling guilty for folding my one-day, all-zone travel pass and crushing Pope John Paul's face

The ITV kids' show *Michael Bentine's Potty Time* –
'Mum, are the patients down the lane potty or mental?'
'Who?'
'You know, like that man who shouts bloody bugg—'
'They're just not well! Now shush and come get your tea'

Sicking up my mashed carrot and turnip after finding a lumpy bit but having to eat it again because my mum couldn't tell the difference between vomit and the original –

'Mum, please, just smell it!'

Trying to imagine being twenty years of age while sitting in the choir at church

Hating the idea of letting go of my belief in Father Christmas, even though deep down I knew I was getting too old for 'that sort of thing' –

'I've seen your presents, Mike – they're in our garage!'

'La la la la la la la la la la la la!'

Throwing a strop on Christmas morning because I had to leave my new chalkboard-painting easel and go to church to celebrate the birth of Jesus –

'Get dressed, now, or this goes straight back to Father Christmas'

'But why? He doesn't come to my birthday!'

'Of course he does, he's everywhere!'

'Well, why can't I play here with him instead?'

'Because he wants you to go to church, that's where the party is'

'Is there cake?'

'No'

'Jelly?'

'No'

'Then what's the point when it's not even a proper party?'

Even the day I nagged Dad relentlessly for an ice cream and he took me outside for a chat –

'I got laid off today. Do you know what that means?'

'I think so'

'Well, then I need you to do me a favour, okay?'

'Yeah'

'Take this quid and get yourself something from the van. Only, make it last and don't ask again for a while'

Stealing all the page threes from the newspapers we collected to raise money for St Austin's Church, and hiding them in a Kwik Save carrier bag under a brick just behind the garages beside St Matthew's Church. Not knowing why they made my giblets tingle but convinced that it was naughty, yet not feeling guilty about their god watching me because they still had their railings they'd held back in the war ...

All of these feelings, each and every moment, were (and are) a part of me. All of them, wittily broadened out, would make perfect anecdotes to fill a cheery book of nostalgia ten times over. But they're paths not travelled by my psycho-Siamese-twin Vegas.

It's along the abnormal, moody B-roads of my mind where I have to search for the first signs of him. Not an easy task, thanks to His scorched earth policy. Carrie Fisher had her postcards from the edge for evidence; Johnny refused to pay the postage.

It's a shame, though. I loved my childish existence with all its harmless ups-and-downs, and I didn't care in the least that nothing at this point in my life felt remarkable. It was innocent and lovely, it was growing up in Hayes Street, Thatto Heath, St Helens. I was eager for a life without incident. I thrived on normality. Or, at least, I thought I did.

PART II
SEEDS OF JOHNNY

2.

THE WHITE FATHER

I made a decision at the age of ten that I truly believe changed everything, for ever. If you think I'm being dramatic, just ask yourself, did you leave home and loved ones at the age of eleven to go and train to become a priest?

No, thought not.

If you did, or if you experienced something even more detrimental, then I'm sorry for lecturing. I just need to make it clear that this book really begins with the planting of the seed of JOHNNY VegaS.

I should understand JOHNNY better than anyone: I created HIM, for fuck's sake. Or so I thought. But in fact He was never a character. He was a stockpile of subconscious anger. He was the Midas touch to transform everything that might otherwise have crushed me.

Something had to trigger it. The subconscious is like a shit safari park on a rainy day: you need something big to come along to tempt the beast out and make it play. That's why my story only really starts at the age of 10 – not at the very beginning, but in 1980.

Everything up to that point was more of a hugely contented false start. But it was from around this time that my feeling of displacement really kicked in – the genesis of what would prove to be an odd lifetime's out-of-body experience. It sounds daft, I know, but the more I retreated inwards, the stronger the feeling of being alienated from myself would become. And the more at odds I'd feel with life's expectations of me.

As a kid, I'd always said that I was going to be a priest when I grew up, but in truth I had never given it much serious thought. I reckon it was down to the positive reaction I'd get from people when I told them that I wanted to go into the Church as a career, or that I had 'a calling', as most believers referred to it.

I'd always felt a little guilty that God had never actually spoken to me directly and asked me to join his team. (Although I'd later learn that presuming an intimate acquaintance with the big man's intentions was a necessary tool for keeping control within a seminary.) Still, as I grew older I kept saying it, and I remember enjoying the response it would get. You could hold a room full of grown-ups enthralled with talk of becoming a priest, or even maybe a White Father? No, I'm not sure what a White Father is, either, but I think they're some sort of missionary – and to the good people of our parish, that ambition seemed even more impressive.

A White Father once came and did a sermon in our church. It was pure fire and brimstone stuff. He ranted from the pulpit about how everyone was in very real danger of going to hell – 'Everyone!' If St Austin's had come equipped with a Tudor priest hole then Canon Tickle (only in unfortunate name, not by nature) would've been hurling women and children out of the way to get in it. When this guy got up a head of steam, you'd be forgiven for thinking the Pope himself was capable of shoplifting an oven-ready turkey – 'That's why John Paul's gone to Iceland!'

I mean it. It was the Spinal Tap all the way up to 11, the *Enola Gay*, the head-popping-out-of-the-boat bit in *Jaws*, the 'Let's get rrrrready to rrrrrumble', the Godzilla, the *Star Wars* Death Star, the space shuttle *Challenger*, the Wall Street Crash, the Hanna Barbera 'Captain CAAAAAAYAYAYAYAAAAVEMAN!', the first lesbian kiss on *Brookside*, the Mount St Helens eruption mother of all kick-ass sermons.

'Stop right now!' he screamed at the top of his lungs. 'What are you actually thinking about right now? WHAT ARE YOU THINKING ABOUT!? And don't lie ... because HE knows!'

I remember my mum, ashen-faced, telling me afterwards that she was doing her maths on the housekeeping and couldn't remember whether or not she'd paid the pop man (we used to have it delivered, even after the daft rumour – probably spread by Soda Stream ponces – that staff used to pee in the vats at the Barton's Pop Christmas party). Fizzy drinks were a luxury never denied us, no matter how tight money got. I think because our pop man wasn't a faceless corporation, I liked him because he looked like Billy Joel from the *Piano Man* album cover. I'd imagine him playing a small Bontempi organ in his cab on quiet days and writing songs about all the discontented housewives he delivered dandelion and burdock to.

Anyway, in the middle of Mum balancing her books, this furious force of ecclesiastical nature condemned us all to eternal damnation. Had it been him in *Footloose*, instead of John Lithgow, he'd have broken Kevin Bacon's legs with his own ghetto-blaster in the opening credits, before pouring quick-setting cement in his ears.

We were used to our local priest's 'softly, softly' approach. But this White Bull in our chaste little china shop was promising us now't but the fires of hell. There was no carrot at the end of his schtick. According to him, none of us would ever be good enough for heaven – even his own soul was in constant jeopardy. And yet, rather than scare me, he left a great impression. It was the first time I'd seen someone in a pulpit and thought, 'If he's that bothered, then he must be on to something.'

It didn't just feel like he was going through the motions: 'Let's get this over with as quickly as possible so you can make the pub, or get yer roasties on!' The grown-ups were getting it in the neck just as much as us young offenders. Unilateral guilt! Like a controversial but brilliant stand-up he was both shocking and mesmerising, with 100 per cent conviction in what he said. Imagine Sam Kinison in a white cassock and you're still not quite there. He wasn't coaxing the crowd, he was tearing 'em apart with his zealous conviction, forcing them to question the pious comfort zone they'd previously taken for granted.

But still, it wasn't enough to make me take my own self-proclaimed vocation seriously, even though back then in St Helens religion was a massive part of our lives.

We got stick – sometimes at school, but mainly at our local youth club – for going to church. We were called 'God squad-ders', and the fact that my dad wore a crucifix openly around his neck made for even more grief. We even had to go to BENE-DICTION. It wasn't even a proper mass! I understand it's about the veneration of the host, the body of Christ, but come on! When you're young and in the middle of a big game of three pops in ... it felt like Lineker being dragged off the pitch by that turnip at the European Championships when my dad announced it was time to go to Benediction.

Lay-kids understood that Sundays involved some form of commitment as a God-botherer. Even glueys sometimes attend-ed midnight mass – pissed, more probably tripping, but present at least. But nobody – no other kids, not even the majority of parishioners – went to Benediction. It was God's way of screen-ing for any potential Ned Flanders.

I actually liked us being a church-going family. There was a real sense of community. It had all the ambition of the middle classes, but with a god that didn't abandon you at the first sign of a fiscal fuck-up. You were encouraged to love thy neigh-bour, not block their extension because you didn't want your garden overseen.

There was strength to be drawn from faith, which I witnessed first-hand through my parents. The death of my nan, Mary, had a devastating effect on my mum. It's an awful thing to see the heart of the family suddenly start to falter as Nan's had. Mum was always the pragmatist who soldiered on no matter what, but for months afterwards the fight had gone, there was no wind in her sails, and she just appeared to be drifting aimlessly from day to day. Grief, depression, apathy, call it what you will, it's agonising watching someone you love drowning in sadness but not having the strength of will to come up for air.

Every week, she would sit in church after mass staring into space, or sobbing, head in hands, as we looked on helplessly, 'till Dad ushered us outside. She had things to say to God, to her deceased mum, things she perhaps could not articulate to anybody else. When the fog eventually lifted, Mum would always attribute her emotional survival to her faith. That was what saw her through her darkest hours.

When Dad was made unemployed and every penny coming into the house mattered (although my parents did their best to shield us from this fact), it was his faith that stopped the pride-crushing struggle to make ends meet from getting the better of him. One hot summer's day, when he'd dragged a huge chunk of scrap metal for what felt like miles on the back of a homemade trolley Uncle Joe had built – taking me along for company despite the fact that all I did was obsess over the ice cream he'd promised me from the profits – I could see the soul-sapping anguish as we got to the scrap-metal yard, only to find it was shut.

It was the point where most folk would be forgiven for quitting, for ranting, cursing and shaking their fist at the sky shouting, 'Why me, eh, why? What more can I do to do right by those I care for? How much more do you need me to suffer before you've proved your point, eh?' That's definitely my default setting. But as my dad hung his head in what I thought was surrender, he was actually allowing himself a little prayer time. And when he eventually looked up, I could see his cheery determination was still intact, despite my stupid determination to point out the blatantly obvious.

'It's shut, Dad!'

'I know.'

'So what are we going to do?'

'Well, I'm not carting it home, that's for certain.'

'So you're just gonna leave it here?'

'I am.'

'But won't someone else cash it in?'

'Most likely, but who's to say their needs won't be greater than ours, eh?'

'So, no ice cream?'

'No, not today, kiddo.'

'Bit of a wasted trip, then?'

'Do you see that hill over there?'

And Dad walked me home via a massive detour telling story after story about him, my uncles and my aunties growing up. It turned into one of my fondest memories ever, and we still laugh about it to this day whenever we pass that way in the car. It was Dad's faith that turned the day around, so why wouldn't I grow up hoping that I'd inherit that same peace and inner strength?

True, a lot of religion was dogma at that stage, but I presumed faith would come through maturity, like a kind of theological puberty, and that one day the once barren landscape of questions would be full of fluffy answers to all of Life's great mysteries, trials and tribulations sprouting up all over the place.

Making your first Holy Communion was a really big deal. It was taken for granted that I'd follow my brothers in becoming an altar boy afterwards. Which I did. And there's no denying there were definite perks to the job.

For starters, you got out of school assembly to serve at morning masses and feast days. It was a free pass to wag off school with the added bonus of spiritual kudos, but it came at a cost. The position tended to carry more weight with the adults as eight-year-old lasses didn't tend to dig altar boys. Any dormant uniform fetishes at that point would've been limited to firemen, policemen, cowboys, astronauts, and maybe the occasional train driver: your basic run-of-the-mill fancy dress stalwarts and stuff of naive junior-school-career fantasies. There were no Pink Ladies, and we sure as shit weren't no T-Birds. No room for wanna-be young nun equivalents to 'dig' where we were coming from.

There were some blokes well into their autumn years still trapped in time as altar 'men'. They wore red under-cassocks as opposed to our black ones. They'd earned their position in their own quiet way, and deserved our respect, yet they felt more like a cautionary tale instead of aspirational figures – like kids held back at school year after year, until the only job they were capable of was caretaker.

So why do it? Yes, the hours were good, and yes, it meant we got a head start on racking up brownie points with old St Peter sitting up there at those blessed Pearly Gates, but the potential payday from a well-served funeral service was even better!

It's an unpleasant truth to confess, especially to those of you who've buried someone dear via a Catholic service, but funerals were a big potential 'Ker-ching!' payday to angelic-looking wee parasites like Simon and me. The passing of a loved one, the distraught anguish, the sombre acceptance of the fragility of human existence, it was money in the bank.

Just as it was for the funeral directors who did this stuff day in, day out, and even the priests who, at times, sounded like they were reading out a shopping list as opposed to the recently deceased's best qualities, death – or at least the spiritual task of delivering some poor soul unto the hands of their beloved maker – was run-of-the-mill stuff to us. It was a job!

And like any job you had to find the fun in it, whilst still projecting a sense of public dignity for those genuine mourners '... gathered here amongst us'. Flashing the reflected sunlight off the big cross we held was a favourite. If you were bold, you might then swish it briefly across the priest's eyes as he was reading, but Simon was a bugger for highlighting the priest's genitals – shining a light on his unholy of holys, and it never failed to get me giggling.

Dimon was the grand master of subtle mischief and could set me off so easily. Too much incense on the charcoal was his favourite: the altar would end up looking more like *Top of the Pops*. And you could sense he was smiling, even when looking straight ahead.

Remember that worst case of giggles you ever had as a kid? Someone sets you off and the severity of the situation just makes it worse, and makes the laugh even harder the more you try to bury it? Imagine that when you're working the funeral of someone with a grieving family who's hard as bloody nails, and you know you've caught the eye of a nutter sitting at the end of the front bench …

If Dimon set me off, I'd have no option but to focus on my feet, hold my eyes open as long as possible without blinking till they'd water, and, whilst working the sniggering shudder in my shoulders into the routine as respectful sobbing, hold my head up at just the right moment to let the light catch a false tear running down my cheek in profile. Let me tell you, the young Ricky Schroder bawling his eyes out at the end of *The Champ*? That kid had nothing on me!

'It feels forced, Ricky daaahling. Remember, keep it minimal, less is more!'

It sounds utterly disrespectful I know, but messing around with your back to the congregation, I reckon, actually gave me enough guilt to achieve genuine sorrow throughout the final procession out of church. And then a quick sniff of the altar wine to take the edge off the agonising wait to see if the funeral director had any tips to pass on courtesy of the grieving family. I wasn't on pocket money like some other kids my age, so £1 or £2 was a small fortune.

There were also the rare days when you got a free pass to piss yourself laughing. Like when the priest dropped the burning charcoal on the new altar carpet, and tried, in a blind panic, to pick it up with his bare hands. It was definitely swearing, but edited like you'd see in an in-flight movie. He started off unintentionally shouting but managed to swallow the end of each curse, kind of like a stroke victim with Tourette's: 'FUrrrgh, SHIheeaah, WANhugh!'

The inappropriate fun we had might possibly have helped blindside me to the extent of the commitment required from anyone genuinely wanting to enter into the priesthood. The sacrifices required simply didn't seem all that daunting at the time.

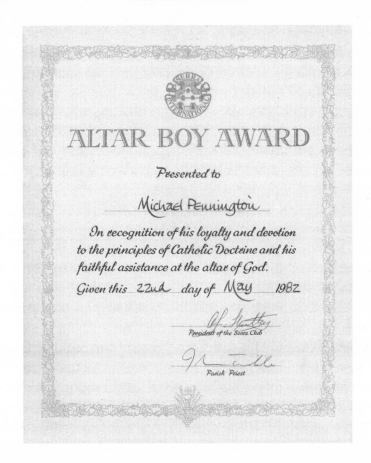

ALTAR BOY AWARD

Presented to

Michael Pennington

In recognition of his loyalty and devotion
to the principles of Catholic Doctrine and his
faithful assistance at the altar of God.

Given this 22nd day of May 1982

President of the Serra Club

Parish Priest

I remember my dad taking me aside after I'd yet again announced I was going to be a priest and saying, 'Are you serious about the priesthood – about following your vocation?' I had no idea what a vocation was. To be honest, I was probably as serious as I'd been about joining the Rebel Alliance after seeing *Star Wars*. In fact, I remember thinking Jedi Knights were basically kick-ass priests, but with swords. With a typical 10-year-old's disregard for the implications of my answer I simply said, 'Yes' and gave no more thought to the wheels that simple little word had set in motion.

My decision to go into the seminary was certainly tough on my family. I knew money was tight, but I now realise the boarding fees must have been a massive burden on my mum and dad.

The diocese used to decide what they thought families could afford and, as a result, my parents had to fork out for this endless list of school-sanctioned uniforms and assorted gym kits, which just about bankrupted them.

Family knitted what we couldn't afford. As a result, I would be permanently posted to the outfield during cricket in case my jumper brought shame on the school. My mum said she'd never spent so much in one shop – not to make me feel guilty, you understand: we just didn't do sprees in our house. My parents never said, 'Do you know what this is costing?' But I had a dawning awareness that they were making huge financial sacrifices, as well as some emotional ones I knew nothing about.

I'd find out later that my mum desperately didn't want me to go. She said nothing at the time, though – she wanted to support me and kept her fears well hidden, but I suspect that they ran deeper than the normal mothering instincts. I believe she was concerned about the potential for abuse at the seminary. Years earlier, she hadn't let me join the Cubs because apparently the then troop leader had instructed some boys that in order to get one badge, they had to run around the Scout hut in their undies!

Because I came from a family of practising Catholics, I think a lot of people thought my parents were living vicariously through me, that I was unwittingly fulfilling their dreams by going to the seminary. I know my dad was proud of me and what he thought might be my chosen path in life, but beyond that, other peoples' criticisms couldn't have been further from the truth.

The material necessities took a bit of sorting out, but otherwise at home – when I think back – there was almost a unilateral denial that the big day was coming. If anything, it was the parish as a whole that made me feel like I was torch-bearer for their collective ambitions in the build-up to my imminent departure. I remember a dinner lady at my junior school taking me to one side and looking at me with this odd expression of reverence. I thought for a moment she was going to burst into tears. Then she said to me, very earnestly, 'What you're doing is a wonderful thing. You know that, don't you?' All I can remember thinking is,

'Well, this is awkward,' because I didn't understand what all the fuss was about.

At heart I remained pretty carefree – like most 10-year-old boys – as to me, the prospect of this new school I'd be going to was all just a bit of fun. But when an ordinarily stand-offish dinner lady hugs you like that, you can be forgiven for thinking she knows something you don't. She made me feel more like a terminally sick kid being given one last treat: 'Am I ill? Why have you bought me a baseball cap? Why do all the adults keep hugging me?'

When I visited the seminary for my entrance exams/orientation day, the place looked positively idyllic. Near Wigan as it was, it had lakes for canoeing and fishing, two tennis courts, even its own nine-hole golf course! Upholland resembled a posh Butlin's, but with priests instead of Redcoats; in fact, I was a little disappointed not to see a mono-rail running around the grounds it felt so like going on holiday.

My older brother Mark had become very protective, and spoke his mind about his misgivings in my build-up to leaving. He was worried that I didn't entirely know what I was getting myself into – and God, he was right. A month earlier, he'd taken me on to the back field by Hankey's Well and said, 'You know where you're going, there's no sex and no booze, don't you? It ain't fuckin' worth it, if you ask me.'

I'd just shrugged. It was the first time this marvellous decision of mine had been directly challenged. 'Well, if you are gonna do it, you're gonna need a vice.' He'd taken out one of his Benson & Hedges, sparked it up and passed it to me. Teenage boys don't tend to be big on sharing, whether it's their B&H or their feelings. Offering me my first full cig, as inappropriate as it might seem, was the nicotine hug he was incapable of giving me himself, and it felt like a monumental gesture at the time.

3.

UPHOLLAND FIRST YEAR: 'UNDERLOW'

It's hard to do justice to just how frightening and real it felt that evening I was taken to Upholland to begin my first term. The last time I'd been there it was bright and fresh: sun had streamed in through the windows of the corridors and class rooms, and it had had a warm sense of tradition to it – proper, solid, wooden desks, and not a whiff of chipped seventies state-school Formica. Had the Harry Potter books been around at the time, then that place would've seemed like the epitome of Hogwarts. (That's why I cringe at J.K. Rowling's romanticisation of the whole boarding-school system. If you're ever in Cineworld St Helens and you hear someone murmuring, 'Stupid, reckless cow' behind you, you'll know who it is.)

In the daytime, Upholland presented itself as a near-magical kingdom – a castle full of potential for jolly japes and *Boy's Own* fun. At night, though, it was just the most imposing structure you could imagine, especially for an 11-year-old from a cosy three-up, three-down terrace. Walking through its huge doors and down its harsh grey stone or dark-stained hardwood corridors for the first time, I was terrified.

I felt completely overwhelmed. There was a feeling of nausea in the pit of my tummy, but the urge to retch was subdued by a tight panic in my chest. My dad was carrying my heavy luggage up endless stairs to the dormitory. My mum waited in the car. We'd said goodbye outside. I don't think she'd have allowed me to unpack had she taken a single step inside that place. And, looking back, I would have begged her to take me home.

My dad was talking away, trying to keep things upbeat, but I didn't really listen to a single word he said. All I was aware of was the awful realisation swimming around my head – like a panic-stricken cat in a washing machine mid-cycle – that was going, 'Oh God. Oh, no. I've made a terrible mistake!' And that's when the catastrophic difference between my first visit there, and that evening, really kicked in: I wouldn't be going home this time.

I was filled with utter dread. But my dad seemed so bloody pleased for me and I reckon that's the only thing that helped me hold it together just long enough to say goodbye without breaking down. That's why Mum – knowing she'd crumble, and thinking she was doing right by me – had opted to stay sobbing in the car.

I have never felt (and doubt I will ever feel) quite as alone as when my dad waved goodbye and closed the dormitory door behind him.

I sat on my bed, drew the useless little privacy curtain across, and cried as quietly as I could into my jumper. There were other new boys crying, but quietly too, as nobody wanted to appear a sissy, I suppose. The buzz of activity, of unpacking and finding a place for everything within our tiny allotted living spaces, was replaced with muffled sobs and snotty noses being wiped on damp woolly sleeves.

Of course it was acute homesickness: all I could think of was the fact that I wanted to go back to St Helens. All those memories, good or bad, had become instantly cherishable. Even the thought of the worst telling-off I ever got suddenly made me yearn for my mum and dad – 'Bollock me every day if you like, but please, please come and take me home.'

One lad decided that there definitely was a going back, and he made a run for it shortly before lights out. They spotted him running round the corridors looking for a payphone, then chased him down the long driveway that led to the front gates.

Diary 83   November

left family and friends behind and am now on the verge of my education that will, if succesful, prepare me for a life in the Catholic Priesthood. At the moment missing home and everything about it....

Have settled in now and yet always seem to be fighting this continual battle within, as do I suppose, all the students in this mutable boat of emotions. An ongoing conflict of wanting so much to be back home, a return to the 'norm'. No amount of family support can help, although according to popular St.Helens myth, I have none as I was sent here with   a religous knife in in my back. Little do they realise that, although I've made my decision to leave, its these same critics that makes my choice much more difficult to excecute. That triumphant send off, along with th continous encouragement of the community is the obligation that burdens me so, giving me such an unwanted self esteem How can I do this to my public? Someone of such social and political importance. Eleven years old with the world, but , more importantly St. Helens upon my shoulders.

The diary might be a fake, but not the sentiment contained within.

They brought him straight back to the dorm, even though he was demanding that a taxi take him home. Years on, I still can't watch that scene from *One Flew Over The Cuckoo's Nest* when Martini's character is dragged away kicking and screaming: 'I want my cigarettes now, Nurse Ratched, now, do you hear me?' without thinking of him.

We all made friends quickly in our year. We had to. There was no getting through the school day then playing with your street mates. Besides, there were only eleven of us. 'Underlow' was our collective name. They didn't mess around when it came to putting us in our place.

Over the next few months I didn't find myself praying for spiritual enlightenment or world peace, but rather for the daily home comforts denied us in some misguided pious belief that it would make us better priests one day. We would wake up and have to go and wash in a stone-cold basement with no warm water. It was long, dank and dark, with a row of twenty or so taps. There were a small number of cubicles with baths in them, and warm water available later in the day, but unless you had spare time during the weekends, the strict Monday–Friday regime meant that you could only really use them later in the evening.

If you did risk a bath at that time, someone might spot you taking the long walk from the dormitory with your robe and wash-bag, wait, and then throw cold water over the top. Or, more likely, lock the main doors and turn out all the lights. The same would happen if you dared to use the toilets at the far end of the cellar in the evening, and it was a bloody scary room to be trapped in when pitch black.

It took years of rehabilitation before my bowels stopped going into lockdown along with the setting sun, because the only alternative was a toilet at the end of our dormitory, slap bang underneath the hatch leading to the bell tower. And legend had it that Betty Eccles, a former resident of the building (I know, she sounds like a bun, but we were only 11, for God's sake!) hung herself in that tower and haunted our dorm. There was even a Betty Eccles night when Upholland legend had it that she left the tower and visited any poor soul situated in one of our dormitory's 'horse-boxes' (these were the beds spaced in the unfortunate position without a window because of a supporting arch, which had no direct natural sunlight as a result).

When that night arrived, along with bedtime, we moved like a Spartan regiment in tight formation up the stairs to our dormitory. We might've looked the part, but lacked the bravery of the original 300. And, as we opened the door to the dorm, this bloody thing sprang at us, howling hysterically.

Eleven kids screamed in pure, abject piss-your-pants terror and tried to leg it at the same time. Unfortunately, it wasn't a wide enough staircase for a mass escape, so obviously there were casualties. I know I trampled and stamped on my new mates and I didn't give a shit. I didn't want to die.

The 'thing' screamed again, but none of us dared turn back. Despite it being dark, I was seriously considering taking my chances jumping through the gap between the banisters. (If you ever find yourself on a flight with me and you notice that I have blagged the extra leg-room by sitting next to the emergency exit over the wings, then it's only fair to let you know now that in the case of a real emergency I would be absolutely bloody useless.)

On this occasion, I used my foot and another kid's head (I think his name was Gerard) as a pivot to prise myself free from the rest of the group. I flew into the wall and was already turning on a tuppence to jump the next full flight of stairs when I heard somebody laughing loud and hard. My instinct to leap was postponed just for a moment: I wondered if maybe 'it' had caught someone and was now temporarily sated in its blood-lust – your brain tends to work bloody quickly in those life-and-death situations.

I had a slight head-start so dared to waste time looking back to see who had bought the farm at the hands of Betty Eccles. Turning around expecting to see a fellow Underlow being dragged back through the door, kicking and screaming (hopefully with a little bit of piss running down his leg too), what I saw instead was a fucking fifth-year lad peeling off a rubber 'old woman' mask while doubling-up with laughter.

'You wankers! Ha ha ha!'

I actually pissed myself a bit more at this point out of sheer relief. I couldn't say anything back though, because my heart was doing a damn good impression of my arse.

'You should've seen your faces! Ha ha ha!'

I couldn't – I was stepping on most of them making my cowardly escape.

'Tossers! Now go to bed and get ready for the real thing! Ha ha ha!'

It actually would've been funny if you were in on the joke, but I had a damp crotch, and my bed was right next door to a horse-box, so I was in no mood for laughter. It sounds awful, but I still can't remember who my neighbour was. I just wished that they would satisfy the ghost and she wouldn't come looking for a chubby dessert.

Jesus, what kind of night those poor lads must have had in the horse-boxes! I was only next door to one and I lay wide-awake, eyes tight shut, my rosary beads wrapped tight around my hand in case Betty appeared over the top of the partition. I distinctly remembered cursing myself for listening to Iron Maiden's 'The Number of the Beast' at Alan Hale's house, despite my dad saying that it was the Devil's music.

I actually hated heavy metal so I was glad to reject it in my soul, but I had looked at the album cover, and Iron Maiden's mascot 'Eddie' was the template for what I expected to attack me during the night. The wife of Eddie. The dead but unavenged grandmother of Eddie. Skin deteriorated and stretched just far enough to show radical gum decay but not quite enough to look like something off of a comically crap ghost train.

I can't remember falling to sleep that night; it was only that complete and utter terror finally gave way to sheer exhaustion. I didn't even egg anyone on into meeting up in 'the cupboard', as I'd already decided – seeing as I wasn't actually in a horse-box – that safety in numbers was a stupid idea.

A daft lad in a rubber mask did more for faith in the Almighty that night than all of Upholland's outdated regimes. I prayed the entire night for God to save me from that fictitious ghost. I made deals with him, including a complete embargo on masturbation, if he would only spare me and let Betty feast on another. A lay student maybe: at least then he wasn't losing a future foot-soldier.

We were allowed access to television only when, and if, our head of year, Father Towers, allowed us to watch it in his room. And then for perhaps half an hour, tops. And what 11-year-old doesn't want to watch the singing nuns tearing up the stage at Notre Dame Cathedral?

Father Towers was one of the youngest priests there; it was his first year. He was incredibly kind and patient, but had a manner to him that was almost permanently apologetic. I often wondered if that was a past seminary's doing, or just his nature. Either way, you could easily make him fidget with awkward questions. Kids can be quite cruel when they sense a weakness like that in an adult, and Father Towers seemed better suited to a quiet country parish somewhere – he lacked the sadistic streak needed to really make a name for himself in his new environment.

I never had a cup of tea the entire time I was at Upholland. And I'd come off the breast and straight onto the teapot as a child. They'd make it in this huge urn, but it was thick with sugar, which made me gag. Like a diabetic Oliver Twist, but asking for less, not more, I timidly requested a little pot of unsweetened tea for those of us unable to handle the saccharine rush. Judging by their reaction, you'd think I'd suggested passing out free condoms to the more promiscuous students dabbling in homosexuality.

And then there was the food in general. Now, in fairness, I was an incredibly fussy eater back then (if only that had stuck to this day). It was a sort of extension of the homesickness – I wanted things cooked the way my mum and dad did it.

I was obsessed with texture and presentation. Apart from morning cereal and sausages, every other meal served there was an ordeal, although tea-time was a jam butty free-for-all. It was help yourself, and I bloody well did. It was meant as a snack before supper but it became my staple diet at Upholland. It was a miracle I didn't get rickets.

My attachment to sausages actually got me into my one and only fight at the seminary. There was a fifth-form prick, a lay-student, whose tan from countless summers in the South of France failed to conceal a pompous ruddiness in his cheeks – probably from generations of in-breeding. He was like a cross between Hawaiian teen-idol Glenn Medeiros and Rumpole of the Bailey. I couldn't stand him. He awoke in me an inverted snobbery that I still struggle to control to this day.

Anyhow, he came over to our table one lunchtime, and started lifting our sausages onto his plate with a big, stupid grin on his face. I saw red and stuck a fork in his hand, hard. He went ballistic, but I couldn't take him seriously because he spoke like someone from *Upstairs, Downstairs* – honestly, you'd think he was bollocking a scullery maid at the turn of the century. He didn't dare physically kick off in the dining-hall, but he made it quite clear that I was in for it later that day.

Now, I was not by any means a brawler as a kid, but I had a strong sense of moral righteousness. And being as unhappy as I was, I can remember thinking, 'Sod him, what have I got to lose?' He waited for me outside my last lesson of the day. I think he thought he'd make me sweat and then bully a squirming apology out of me. But I just flew at him. His four years of seniority and height advantage meant nothing to me; I couldn't care less if he did give me a 'ruddy good hiding'.

He obviously wasn't expecting it, because I got a good few punches in before he swung back at me. My dad used to say, 'It's not the size of the dog in the fight; it's the size of the fight in the dog.' Well, I'd found the perfect outlet for all my discontent with Upholland and was not about to give up, even though I could feel these heavy thumps hitting the back of my head.

My face was buried in his chest as I swung away madly at him. He pushed me away, trying to get a decent angle at which to hit me, but I just ran at him again. I was ape-shit furious, out of control. I wrapped his tie around my left hand and yanked him down so I could smash his stupid face in with my right. He ploughed into my forehead as I was looking up at him, desperate to land one square on his nose.

I belted him good and hard, but that only seemed to make him angrier. He grabbed my hair, trying to manoeuvre me again into a perfect striking distance. I shook him free and threw punch after punch until there was nothing in front of me but red mist.

The next thing I knew, we had been yanked apart by a passing priest and were being made to stand against the wall outside Father Samuel's office. My adversary was fuming, but it was the best I'd felt since I'd got there. The swelling over my left eye and the headache from the blows to the back of my head barely registered. I was experiencing something very like euphoria – better than any cry under the covers in the wee small hours. Part of me had managed to say, 'Enough is enough' and I was buzzing off it. That's probably why I wasn't anywhere near as nervous as I should have been when we were ushered into Sammy's office.

You know in war films when you think the Nazis are bad enough, but then the SS turn up and make them look like a bunch of bed-wetters? Well, Sammy had that very same effect. He was the last remnant of the Spanish Inquisition. He was Darth Vader. He had his own terrifying theme tune that played in your head as he walked by.

He was short but no less intimidating for that, and walked in that quick, determined manner that so many little people tend to. Behind his glasses he had keen, mean, piercing eyes that made you feel like you'd been captured on CCTV. He watched you intently, like a bird looks at a worm before dragging it out of the ground, waiting for any sign of weakness, his head tilting in a sharp, short move when he suspected something was rotten in the state of Upholland.

That man was a human lie detector. And when he wasn't scrutinising you, he had a way of completely dismissing you – like a crap doctor who conducts an appointment with a couldn't-care-less tone whilst staring out of the window the entire time, making you feel unworthy of the most basic common decencies, such as eye contact. Father Sammy reserved this for the times when he knew a gripe was genuine, but had no intention of resolving the matter. He could be menacing and then instantly casual. It was like being 007 in Goldfinger's lair – you knew he expected you to die, and he couldn't give a toss.

Father Sammy managed all of our finances. Our pocket-money was given to him, and he in turn would decide if your individual request was deemed worthy of releasing funds. Some kids used to hide cash in the dorms, under mattresses like teenage pensioners, but you were for it if it was found. It was claimed it was to stop us abusing the once-weekly tuck-shop facility, but really it was just another means of control.

After all, who needed Mars Bars when you had cups of tea that would make Willy Wonka OD? No, Father Sammy was an accountant, not a spiritual guru. I had to virtually beg him for my own cash so I could send away for a calligraphy set. (Oh aye, I was hardcore! I had me some mad scribing skills going on.) You would think he suspected I was buying smack the way he questioned me. What could possibly be detrimental about fountain pens with a slightly broader nib? 'That curve on your peculiarly detailed capital R, be it a devil's tail? Burn the witch!' God, it really bugged me. There I was, trying to get through the days with a hobby that would make any state-school teacher spontaneously combust with admiration, yet all I got from Sammy Scrooge was a seething reluctance to part with my own pocket money.

One thing was certain. Neither the fifth-former nor I was coming out of this particular encounter any the richer. As we stood there awaiting judgement in his office, Sammy asked if we had anything to say for ourselves. The man was normally a human laxative where I was concerned, but I was still on my adrenaline high. I knew I could hardly pipe up with, 'This has easily been my best day here so far!' so I just shrugged.

Posh-Boy Pob cracked, however, and tried to claim that I had been taunting and bullying him. Sammy turned to me but I offered nothing more than my 'As if?' face. For me, for once, whatever punishment would be served seemed well worth the crime.

Sammy studied both of us for what seemed like an age but I had nothing to hide. Eventually, he turned back to his big book of numbers and delivered judgement in a very matter-of-fact manner: 'If this boy is capable of bullying somebody your size, then perhaps you deserve to be bullied. Now get out of here, the pair of you.'

This left me with a grudging respect for Father Samuel. I mean, he remained for the best part a by-the-book disciplinarian/disciplinary dick/douche-bag, but that felt like the first time I'd seen common sense prevail in that place. And as the years have passed, although I can't quite qualify this beyond a gut feeling, I've come to believe that he was at odds with some of the goings-on at Upholland. I think he did what he believed was best by us in a mean-minded, bureaucratic kind of way but, overwhelmingly, he hid behind the day-to-day economics of running such a big institution: not so much a collaborator, more an anguished passive enabler to the system. I think lots of decent priests found ways and means of distracting themselves from some of the more distasteful realities of Upholland in this way.

Outside Sammy's office, my bouffant aggressor made it quite clear that our feud was far from over. I offered to go again straight away as my blood was still up, but he strode off with all the camp menace of a semi-beaten *piñata* donkey. Still, I knew I couldn't rely on me being able to lose my rag as effectively as I'd done earlier on any other random day. So I called in the big artillery.

I'll never forget the weekend our Mark accompanied my parents up for a Saturday afternoon visit.

4.

ORWELL'S WORDS WERE MY SILENT LULLABY

There were some pretty rich lay-students at our school, and some quite amazing cars would glide up the driveway on those days: one or two even had those dignitaries' mini flags on the front. Which is what made my family's entrance all the more spectacular in our turd-brown Mk II Ford Cortina estate that someone had given my dad because it was cheaper than paying to have it towed away as scrap.

The clutch was knackered, and the handbrake was well on its way out, so Dad had to plan his routes carefully in order to avoid any hill stops. The car was burning oil and would let out big, black clouds through the exhaust as it jerked its way into parking spots like a geriatric clown car.

I never felt any embarrassment over it, though: I was always just too damn pleased to see my folks. It was the most precious few hours in my fortnight. And as decrepit as the car might've looked, nothing was cooler than watching my brother Mark climb out of the back dressed in full 'fuck you' Mod uniform.

Eat your heart out Harry Potter. Although on closer inspection there was little magic at work behind those imposing stone walls.

At this particular moment, he was my Ace Face. He lifted his shades and gave the building a brilliantly disapproving once-over. He wanted onlookers to be in no doubt about his immediate disdain for the place. After big hugs and hellos with Mum and Dad, I took Mark for a tour of the seminary, knowing he was dead keen on sorting out our bit of business.

'Right, where's this gobshite who's been giving you grief?'

There were a couple of likely places he'd be. We checked there, but no joy. Then, as we walked through the double doors near the refectory, I saw him walking towards us from the far end of the corridor.

He stopped, I pointed. 'That's him!'

The gobshite realised immediately what was going on, because I'd told him my brother was going to come down and paste him. He'd scoffed and made naff threats, but had at least not made to hit me again after that day in Sammy's office. Now, he bolted and our Mark went after him like a whippet.

I gave chase, mad keen to see the carnage for myself, but I couldn't keep pace. Our Mark was a fast scrum-half, and Moulin Rouge-chops was running like he had the devil on his tail.

Mark came back about twenty minutes later. He'd lost him up in the woods by the golf course. He told me how he'd shouted at the top of his lungs exactly what he was going to do once he did get hold of him. Rag Dolly Anna must've heard him, because he never came near me again.

I suppose it was for the best that Mark had to leave it at verbal threats. He was lean and wiry and could punch his weight painfully well. I might've been expelled had he actually caught up with his quarry that day (maybe that's what I was inadvertently after).

Afterwards, we had a smoke around the back of the big trees on the far side of the lake. I didn't feel the need to put on a brave face in front of our Mark. He was at an age where he felt it absolutely necessary to be anti-Establishment. He was listening to *Quadrophenia* and brawling every other night, whereas playing Wham's 'Bad Boys' in the common room was my revolutionary highlight. One lad even got carried away enough to smash his mug of hot Bovril off a wall.

We couldn't hope to compete with the kind of riot enjoyed by the inmates of HMP Strangeways, but it was still a gesture that suggested I was not the only Underlow aggrieved with the regime – not quite a dirty protest, more a meaty liquid remonstration in tribute to George Michael's determination to say enough was enough. How far short I was falling of my brother's example was clear evidence of how institutionalised I was becoming.

It wasn't just Mark who was putting me to shame in rebelliousness terms, either. There was also a fellow inmate's mum, who was a living legend as far as we were all concerned.

'Where's that fucking Father Sammy? I wanna word!' We could hear her screaming from a mile away. She was the only person who used our private nickname as an official title. Well, she added the 'fucking' bit, but we all thought that a bold stroke of genius. Sammy hated the banshee, you could tell. He couldn't intimidate her, and he certainly couldn't reason with her. And she wasn't deterred by the dog collar. She'd call him all sorts.

'You're a bully, you poisoned little dwarf, you!' You could've sold tickets for the spectacle, had anyone been brave enough to stand and watch – most students hid around corners but still within earshot. And you were basically within earshot anywhere within the seminary walls. Eventually, Sammy started finding things to do away from his office on those Saturdays.

You had to find fun where you could at Upholland. And we did. It was a survival technique. Plus we were eleven, for God's sake. I used to try and get all the other lads in my year to meet up after lights out. There were these huge linen cabinets in the centre of the dorm, and two cupboards at either end could easily accommodate six or more of us.

I know it all sounds a bit *Dead Poets Society*, but without access to a mate's house whose dad kept a poorly concealed stash of porno films back home, this was the only alternative. We didn't play Wank on a Biscuit or anything like that – all we had was a baking apple. We'd just sit up whispering – breaking rules and dodging the dorm monitor.

To the rest of the lads this was just a bit of fun, but to me it was essential. I couldn't sleep at Upholland; I could never just climb into bed and nod off. There was too much time put aside there for contemplation, and it was hard to stop my mind racing at the end of the day.

Insomnia wasn't recognised as a genuine affliction, and I certainly didn't understand it as a condition back then. I was merely labelled as disruptive because I wanted everyone to be awake when I was: like Bagpuss, they could only go to sleep once I had. I envied tiredness in others. Sitting up late in that cupboard, even on nights when nobody else was up for messing, was always preferable to lying in my bed thinking sad or scary thoughts.

I tried reading, which I loved. Had they allowed me a lamp I'd have happily read throughout the night, but 'lights out' meant lights out. I was eleven at the time, and getting to grips with George Orwell's *1984*. Now, I can understand why that book might have been considered subversive in a seminary setting –

in there the anti-regime rhetoric felt like a true God-send – but nobody ever bothered to ask me what it was that was holding my attention so successfully. Their only concern was the fact that I was reading when I shouldn't be.

Deprived of light and the relative sanity of gifted authors, my head would embark on an evening of relentless self-interrogation. *1984* had been light relief in contrast to the tortures my own mind would concoct. Orwell's words were my silent lullaby, with thoughts of rats gnawing through a victim's cheek providing sweet relief and the chance to dupe my wired brain to sleep.

I've heard people use the phrase a lot since, but that was the only time in my life that I actually devoured books. I read *Animal Farm* in the same year that I heard whoops and hollers from the quad because FUCKING MARGARET THATCHER had got back into power. I knew that my dad would be knackered for another four years as a result, and we were stuck with the clown-mobile for the foreseeable future.

As spring dragged into summer, I made the most of the natural light. I read *The Road to Wigan Pier*; Orwell's sense of social injustice struck a real chord with me. And although much of the book might've gone over my head, I still felt this overwhelming frustration. Why did things at that place – much like in this bloke's books – have to still be the way they were, just because someone, at some point, had said so?

Christ never mentioned telephones in the Bible. So why were we not allowed to call home and talk to the people we loved? Why? Because God needed anguish to prove that we loved him? How could it be that they had misinterpreted his message so badly? Where was the love? Had they just flicked through the Bible and missed the bits concerning compassion?

By claiming it was all about God and his will, 'they' had squeezed him out of the moral equation altogether. The desire for free speech, the notion of debate, was treated like a sickness, and the place felt more like a Victorian asylum for the 'treatment' of emotional and spiritual awareness. It was all about stripping away your individuality to make you unthinkingly accept a regime that entirely contradicted my upbringing (my Catholic upbringing! That was the irony of it).

What Upholland tried to drum into us was that it wasn't our place to question such fundamental issues. They wanted blind obedience, and that flew hard in the face of my natural inquisitiveness. In so many sermons I'd heard of awakenings, of folks' eyes being opened to the wonder and glory of the Lord. So why, in training to become his representatives here on earth, were we being taught to close our eyes tight shut and ignore these nagging doubts?

I got quite pally with some of the sixth-formers, partly to see how they were dealing with these tricky issues, but mainly because one of them was a St Helens lad, Mousey, who knew my family back home. They soon realised that I was up for the *craic* and didn't blub, so they rolled me down four flights of stairs in a bin one day, just to see if I'd puke. Trust me, it wasn't bullying. They dunked me in a bath and threw me into choir practice sopping wet, but I was laughing as they did it. I remember enjoying the notoriety of getting a detention for dampness.

Detention? It was pointless! We did two hours of forced silent study in the prep hall every weekday anyway! I'd finish my 'not-at-homework' in twenty minutes and doodle. Nothing they made us do made much sense. I didn't need to study under duress: I was up there in the top two of our year, grade-wise. It was like they were punishing you with further silence for being bright. I missed comics, so I drew my own. It was mainly sci-fi stuff, inspired by *2000 AD* – a comic I had maintained a healthy obsession with since an early age.

The sixth-form block was a no-go area. But they had a payphone: telecommunications and a private room were their privileges for sticking it out that long. I would go without my weekly chocolate fix and use the money to call home instead. Now, if you got caught, you were knackered. Some of the sixth-formers took a sadistic pleasure in policing it, but that just involved a slap. The greatest threat was a passing priest.

Still, I'd sneak in there and ring my mum. For the most part nobody bothered with me. I'd call and tell lies about how everything was fine. I just wanted any news regarding home life. The trick was being able to cry instantly if a priest came striding down the corridor.

I soon learnt to sob on demand. It wasn't hard: as soon as I heard my mum's voice I'd have a huge lump in my throat, anyway. I was bloody convincing. I would start blubbing and pretend that I was unaware of the priest's presence. Ordinarily they'd put this down to homesickness and yank you off the phone. The trick was the delivery of the line, 'I can't believe she's dead!' Cue more fake sobs.

Mum was used to these random outbursts as she was in on the scam. She'd talk about how bingo had gone while I put in an Oscar-winning performance on the other end of the phone. The priest would think better of interrupting me, and walk away. The amount of imaginary relatives I lost during my time there, you'd think the Black Death had struck St Helens.

They were just daft ways of bucking the system, but they were still important to me. They helped me deal with my growing discontentment. Like an escape committee in a POW camp, I felt that any disruption to the routine was worthwhile.

It was only my jam-butty hips that stopped me digging a tunnel.

5.

THE VATICAN DIDN'T STAND A CHANCE FROM THAT MOMENT ON

Once I managed to blag a cigarette from a fifth-form lad. I can't remember if it was Elliot or Enzo – they were two Italian twins who were a great laugh and only too happy to oblige. They had even less fondness than me for Wooster the sausage thief, and loved the fact that I had gone toe to toe with him. I remember them telling me how their dad had caught them smoking and made them eat a packet of fags, so their only stipulation was that I had to say 'the fag fairy gave it to me' should I get caught.

The handover felt suitably dangerous and over-dramatic. I had agreed to meet another Underlow, Peter, to smoke it in the linen cupboard down in the basement wash-room. There was a push-up plywood flap in there that gained you entry to a tiny annexe, like a mini attic.

The intention was to kick back like a couple of stoners, but we actually smoked it in record-breaking time. We were bricking ourselves. Four flushes later the last bit of evidence was gone. We washed our hands, brushed our teeth and made our way back to the common room. We hadn't got through the door before Sammy called our names from outside his office in a tone that told us we were busted.

Apparently, we were the only first-years to get caught smoking in Upholland's hundred-year history. Somebody must've grassed us up, but I couldn't work out who; Sammy wasn't telling, he was enjoying the interrogation too much. And there was no point in denying it when those eyes were scanning you. I could do nothing but nod and pull my best 'regret' face.

Peter seemed quite chuffed at being charged with a seminary first. Maybe it was just a nervous grin, but Sammy wasn't impressed. I was determined not to tell him where I'd got the coffin nail from, but he didn't actually bother to ask. It was more about us letting down the principles on which the college was founded, letting ourselves fall victim to a heinous and harmful temptation and blah blah blah. It was only when he asked us what our parents might think when he told them that my arse completely collapsed.

I'd been juggling my quiet contempt for the place with a glowing trainee-priest presentation to my mum and dad. And while our Mark had made smoking cool and anti-Establishment, I didn't want to break my parents' hearts. Smashing the system was one thing, but bringing shame on those you loved by fucking up like this was a different matter altogether.

I stood there back in that office like a junkie desperate not to do hard time. I begged Father Sammy not to phone my mum. And that's when he knew he'd found my weak spot – he even had his hand poised over the phone, the devious git. In the space of a few moments I went from cocky rebel to desperate witch at Salem screaming for mercy. He had me just where he wanted me. It was more an initiation than a bollocking: standing in his office pleading with him, I became a dues-paid, card-carrying member of the please-don't-tell-the-outside-world brigade.

'Please, please, please don't tell my mum!'

My parents' love and respect was all I had to help me get through my time in this horrible place. I desperately didn't want him to tell them I'd become a bad kid. I felt lost and ill at the prospect of being morally abandoned. They had replaced the Church in my private sense of worship. They were all I had faith in. If he called home and dropped this bombshell, he would shatter my belief system.

'I'm sorry. I'm really sorry. I won't do it again, I promise. Please don't call my mum and dad. Please.'

In the end, he didn't call them, but not because my begging had swayed him. Instead, he held that threat over me for months. Sammy had found the chink in my armour. I actually prayed that he'd have a stroke and be rendered speechless. I tried to imagine him shaking his head in my dad's direction on a visiting Saturday as I silenced him with big fat spoonfuls of yogurt . . . yogurt I'd peed in, after eating a field-full of asparagus.

We earned ourselves a mention at evening prayers in the main chapel. Well, a very obvious reference to the evils of tobacco, and a couple of hundred heads turning to stare in our direction. The old me would've thrived off of the kudos had Sammy not found my Achilles heel. Still, beyond my personal fears, I couldn't care less about the silent moral outrage of the rest of the college.

I think that Peter, being a lay-student with no desire what-soever to go into the priesthood, actually enjoyed the notoriety of our scandalous behaviour. He was just a naughty boy. I was the future head of a parish and therefore should know better. I always felt sad for lay-students. I mean, us students who'd heard the call to do God's work had put ourselves in that place. I don't think I could've forgiven my parents had they sent me there to get myself a 'proper' education.

Maybe that was what gave Peter such an obvious sense of satisfaction, maybe not. Still, God love him, he sat through evening prayers with the same big fixed grin that he'd had in Sammy's office.

As summer came, things improved at Upholland: there were more outdoor activities available; it stayed light till much later so I could read more in the evenings; and the whole building warmed up and the trudge downstairs to wash in the morning was a much more pleasant exercise. I'd got to grips with the day-to-day routine and had settled into the idea that this was my life from now on. Anger gave way to a faint hope that I could make a go of this priesthood lark.

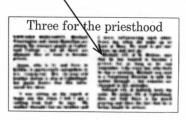

Michael (12), of St. Helens, says that he has wanted to become a priest for as long as he can remember. Like every boy who feels he has a vocation, Michael was sent to a Vocational Director to talk the matter through — but remains unchanged in his attitudes.

Three for the priesthood

The poster boy for the next generation of clergymen!

I had made a really good friend in Simon, a Geordie lad in Underlow. He was a bright kid and great *craic*. I think his dad worked away and his mum couldn't always make the home visiting days, so he would come back to St Helens with me on those precious Saturday afternoons out. We'd nick off over the field for a fag with our Mark and eat our own body weight in whatever treats my mum had got in. Simon was 'proper' working class in my eyes. We were both from backgrounds that didn't have a great deal in terms of money, but made up for it in pride.

I could never understand why pride was considered a sin. It's what gave most folk I knew back home the strength to endure through difficult times. And, under the Thatcher government, it was the worst of times.

We liked to dress smart, even in the absence of lasses to impress. I took to wearing shirts with tiepins in them. Burton's finest. God, to think I thought them so smart. I'd hit that age where I wanted clothes for my birthday: Slazenger jumpers were the epitome of cool as far as I was concerned. It was the time that I was first becoming aware of gaining weight, and I think dressing to impress was a way of combating my growing self-consciousness. My burgundy Slazenger helped hide a multitude of sins, but others proved more difficult to conceal. Puberty was upon me, and you couldn't be in a worse place when those hormones started raging than a seminary.

My first interview day at Upholland! You can see in the background they're going all out to pitch the place as an upmarket Butlins.

You see, ten-year-olds sitting their entrance exams don't tend to think in terms of long-term consequences. It had seemed perfectly acceptable that marriage was banned within my future career. Sex wasn't on the agenda then. Back home at St Austin's Junior School, I had wanted a girlfriend as a status symbol, but there were no real base urges involved beyond snogging, so what big sacrifice was there in celibacy? How was I to know that within the space of a year, the fairer sex would be dominating all my waking thoughts (not to mention my nightly indiscretions)? Ten was a crazy age to seriously consider going celibate.

In the last few months before I'd left for Upholland, I'd started to fall prey to random and demanding 'stiffies'. I had to relieve myself. I couldn't discuss it with anyone because I was plagued with guilt. It felt so damned good, it had to be wrong. Either that, or I was a unique medical phenomenon, because why else would nobody have ever thought to forewarn me of this? If this was normal, then surely somebody would've taken the time to explain to me that the contents of my Y-fronts would turn into the orgasmic equivalent of Blackpool Pleasure Beach?

I actually thought I could be a freak of nature who might be paraded around medical seminars the world over should my dirty revelation ever come to the attention of others. Or maybe I'd invented it? Just like Darwin, I was torn between my responsibility to disclose one of mankind's greatest ever discoveries and my fear of incurring the wrath of The Mother Church.

I kept telling myself, 'This can't go on. When you get to Upholland, it'll have to stop.' Before leaving for the seminary, I went hell for leather to get it out of my system. One night, I threw my penis what can best be described as a wild going-away party, and beat the poor thing half to death in the process.

I actually thought I'd broken it. I had a panic attack, convinced that I'd done some permanent damage. I sat downstairs with it resting on a bag of frozen peas, terrified in case anyone else got up in the night. I was a wanna-be lover, not a fighter, so how did my genitals end up looking like Sly Stallone at the end of *Rocky II*?

I sat there into the early hours, too ashamed to pray for help, and too embarrassed to dare think of seeking medical assistance. I eventually went back to bed, slept a little on my back with legs akimbo, and left for school the next day walking like a chimpanzee that had just had a vasectomy.

But even that terrifying ordeal didn't manage to purge me of the urge. You'll never have a more guilt-ridden moment than your first 'self love' session at a seminary. You're waiting for sirens to go off and a gang of priests in riot gear to come charging in, restraining you with a tight bed sheet like that scene from *Full Metal Jacket*, before smacking you with multiple bars of Pope-on-a-rope soap wielded in towels.

Occasionally, on a Saturday, the priests would take us out of the seminary for a swimming trip. They'd leave us at Skelmersdale Baths, but we'd wait for the minibus to leave and then go straight out to the shopping centre to follow girls around. (We'd wet our hair later in the sinks so as not to raise suspicion when they collected us.)

We were so socially inept, but, temporarily free from our all-male environment, we were desperate. It must have been terrifying for those girls to be followed around Topshop by a group of eleven-year-old trainee priests, capable of nothing more than gawping at them, slack-jawed, eyes burning with wonder and desire, desperately storing up memories of the female anatomy for our respective wank-banks.

I apologise to any of my unwitting fantasy co-stars, but anything was better than the night I found myself 'getting off' over thoughts of the seminary's dinner lady. She must've been in her sixties at least. No offence to her, she was a sweet old gal, but it was the adolescent masturbatory equivalent of drinking your own urine when cast adrift at sea with no fresh water. And it was an agonisingly slow walk of shame taking my plate back to the kitchen hatch the following day.

If I wasn't lying awake at night feeling homesick, I was busy exorcising my unholy urges. And I was genuinely worried that this might impede my chances of making a half-decent priest one day. Was there a technique for keeping your hands north of the elastic pyjama border, which they would share with us at a later date? This was a basic instinct that was growing in its intensity whilst they just seemed to expect us to ignore it.

I tried going cold turkey, but then wet dreams kicked in – and my subconscious had a far filthier imagination than me. Up to that point, my indiscretions had been low-budget Dogme-inspired short movies. My wet dreams were multi-million-dollar summer blockbusters with an A-list line-up and a supporting cast of hundreds. I was damned if I did, and damned when I didn't.

That's why I was so excited when Father Cornforth, who had been a parish priest local to Simon's home town, but who was now teaching at the seminary, offered to take him and a friend away for a night at an orienteering hostel. A school from his old parish were there on a trip, and he was going to go and say mass for them as there was an upcoming Holy Day of Obligation. Simon nominated me to go along with him, and not only would we get away from Upholland for two days, but girls would be there too!

You can't know what a mind-blowing proposition that was for two wanton overnight escapees from God's borstal. I packed my coolest jumpers and my tiepin with the over-tie chain. We were so excited driving down there. Tony – Father Cornforth was cool enough to let us drop the 'Father' title during the journey – was great fun. He didn't stand on ceremony and talked to us like we were young men, not Underlows.

There was nothing pious about the guy and he didn't have that underlying bitterness that a lot of the other priests seemed to have. I always imagined Tony was one of those at constant loggerheads with Church bureaucracy; he was a different breed who seemed to understand the need to connect with students rather than throw the rule-book at them. He was also proof that you could serve God and still have a sense of humour. Plus he taught judo, so he was also kick-ass. The man could do no wrong in my eyes. I can honestly say that I might be sitting here writing Sunday's sermon right now had Upholland had more priests like him.

We got to the hostel in time for the evening meal. The other boys there must have thought us soft arses, but Simon and I were in seventh heaven sitting in amongst a gang of girls talking away to them. God, it was great! We were a bit of a novelty item and got bombarded with questions about life at the seminary. I felt so normal, despite our minor celebrity status, and that was the lovely thing about it. The other lads didn't seem to have a clue what they were missing out on, so there was zero opposition. Then the question of girlfriends came up. There was one girl in particular who seemed astonished at the idea of no relationships with the fairer sex.

'Not even kissing? But you're not actually priests yet!'

'I know, it's rubbish, innit?'

'Not at all?'

'Not even on your birthday, or really sunny days!'

Her name was Lynne. She had this gorgeous, tight bubble-perm and a real cheeky smile to her. And she was the easiest lass to talk to. Attitude-wise, she was classic tomboy, but nonetheless beautiful for it.

It might sound corny, but chatting away to her I felt like I'd known her for years. She was so matter-of-fact and there was no awkwardness with her. I loved the way she seemed to understand my frustration with life back at the seminary. It was a killer when we had to break it up and go to our respective rooms. I didn't want that evening to end.

The room with the boys' bunks in it proved itself an odd revelation: while it was a real novelty for them to be spending a few nights away from home, for Simon and myself it was the unfortunate norm. They thought it great fun, chatting away till their teacher would stick his head around the door and rollock them.

'Now this is your last warning. Settle down and get some sleep! Try taking a leaf out of these boys' books.'

He was referring to me and Simon, of course. We were roughly the same age as the other boys, and they were a decent enough mob, but there was a massive intellectual gap between us and them. I felt like I was umpteen years their senior – not in any condescending way, but I just couldn't get rid of a nagging suspicion that they knew nothing about the bigger world beyond their front door. All the things they were slagging off, everything they thought was lame or unfair, I yearned for on a daily basis. It was the first time that I realised my childhood was slipping away from me at an alarming rate. I lay there feeling cheated of something. I wanted to not give a shit, just like the other lads in that room, but I couldn't.

I was 11 going on 40. I had lost the innocence that they all so rightly took for granted. I could've cried, but how embarrassing would that have been? Instead, I turned my thoughts to the beautiful tomboy and fell asleep smiling at a daft dream that I was heading back home to their school with her the next day. And there was no stiffy. Suddenly, I was all about the romance.

We went down for breakfast the following morning and the girls had reserved us spots on the benches next to them. This place was a dry dream come true! We ate and talked and already I was dreading leaving later that day.

My bubble-permed beauty and her friend asked if Simon and I wouldn't mind nicking off for a wee while, as they wanted to show us something outside. They made it sound very matter of fact and harmless.

'Yeah, 'course.'

Would I mind? I'd have shown my arse to the archbishop if that gorgeous gal had asked me to.

We excused ourselves from the table with a demeanour as studiedly casual as Jeffrey Archer hooked up to a lie detector. Not that we actually thought we were going to get up to anything, but because just the four of us left, it felt almost like a mini double-date.

We left by a side door and then Lynne actually took my hand and led me around to the back of the big stone building. There was a rickety doorway leading into a small lean-to where muddy shoes and wet coats were kept. I turned around to say something to Simon but the other lass had led him around the far side of the structure. My heart was thumping nineteen to the dozen.

'Listen, Michael. We've been talking, yeah? And we've decided that it's not fair that you don't get to kiss anybody.'

I could barely speak but just about managed to croak, 'Um, yeah, like I said, it's, erm, it's a bit rubbish.'

'Well then, now's your chance.'

And with that, Lynne put her hands either side of my face and kissed me. I mean she properly kissed me. Full lips and open mouthed.

The Vatican didn't stand a chance from that moment on.

My head swam with all these new incredible sensations. I raised my hands and let my fingers hang in the soft, tight curls of her perm. Our noses rubbed gently together as we switched sides mid-kiss. I'd never, in my entire life up to that moment, experienced anything as wonderful as those lips.

For all my dummy-runs late at night back at the seminary, I was not prepared for this. And I'd have never dared go in for a kiss myself. But, thankfully, Lynne had initiated it, and she definitely knew what was she was doing. She made reciprocating that beautiful gesture just as easy as talking to her.

That first kiss seemed to go on for ever. I can remember to this day the waves of pleasure as she stroked her thumbs across my cheeks. I was trembling slightly from the adrenaline rush and thought my legs might give out at any point from swooning.

It was the greatest payback for what had, in fairness, been the crappiest year of my life.

I couldn't tell you how long we'd been kissing for, and I doubt it would have gone any further than that, but we'll never know because that sublime moment was brought to an immediate and incredibly embarrassing end when a teacher suddenly appeared and bellowed, 'And just what in God's name do you two think you're doing?!'

Simon and his new friend were standing behind her looking sheepishly at their feet. I froze on the spot and couldn't think of a word to say that might answer her question.

We were marched back into the communal dining room that was now being cleared for mass. She motioned to the girls. 'You two sit there and don't move! I'll deal with you later. Now, you two, come with me.'

My partner-in-kissing-crime actually winked at me as we were dragged off to see Father Tony. She'd had a bit of a smirk on her face since we'd been busted. Lynne was great. It felt just like the smoking incident back in Sammy's office. I mean, this was a serious misdemeanour, but my heart now ruled my head and I was already rehearsing my 'I regret nothing!' speech.

Tony was dressing for the service as the teacher stood there telling him all about our scandalous behaviour. She really did go on and on, so I think it was relief for all three of us when she finally said, 'I don't know about you, Father, but I'm at a loss for words.'

I wished!

'It's disgraceful behaviour. You must be so disappointed with them.'

Tony looked at us briefly.

Sod the speech, my face said I regretted everything.

But then something absolutely brilliant happened. He turned back to the teacher, and in a very matter-of-fact manner said, 'Nah, not really. I'm proud of them for getting stuck in!'

I'd pay anything for a photograph of the smiles that broke out across my and Simon's face at that moment. And, thank God, for the first time words did fail her as he continued, 'Now, if you'll excuse me, I've a mass to prepare for.'

That was Tony's way of dismissing all three of us (and there's no denying that as pay-off lines go, it's a killer). Simon and I strode out of that room like studs. The teacher followed on, still in shock. I even managed a wink back in Lynne's direction as we were seated on a bench as far away from the girls as possible.

Word had travelled quickly and the other boys were already having snide digs at us for snogging lasses. Unlike the night before in their room, I now enjoyed feeling ten years or so their senior.

We had come to that place as boys, but Simon and I would be leaving as men.

After mass, the kids were going off to do an orienteering session and we were preparing to head back to the seminary.

The teacher was watching us like a hawk, but my resourceful co-conspirator still managed to slip me a bit of paper with her address on it. 'Here, you can write to me if you like.'

And with that, Lynne winked at me one last time before running back to her giggling mates and walking away down a steep hill nearby the hostel. 'Write to you?' I thought. 'I'm gonna bloody marry you!'

The whole drive back I kept replaying everything over and over in my head. Father Tony never once mentioned our fall from grace, but we couldn't wait to get back and tell the rest of Underlow about our star-crossed lovers' escapade. Oh yeah, following girls around the shopping centre was for amateurs – you were now looking at the professionals!

I wrote to my initiator into the pleasures of kissing the very first day after we got back. I had a slight panic going to Sammy's office to buy the stamp out of my pocket money as I wondered if he might fix me with that gaze of his and somehow know that this was a letter full of forbidden love: a symbol of everything he had taken an oath against; a passion that I was supposed to turn my back on in favour of a life spent in servitude to Jesus Christ our Lord.

He just asked me if I wanted first or second class, and so the epistolary romance of the century began.

I lived for those letters. I loved receiving any mail whilst I was at Upholland, as anything connected with the world outside that place helped keep me going. My heart would sink at breakfast if there wasn't an envelope with my name on it plonked on our table. I even took to writing to random companies for literature concerning their products, just to know that somebody, some-where, was aware that I was here.

Car manufacturers always gave good mail, as did Scotch whisky distillers, funnily enough. I can't remember why I chose to start writing to them, but they went out of their way to send tons of stuff. I suppose requests like mine were few and far between. Anyway, they didn't seem too concerned that an 11-year-old trainee priest was taking such an ardent interest in their product. I don't know, maybe they just thought I was getting a head start on my drink problem? Perhaps their post-bag was busting at the seams with letters from the clergy wanting to look into alternatives to altar wine? Whatever their reasons, they were more than happy to send label samples, brochures and breakdowns of the distilling process. Had I stayed on at Upholland, then I'd have had all the necessary know-how for building my own still and brewing up some kind of moonshine, which would've appealed to the other students. Sammy could've played Eliot Ness and eventually busted me for calligraphy tax evasion.

But nothing meant more to me than a hand-written letter from home, or especially from Lynne. I would read them over and over and over again. They were my most treasured possession at Upholland. It's probably why I still write letters to this day, and take so much pleasure in receiving them. I don't care that an email is a trillion times faster and costs you nothing: there's no soul to them. A hand-written letter or card tells a person they matter. And I desperately needed to know that someone cared enough to make me feel that way.

I actually started making the most of seminary life towards the end of the summer term. I had what I considered to be a girlfriend (calling us 'pen-pals' didn't do justice to how good she made me feel), and I was still coasting it, grade-wise.

I was also in the fishing club – an activity I'd really missed, and I even offered to captain our tennis team in an upcoming match with another school. It was a quiet back-up plan of mine to turn pro and one day win Wimbledon for my mum. That would be the only way I could make it up to her for abandoning my parish to marry a girl I'd met at a youth hostel at the age of 11. After that, all I had to do was drop four stone and win the Grand National to get Dad back on side. Simple! What a difference a kiss makes.

But my opponent was less than dazzled when I stepped onto the court and delivered a wanky 10mph underarm serve. It was a whitewash. But you know what? I wasn't bothered. For the first time in what felt like an age, I wasn't carrying the weight of the world on my shoulders.

I didn't even kick up a fuss when they took my life-sized cardboard cut out of ET off me. My sister Catharine had swiped it from a promotional display at Argos, and I was the envy of the dorm for the brief time that it was displayed there. However, it apparently represented 'a false idol' and wasn't 'in the image of Christ our Lord'. I remember mumbling a few words of protest as it was carried away but, to be honest, my heart was no longer in it as far as rebelling was concerned.

Just like Fletch in *Porridge*, I was happy to do my stir and keep my head down. The summer holidays were coming up and I'd have six full weeks of tea, proper mashed potato and kicking back with the Hayes Street mob. I'd come a long way since sobbing myself to sleep the previous September. I was now the new poster boy for the priests of tomorrow. Soon, I would take my case to Pope John Paul, explain to him why vicars had it sussed when it came to loving both one woman and God simultaneously, and return with reading lamps for all.

6.

A DECANTER OF SHERRY

I would have ended that year a model example of an Underlow student had it not been Upholland's centenary, and had they not celebrated by putting a decanter of sherry on every single table during a commemorative lunch one day.

This was a big mistake.

We sat there waiting for somebody to realise and come to clear it away, but they didn't. So I decided to try a glass. I offered it around but there were no other takers at the table. No seniors noticed as there was so much going on in the hall that day – there was a big top table with special guests and religious dignitaries tucking into the good grub they'd put out to mark the special occasion.

I drank the first glass fast and gagged slightly at the bitterness, but then felt a warm glow in my tummy like liquid Ready Brek. Still everyone else was face down, focused on their plates. So I poured another and took my time with this one. I started to feel a bit light-headed after that, and uncontrollably giddy. Anything that was said by the lads at the table seemed absolutely hilarious, and my new-found sense of humour made them laugh in return. Then they egged me on to have another glass, which I did.

The rest of that meal is a bit of a blur, but I remember realising that the decanter was empty, and that the world was a really fucking funny place. I was giggling through all of the speeches – with my arms folded and my head buried in there trying to muffle the laughter – and clapping way too enthusiastically at the end of them.

I might have got away with it if I'd just gone up to the dorm and slept it off, but a priest came to our table and announced that there was a centenary round of golf to be played and they were looking for a student from each year to represent the college versus our visitors. Without any hesitation I stuck up my hand.

'I'll do it!'

'Do you play, Pennington?'

'I'm brilliant at it, honest. The golf course here is the main reason I joined the seminary.'

I'd never played golf before in my life. But I was peaking in the drunken bravado department and figured how hard could it be?

'Don't be smart. Be by the quad entrance at 4 p.m. Do you have your own clubs here with you?'

'No, they're at the cleaners.' I thought I was hilarious.

The look the priest gave me told me he wasn't amused.

'No, I don't, Father.'

'Well, we'll have to see if we can rustle some up for you. Don't forget, four o'clock.'

In the time between then and four o'clock I went from being ridiculously happy to absolutely smashed, and my smart-alec remarks were replaced with barely comprehensible slurring. Father Cunningham, our science teacher, gave me his old set of clubs to keep. They were pure *Antiques Roadshow*, and actually made from bamboo cane. Still, it was incredibly decent of him, but in my drunken state I might have overdone it a bit on the old gratitude front.

The would-be golfers were broken up into groups of four. For the most part it was two guests, a student and one of the seminary's priests. We were to play a round of nine with no handicaps. (Which meant absolutely sod all to me – though I had a booze-induced handicap of my own to contend with. Plus, on top of that, there was the fact that I couldn't actually play golf.)

A priest and I were up against a bishop and some other guy. I wasn't really bothered because my head was swimming. This was a really bad idea.

They must've thought it was the weight of the clubs making me stagger so haphazardly behind them heading to the first tee. My balance was completely banjaxed, and I just wanted to lie down on the grass and watch the sky until the bouts of queasiness passed.

Whenever anyone spoke to me my head would do this 360-degree bob before coming to rest at an angle that suggested a broken neck. 'Yes' and 'no' were the only words I was capable of forming. When it was my turn to tee off I couldn't even place the bleeding ball. There were two of everything and whenever I leaned forward I thought I was going to be sick. I know you're meant to swing the club, but leaning on it was the only way I could stop myself falling arse over tit.

If this had been a movie we would have now cut to a montage of the absolute worst round of golf you have ever, and would ever, see again. They weren't divots I was whacking up that day: I was like a JCB earth mover out on that course. Not a single clear strike of the ball! And my putting was no better. If you could have followed the line of the ball from an aerial view it would've resembled an angry doodle done by a three-year-old high on Calpol.

The bishop and his guest were doing their best to be polite as everyone else played around us. 'I'm sure he'll settle down soon. It's just a matter of getting your eye in, isn't it, Michael?'

'Tighten your grip but relax with your swing.'

Getting my eye in? I could see bugger all. Then the last glug of sherry kicked in and I couldn't even feel my own hands. Half the time I didn't know if I was holding the club or not, and when I was, it tended to go further than the ball. You could sense the fear whenever it was my go and my group retreated to wherever they prayed I wouldn't manage to throw the club. I swore a couple of times too, when the fog briefly lifted and I really tried to concentrate on a shot, but luckily I wasn't coherent enough for them to make it out.

My team partner – Father something-or-other – wasn't quite so supportive. In fact, he was furious. He kept growling at me whenever the other two were out of earshot.

'What the hell is wrong with you?' or 'Next time, just pick it up and throw it, do you hear me?'

What finally did it for him was my staggering off like a town centre drunk to have a pee against the bushes. I was bursting and way too gone to worry about golfing etiquette, and it was a crap game, anyway. His gritted teeth could barely contain his anger. He reminded me of the Jack Russell dog on *That's Life* that used to say 'Sausages.'

'You ... grrr ... are an absolute disgrace. Just wait till ... we get back ... grrrrrr.'

Apparently it was a small course by club standards and everyone else finished in an average of around an hour and a half; we arrived back almost four hours later. I was green to the gills and sent straight to bed as apologies were made on my behalf to our patient fellow competitors. The day finished more like a stag party than a centenary celebration for me: I slept in my clothes and possibly peed in the linen closet during the night.

Surprisingly, I felt pretty robust when I was summoned to Sammy's office the following day (again!). I actually think they realised it was their mistake giving out booze to kids because the bollocking seemed pretty tame considering my behaviour. No fire and brimstone, just a lot of fluff about my being an ambassador for the college at all times, and how I conducted myself was a direct reflection on Upholland itself.

'Yeah, well, you gave me a big jar of sherry, and I drank it and got drunk!' Now, obviously I didn't say that, but I'd have been well within my rights to do so. I think it's what the law would call 'a technicality'.

Sammy had to get his pound of flesh somehow, so he confiscated my clubs. According to him, it would be selfish of me to keep them for myself when they might be made available for the whole of Underlow to use. And so they went into storage under his supervision and were never played with again. It felt petty, and a wee surge of my old resentments started rising again. After all, they were a gift given to me. Their fate wasn't his to decide! But then I remember thinking, 'I fucking hate golf, anyway. Let the baby have his rattle.' Plus I had been expecting to get suspended or, worse still, expelled, so all in all I got off lightly.

And then the summer holidays finally arrived. Back at St Austin's, there would be a buzz at this prospect, but at Upholland it felt more like Mardi Gras. I don't know if I've ever been quite so excited at the prospect of packing a suitcase – like a toddler going to Disney World, my mind was racing with things I wanted to do once I got back.

The simplest things, the home comforts I'd longed for, felt like eye-popping, upcoming attractions at a theme park. Cups of tea, my mum's homemade quiche, my bunk bed that Dad had built, watching telly whenever I wanted, staying up late, our fridge, Barton's pop, playing out over Hankey's Well, or playing 'Kerbie' in the street until it got too dark to see the kerb properly.

The Fords, the Leylands, the Croppers, the Barnets and the Rodens. Alan Hale. Bryan Davies. Martin Hurley, and of course my cousin Dimon. I would play out with all of them, even the girls, despite considering myself officially spoken for.

Good job really, as I wasn't considered any kind of catch in our street and coming home from 'that priest school' didn't help matters. God, it would've been great if my wife-to-be could've come to visit me, or vice-versa (but in those days the price of a train ticket, and the prospect of travelling to the North East all by myself meant she might as well have lived in Australia).

I could kill a lot of trees with pages and pages full of daft little details, routines and pals from my former life that I was dying to re-acquaint myself with. It was almost like the excitement of my homecoming had thawed out the kid in me after a long frozen winter of discontent. I had six weeks ahead devoted to real carefree fun, as opposed to merely making the best of things. Many of the Underlow lads were going off away on different holidays during the break. Some of them sounded pretty exotic, but I didn't care. I didn't want to leave our house for any longer than it took to go to Metcalf's for a sherbet dip.

When my dad arrived in the car I was practically banging the roof and shouting, 'Go, go, go!' like I'd just robbed a bank and the contents of my huge case were unmarked bills of assorted tens, twenties and fifties. Had I actually hit the car then something probably would've fallen off, so I opted to help Dad push-start it instead.

We jumped in as it hit the downhill gradient of the drive and I sat kneeling on the passenger seat with my chin resting on the back of it and watched Upholland College get small and insignificant in the rear-view window. The engine reluctantly coughed into action so I turned round in my seat, buckled up, smiled at my dad as he gave a relieved puff of his cheeks before smiling back at me saying, 'Thunderbirds are go!' With that we pulled out through the gates and headed home for the summer.

Some might say there's now't spectacular about the St Helens skyline, but Lowe House Church, Beecham's Tower, Pilkington Glass's old head office and their huge chimneys spewing out dodgy, multi-coloured smoke between twilight and dawn like fading Roman candles were all the wonders of the world to me whenever we crossed the border into Woolyback territory. In years to come, my art teachers would drill into us the importance of stepping back from your drawing so we could get a decent sense of perspective. I always felt that those few folk who slagged off their hometown of St Helens hadn't spent the necessary time in exile to appreciate it.

I had, and I loved every single stone of the place. I'm not just paying homage to my hometown for sentiment's sake. I'd missed it like an amputee might miss a limb. St Helens – and Thatto Heath in particular – were as much a part of me as my DNA.

God, it felt so good when I first got home. I indulged myself in all the privileges that being back provided. Mum seemed particularly chuffed to have me home again and made that kind of fuss that only mams can.

Other parish members did similarly, but the big difference being that my mum was pleased to have her own flesh and blood back where I belonged, whereas I felt they were just keen to check on their investment. Maybe I was being overly cynical. A seminary education'll do that to you. They were all mad keen to compliment me on my progress. Apparently, I was such a lucky boy. A year ago I'd have been dumb enough to believe them, but I'd come a long way since the previous September.

'Oh, it must be marvellous there. Your dad was showing us the photos.'

'Has it been a year already? Hasn't that flown by?'

'You'll be getting bored back here before you know it, won't you?'

'Your own private fishing lake? Blimey, you've the life of Riley there, haven't you? Might have to sign up myself! Hang on though, I'm married aren't I? Eh, now that's not fair … ha ha ha.'

I remember thinking, 'You lot don't have a fucking clue, do you? If it looks so idyllic, how come you don't live there?' They were more naive than those boys back at the youth hostel!

If I was so special, why did most of the staff at Upholland treat me like shit on the bottom of their shoe? I had ceased to view the majority of its wardens as priests. They were – with the odd exception like Father Tony – bureaucrats, number-crunchers, academics, or monumental pricks; as morally corruptible as the rest of us, but a law unto themselves. I'd been to the coalface. I was living on the production line and understood why there were so many flaws in the finished product that this lot worshipped on a weekly basis.

I could have shattered their faith in all that they claimed to hold dear there and then. I could tell them all about life beyond its idyllic lakes and nine-hole wanking golf course. I had all the inside info on their precious belief system. I could pull back the curtain and reveal their Wizard of Oz. I could blow the lid on the whole sorry system. But I didn't.

Photo from a rare family holiday during the Thatcher years. Mum, cousin Julie, moody me, Rob and Mark doing a damn fine impression of two no-nonsense detectives who get the job done and dad, their weary police commissioner.

My sister Catharine, Mike Fairclough and I on our bad taste fashion night out around St Helens. Before you ask, no, the girl on the right was not with us.

It's either my first holy communion, or an early audition for that 70's TV show *The Comedians*.

Even as a baby I was a natural at the old pint and a ciggie grip.

So that's why we never went abroad for holiday! Dad would only pay for one passport photo between all of us!

We took casual Fridays seriously in Hayes Street. Hang on, my mistake, it's our Silver Jubilee street party. I'm Noddy on the right.

I'm doing my best to look disinterested in the lovely May Queen but, ask yourself this, what's the crown hiding?

The day we all dreaded, when summer was over and it was time to go and get fitted for new school shoes.

Ah, the Holkers and I cruising on the Thatto Heath Riviera. Aunty Kath has just announced it's Pimms o'clock.

How was I not offered the lead news anchorman slot on BBC's *Look North West* after this headshot? Gordon Burns, did you shred my CV?

Michael age 10.

My sister Catharine perfectly captured the ravages inflicted after Thatcher took away my free school milk.

What can I say? It was a
drinking culture.

Faith was all some of these people had. No, they hadn't been denied the basic privileges outlawed at the seminary, and yes, that meant they took a lot of what they did have for granted, but that's the life they'd chosen. And I had chosen to go to that god-awful place. Me. I had dared to climb down that rabbit hole. So it would remain my dirty little secret as I nodded, smiled and answered all their questions politely.

Something was irreversibly different about me. I didn't connect with all the kids in my street like I'd longed for. I felt like I had some contagious disease. It wasn't a conscious indifference on their part, but a year away had stripped me of childish concerns. When some kids made the sign of the cross and comically genuflected in front of me, I wasn't really bothered.

'Ey up, it's Father Penno!'

What killed me was the thought that I no longer had a single thing in common with them. All my suspicions from that night bunking in with those boys back at the youth hostel were confirmed. I was different, and all the kids back home somehow knew it. I was like Red in *The Shawshank Redemption* when he tries to adapt to life outside prison. It truly is an awful feeling when you accept that you've been institutionalised.

I tried playing out as much as I'd promised myself that summer, but I was like a ghost amongst my former childhood peers, the Betty Eccles of Hayes Street. Part of me actually fucking missed the acceptance of the lads back at the seminary. I hated the place and yet I could no longer function in the town that I had so painfully longed for and cried myself to sleep at night over.

Something inside me had died. I had left my childhood cake out in the rain and couldn't for the life of me remember the recipe. I felt completely and utterly removed from who I used to be as I hid over Hankey's Well, crouched in the long grass, weeping at the fact that there wasn't a single soul on this earth who understood how shit it felt being me.

7.

UPHOLLAND SECOND YEAR: 'LOW FIGS'

Had that summer gone to plan, I doubt I'd have returned to Upholland. But it didn't, and I just kind of drifted back to the place. There was no pomp or ceremony this time around: no big shop beforehand, just patch, mend and the letting down of my trousers by an inch or so. There were no hidden tears on my mum's part, and none on mine either. Nor was there any big wave off to my mates in Hayes Street.

In fact, it was getting dark as we left and the summer evening buzz of playing out late had run its course for even the most devoted 'Bung-off' fan. The street was empty, and my journey back to Castle Grayskull felt equally hollow. Like an illegal immigrant being deported, my destination held no uncertainty, just certain disappointment and a probable desire to flee again soon after my arrival.

I think in a way my biggest problem with Upholland was that it was all about academia. There was a lad there in the fourth form whose continuation on to the sixth form, and ultimately

Ushaw College (the Geordie finishing school for future priests that people went to after Upholland), was called into question because of his intellectual grades.

Now, let me tell you, this lad had an emotional maturity way beyond most others at that place. There was an innate decency about him, and he always had time for everyone, no matter what year they were in.

In the second year we were given a room with huge drawers where we were allowed to store treats brought from home. But mice had gnawed through the back of the cupboards years earlier and so regularly ransacked our precious booty as soon as it was placed in there. We tried to raise the issue with Sammy, but he couldn't have cared less. The fourth form lad taught us how to catch mice with digestive biscuits rather than cheese when they infested our tuck cupboards – 'You've all been watching too much *Tom and Jerry*, you lads!' He was the only person in that place who was arsed enough to try and help us remedy the situation (my dad quickly built me a tuck box to fit in the drawer, which resolved the problem temporarily, but that again was made of wood and within a week there was evidence of vandalism where the mice had gone after my pickled onion Space Invaders). He had time for everyone. He was decent and generous with his knowledge of life. He should have been at the very top of their wish list for future community leaders within the Catholic Church, but he wasn't considered academically bright enough? Idiots! You had faith in him as a person, so if he were to represent God in some future parish, then wasn't that surely the best starting point?

Years later, I was amazed to see a fellow Upholland student, Jason, turn up at my sixth-form college. He had something like nine O-levels and told me how he had hated the seminary but had decided to stay on for the education. In fact, he revelled in telling them he was agnostic when they asked him about his thoughts with regard to progressing on to sixth form. A payphone and a private bunk weren't a big enough bribe to sway him.

Most of the recruits they were after were too bright not to see through their bullshit, and by judging the rest on what they knew about the melting point of mercury or gender roles in Shakespeare's problem-plays, they actually diddled themselves out of producing decent priests by ignoring the finest qualities in folk. That poor lad was too genuine to play the game and, as a result, he never made it.

To this day, some of the best priests that it has ever been my privilege to know have entered into the priesthood later in life. Like mature students, they have lived in the real world and fully appreciate the sacrifice they are making. They entered into priesthood with a practical and wonderful insight into the very people they would be serving on a day-to-day basis. They could connect, just like this lad, with folks' daily needs as well as their spiritual yearnings.

The only different thing about this new school year was that I started the first term a few days later than everyone else in 'Low figs' (the Upholland name for second year). I was so bloody apathetic at that point that I can't even remember why, now, but I think I'd maybe been shown off around some religious retreat my dad had undertaken.

Ordinarily, a few stolen extra days away from that place would've been manna from heaven, but the acceptance of inevitability was another symptom of loss of innocence, and it didn't really matter to me when I went back, as long as I went. Like a wrestler waiting backstage to go out and fight a championship bout when the outcome has already been decided months earlier by his manager and the promoters, I just wanted to get it over and done with.

The boys from my year seemed genuinely chuffed to see me, especially as my late arrival had spawned a rumour that I had bailed out of Mother Church's boot camp during the summer. It was odd, really. We had all spent a year living in such close proximity – a makeshift family in the absence of our biological one – and yet, once the summer term ended, we had all instantly severed links with each other for the full six weeks. Or at least

I did – even with my best mate, Simon. It was almost as if I'd packed them away with the same kind of relief I had my college uniform. They'd been kept at arm's length, like members of a school swots' chess club that could cause embarrassment in rougher kid's company.

To this day I have a horrible knack for vanishing acts. Sadly, many former friends will testify to that. People I've forged close bonds with have found themselves wondering how 'out of sight' could lead so quickly to 'out of mind'. And so have I. Because despite my many faults, I've always considered myself quite a genuine person, and I don't know if I was born with this sad ability to treat folk like a boxed-up relic at the end of *Raiders of the Lost Ark*, or if it's a defence mechanism that over-developed as a result of my time at Upholland.

Either way, for a long time now, I've been self-diagnosed with attention deficit syndrome. Laymen, teachers, ex-partners and publishers have called it 'fucking laziness', and I (appropriately enough) can't be arsed to explain the subtle differences to them. But I do loathe the fact that my 'condition' often extends into deadlines, and impacts on friendships that I sincerely do – or did – hold dear. It'd be a pretty poor showing if *This Is Your Life* ever tried to get my past gathered together in one room. Sadly, a broom cupboard would probably do just fine, and it would all be my own doing.

Anyhow, on this occasion I was pleased enough to see everyone when I got back to Upholland. Even if it did mean that I kind of belonged there now. The biggest news the lads seemed keen to relay was that there was a new addition to our year, and he'd been throwing his weight around a bit. It seemed he fancied himself as the new 'Daddy' of God wing.

I wasn't a natural-born scrapper, and with the exception of the sausage snatcher, I can't remember any of us coming to serious blows with each other back in our Underlow year. One lad had squared up to me once. To be honest, I wasn't dead keen on the thought of fighting him, but he had insulted my rendition of 'Chitty Chitty Bang Bang' on the trumpet, and knowing what the lessons were costing my folks, I had felt I had to justify the expense by taking a stand. It had turned out to be your harmless, run-of-the-mill, brass-section-related male adolescent posturing, and we were mates again before you knew it. That's probably why this new boy with the attitude had caused such a stir: he obviously hadn't yet realised that, 'The fight was out there, man ... out there!'

For all the impressive facilities that were supplied to make life more bearable at Upholland, we still lacked a snooker table. So with nothing really substantial enough to fill a sock Ray-Winstone style, I opted to go on the verbal offensive. Something along the lines of, 'Oh, yeah? Tell him I'd like to see him try that on with me.'

Oh aye, the system had produced a right sociopath in me. Still, my aggressive response had the desired effect, and the word quickly spread of an imminent showdown.

I wasn't that fussed. Oddly enough, that's something from my time there that I remember with genuine fondness – beyond a few possible cuts and grazes, the prospect of fighting in that place often failed to summon up the normal fear of any real harm being done. In those days, you walked away from fights like that with a severe bruising of the ego being the worst possible outcome.

As an adult, I hate violence and avoid it whenever possible, but back then it kind of felt like a harmless pastime. It felt more like something that would happen in a song by Pulp – an enjoyable symptom of having little left worth losing, if that makes sense. That's why working-class town centres are full of blokes – and lasses – knocking seven bells out of each other on a Friday/Saturday night. It breaks up the monotony.

As for my projected adversary, he was biggish – not huge, and certainly not muscular, but big enough to pass for a third year. I instantly disliked him. It was his cheeks: reddish and ruddy, just like that arsehole from the previous year. He reminded me of a poem from junior school: 'Augustin was a chubby lad, fat, ruddy cheeks Augustin had.'

Now, he wasn't posh, but his weight, his long, straight hair – almost a bob in length, with a fringe perfectly parted salon-style – and those cheeks made him look more like an effeminate dessert than a serious threat to the status quo. He was a walking meringue of malcontent, with black cherries for eyes buried deep within his big, fat head. His whole 'look' made him appear harmless to me, more a laughable nuisance than a threat, like folk who take their cats for walks on leads whilst talking loudly to themselves.

Simon, who kind of kept out of class politics, had told me he'd already tried coming on cocky with him. He'd told him in no uncertain terms to fuck off, which he had. So he didn't strike me as the type to hit first and ask questions later. He did his best to walk the walk, but now, as he came closer and I got a good look at his fruity face, you could see the complete lack of conviction behind his talking of the talk.

'Are you Pennington? I heard you've been gobbin' off about me?'

I didn't say anything. I was still clocking his expression. He was half-heartedly squaring up, but he looked like he might just as easily burst into tears at any moment. And that's when the penny dropped. He was scared shitless. Not of me, but of this place.

'You looking for bother, are you?'

The rest of us were all a year in to our stretch, whereas he was fresh fish, and every bit as afraid as we'd all been in those first few weeks, twelve long months back. But the big difference was, we'd done it as a team. We'd been cast adrift, but at least we'd had each other to cling on to, metaphorically speaking. He might've put himself across as a bit of a knob, but you could see it was all in the name of self preservation. I was only twelve but, as corny as it sounds, I felt like an old bloke looking back at himself when he was a young whippersnapper.

'Well?'

The younger me would've taken this into account and tried to reach out to this petrified lummox somehow. But a lot had changed in a year.

'Nobody here likes you. Do you know that? Nobody! And it's not because they're scared of you. It's 'cos you don't belong here, and you never will. So fuck off!'

And then I just stood there staring at him. I could've carried on and gone for the full bottom-lip quiver, maybe even tears. He might've struck out had I done so, like a distressed heifer in a cake shop. But as I said, that prospect didn't scare me, and I think he could see that. And I wasn't going to hit him. I'd already hurt him the best way I knew how, by exposing his sense of loneliness. Misery likes company as the saying goes, and homesick boys are each other's lifeline. I'd just severed ours good and proper.

I could lie and say that I did it out of my innate hatred of bullies, but the truth was I resented him for falling for the con and winding up there with the rest of us, and I despised the fact that he reminded me of myself twelve months back.

'You fuck off!' He parried, weakly, and with that he turned and stomped up the stairs towards our dormitory. No doubt to cry. Some of the small crowd of onlookers seemed disappointed that things hadn't got physical. One or two actually seemed disapproving of me, as if I'd over-stepped the mark. And they were right. I had, really. A good old-fashioned bust-up is what he needed – something he could use to prove himself within the troop.

It's hardly an original thought – the pen sometimes being mightier than the sword and all that – but it is an incredibly empowering discovery that you can floor someone with words. I don't mean the simple skits that all kids instinctively know how to use. They're just born from obvious physical quirks, or tried and tested myths designed to embarrass their victim:

'You stink!'

'You pee your bed!'

'You got that coat from the jumble sale. It used to be our kid's!'

That was all amateur stuff. I mean seeing something 'in' a person, something that they thought was securely buried, something true that they'd rather not share with the world. Seeing it and revealing it for everyone around to see? Now, that was powerful stuff. Although you can also get your head kicked in when trying this approach in the wrong pub or club. Like comedy, the trick to cruelty is all in the timing.

8.

FUCK CATHOLIC GUILT!

or

The Dynamics of the Communal Shower

The dressing-down I gave Sara-Lee-face was wrong of me. Morally speaking, I came from better stock than that. But in just one day of being back at Upholland, I'd already surrendered another little bit of the decency that back then I believed made me who I was. And, sadly, it felt necessary, even right.

If I could go back now, I'd ask him where he was from and warn him not to use the loos or baths in the basement after supper because an older kid would definitely lock the door and turn off all the lights. I'd tell him to write to anyone he knew because letters back reminded you of what our priestly teachers were trying to replace with dogma.

If religion was founded so strongly on personal faith, rather than definitive straight answers, why were we forced to live in such a regimented, 'Do as I say, not as I do!' day-to-day existence? If I was cut out to be a priest that deserved the collar, and the unquestioning acceptance of a parish one day, then I would have helped him. I would have reached out to him as a Christian – as I'd been raised to do by my wonderful mum and dad, and not these god-awful step-parents with the emotional reach of a T-Rex.

That's what was so wrong with them. They wanted to wipe your personality like they were deleting some fucking files on a PC. But the one thing they couldn't wipe – the very thing that they claimed they wanted to use in order to bring you closer to God (who had by that point become some huge, mystical personality shredder thanks to them) – was your soul, your hard drive. That irreconcilable force that whispered the difference between right and wrong, whether you chose to listen to it or not.

Try drowning it out with Guinness, I dare you. It floats.

God gave me that soul, not Upholland. God allowed me to fill that soul with love, pain, regret, hope and – yes – faith. The soul is the only honest processor of our self. It's the one doorstep you should never shit on. It registers all our faults but constantly turns us towards a peace that those middle-men in black would have us believe we don't deserve.

FUCK CATHOLIC GUILT! Guilt is their design, their hooked line, not God's. God never meant us to entrust our souls to anyone but ourselves, until we die, when they're returned to sender. He had faith in us, Upholland didn't.

It was like some twisted sanctimonious game show in which we were all playing for the star prize: a house of God, a house of our own, a congregation to lead and a Papal guarantee that we would see heaven, just so long as we 'saved' enough souls along the way. And all we had to do to play was surrender our own in the process.

That's why I fucking loved reading George Orwell. Show your arse to the twats in charge but save your smile for God and those who can recognise the difference between defiance and genuine devotion. It's now't more than a sly twinkle, but to those who are already dead behind the eyes, it's a flare gun that threatens to shine. I'll answer to my maker ... not the fucking salesroom rep trying to claw in his tatty bit of commission.

Believe you me, without faith I would have killed myself back then with no more fear of losing my mortal soul than of losing tuck shop privileges (the latter being no mean threat to a depressed kid gaining weight and abusing the chemical similarities between a cocoa rush and a shared orgasm). We weren't allowed to call home, but at least God was omnipresent. He knew – He had to know – that although my heart had taken a beating, my soul was still intact.

That's why despite all the wanks and the sniggering during prayers and the indifference towards his earthly appointed soldiers of ecclesiastical fortune, had I thrown myself off that big green copper observatory dome that sat on top of one of the college's four main towers, had I fallen from grace and to my death, He would still have let me into heaven. He'd have welcomed me with open arms and whispered in my ear, 'Kudos to you, you wee scallywag, you kept the faith. Now pass through these gates. We've a huge pot of tea waiting for you ... sugar free, just as you like it.'

But yet again I digress from my own story with theories on the soul. I do apologise, but I had a lot of time at Upholland to sit around and consider this stuff, and there was a lot of resentment that this poor lad obviously became the focus of.

Things should have settled down between us after that, but they didn't really: he remained a channel for my frustrations with life at the seminary. I didn't bully, I just made a point of blanking him. He settled in all right with most of the other lads, but not really with the regime, and definitely not with me.

I could excuse myself by simply saying I didn't like him, but the truth is I didn't like myself. Yes, I 'couldn't take to him' as my mum would say. His frustrations leaked out from time to time in mini thuggish tantrums, whereas I did my best to bury mine in self-loathing and quiet resentment. The more I managed to conform, the deeper my anger at myself festered.

Over the past summer I'd managed to forget just how bloody cold that place could get in the late autumn and winter months. Miserably cold! There was every chance of finding Walt Disney's head in that basement wash-room. There were mornings when it was a toss-up of what might ultimately get the better of me – SAD syndrome, or frostbite. The only time I didn't feel like I should have a lolly-stick stuck up my arse was in the hot showers after rugby. But even that experience came with its own setbacks.

I don't mean the rugby. I loved playing that. And what I lacked in natural talent I made up for in determination and my 100 per cent commitment to the tackle. Ever since I was a young lad, our Mark had taken me out every Sunday and spent a good hour or so running into me at full pelt. Both Rob and Mark were good all-rounders sport-wise, but Mark had a real knack for rugby union.

Although St Helens can boast, in my humble opinion, the best rugby league team in the world – and every young lad held an ambition to one day pull on the red V of the Saints shirt and play for their town – we were stuck with a national curriculum in schools that dictated we play rugby union. Mark was a feisty scrum-half who, in his youth, was fast as spit off of an iron, could take punishment for the sake of laying a ball off just at the right time to break, and would then most likely give back at least as good as he got.

He taught me the basic physics of tackling. If you're standing still, it's going to hurt. But if you're moving at roughly the same velocity as your target then that actually softens the impact. Hit them at the waist, with your shoulder, get your arms wrapped round them, and then slide down towards the ankles. Our Mark drilled it into me every time he ran at me.

'What can't a player run without?'

Thump!

'His legs!'

'Correct. Now get up, we'll go again.'

When I played at Upholland, our PE instructor created a new position for me to play in as a result of my having all the pace of a potted house plant. I was a kind of secondary full back, but left to drift, slowly, from wing to wing, the strategy being that if my teammates could chase an opposing player who had the ball right down the touch-line, with no place else left to run – not even a side-step, only straight at me – then I would be there to stop them.

Limping back across a rock-hard frosted pitch after a games session of solid scrogg and bash, the boiling hot showers that awaited us had always felt like a real, hard-earned treat. A chance to warm your bones for ten minutes! But the dynamics of the communal shower had changed in this second year.

The boys of Low figs were turning into young men, and some were accelerating far faster into puberty than others. Unfortunately for me, my biological clock had no more pace to it than my legs did.

It wasn't fair. Even Monsieur Eclair-face had sprouted a meagre crop of pubic cress. I had become self-conscious about my slowly expanding waistline where the fairer sex was concerned, but for the first time ever, I had real issue with the way my body looked in comparison to my fellow rugby-players. Not that I'd ever gone into the showers shopping for compliments, but I was absolutely convinced that the ominous bald patch above my hell, fire and brimstone compass was a source of awkwardness for everyone else in there. And because I wasn't in on Play Doh-face's 'pubic barber shop in my Y-fronts' phenomenon, it never struck me that their awkwardness might actually be a result of the very changes they were obviously going through. My ego had decided that my slap dick was the cause of low morale.

I quickly became obsessed, and extremely impatient, with my genitalia. This former source of shameful pleasure had become singularly embarrassing. A shiny badge of manly dishonour! Had God sprayed me with some ecclesiastical strain of Agent Orange as punishment for all my wicked deeds? Was there nothing I could do to encourage the curly little blighters out?

9.

MADAME HAD REAL CLASS

I had another reason for wanting rid of the miner's helmet in my pants. Although I was still writing to Lynne, and loved getting letters back from her, I, like a vast majority of the inmates there, had become infatuated with the new college French teacher.

She was Scottish, and a lot younger and prettier than the dinner ladies who had made the odd guest appearance in my nocturnal fantasies. She was my Venus de Milo, my Princess Leia stunt-double. I was still quietly determined to marry Lynne some time later down the line, raise a family and grow old together – my calling to the priesthood waning with each passing day and every night-time fall from grace – but on a day-to-day basis, I couldn't deny the charms of the Celtic temptress.

I only really thought of Lynne in romantic terms: her smile, her laugh, and that wonderfully innocent kiss! She was a friend with future benefits. My French teacher, on the other hand, I only thought about naked. Always naked and ushering me into her boudoir, ignoring my feeble protestations as she placed my hands on her perfect breasts and made good on her fantasised promise to tutor me in the Gallic grammar of love. I never got much further than that before the inevitable 'Fire in the hole!'

Oddly enough, even in my made-up scenarios, I never got to the point where she undressed me. I didn't want my self-consciousness butting in and ruining the mood by imagining her face when she pulled down my pants and saw I had the anatomy of a highly buffed but not fully ready for 'action' man. 'No baby oil for me, ta, just a light going over with some Mr Sheen and a terry cloth!'

I hadn't a single sock that didn't crunch underfoot from the hardened illicit discharges she would prompt on a nightly basis. I eased my conscience by telling myself that when we actually consummated our 'relationship' for real, I would only be practising for mine and Lynne's wedding night. So that she would have the man, the lover, she deserved, rather than this clumsy, hairless boy capable of nothing more than penetrating his woolly size 2s.

It must've been odd for 'Frenchy' coming into that huge institution, so outnumbered by sexually frustrated men and boys of all ages. I often wonder if she was aware of just how many corks she was popping as the lights went out and the college-wide celebrations began beneath the sheets? There must've been an inkling, because she seemed very careful about who she allowed to access her private quarters (not a euphemism).

Lay-teachers lived on site much like the priests and, of course, us students, but she didn't operate the same, 'My door is always open to you' policy as the rest – there'd have been a line twice around the building had she done so. Plus I suspect some of the elder members of the faculty would be highly suspicious of a vibrant, pretty young lady distracting the students from a life otherwise devoted to navy wanks and endless acts of Contrition.

I came up with one lame academic excuse after another to try and gain an audience with Frenchy back at her place, but she always managed to resolve my issues within class time, and she made it quite clear she was not up for students turning up without a prior appointment. There were, however, two boys from Low-figs who seemed free to come and go almost as they pleased.

Now, throughout Underlow these two lads had displayed quite a prominent camp streak, and it hadn't lessened in our second year. They spent a lot of time in each other's company, and I reckon Frenchy – like the rest of us – had presumed they were perhaps an item, and therefore had no ulterior motive for wanting to spend their free time with her beyond admiring fabrics or listening to Charles Aznavour albums.

It was common knowledge at Upholland that some of the older boys, like a great many guests of Her Majesty's Prisons, grew weary of DIY damnation and would take to making conjugal visits to other willing participants on their dorm. It had spread like wildfire that a lad in High figs had been caught with another boy in the deserted shower-block putting into practice the principle that one good turn deserves another. We all enjoyed a quiet giggle at his expense, but it wasn't the kind of career-ending fumble that might destroy a reputation at a state-run secondary school.

That this kind of thing happened on a fairly widespread basis was pretty much taken for granted at Upholland. I think we all understood how lonely and/or sexually frustrated a soul could feel in that place at times. We were denied so much for the sake of a proper Catholic education, for our calling, and, as far as I was concerned, my fellow pupils had to grab whatever comfort came their way and to hell with their rules.

Acts which I might've considered unthinkable a year earlier – only through naivety, not outright homophobia – I now accepted as human nature daring to defy the fear-mongers. Like a weed forcing its way through unforgiving tarmac and daring to reveal itself, the decision as to whether to view it as something ugly and destructive, or a miracle of nature, was entirely in the eye of the beholder.

As it happened, I hadn't felt the urge to turn to anybody but Frenchy for sexual liberation. I had Lynne as something to hope for on the outside, and as empty as I might've felt at times, a cuddle from anyone but my mum would have failed to fill the void.

Still, I'd changed so much already during my time there, how could I sit here now and say with absolute certainty that I wouldn't have needed something more myself had I resigned myself to serving out my full seven-year stretch? It's well-documented that many straight people have reached out to same-sex 'partners' for comfort in single-sex boarding school environments, a large number of them knowing full well they're straight, yet just being desperately lonely, or inquisitive about these brand new feelings that their privileged education failed to provide explanations for.

Oddly enough, the powers that be seemed to turn a blind eye to this – as they did to a great many things that had started to matter far more than earning their approval – possibly putting it down as collateral damage in the war against our inevitable attraction to the fairer sex. Or maybe they were just hell-bent on keeping it in the family, like travellers gambling only amongst their own kind. Perhaps they were lenient because having gone through these rites of passage themselves, they remembered the biological maelstrom, and understood why boys would dare to break the rules in such a way. Or had dwindling numbers of young boys entering the seminary (Underlow consisted of only four students in this new term, as opposed to us eleven hopefuls when I first arrived) led to an unspoken U-turn on their policy in this contro-versial area? I remember thinking that might make them a little more humane, and if so, then maybe there was hope for all of us.

I should say at this point that I know a great many ex-students from Upholland whose fond memories of the place far outweigh any negatives. I apologise to them that my recollec-tions are tinged with so much bitterness. It's true that we were a resilient bunch when making the most of whatever mischievous opportunities presented themselves – we had fun!

I'm sure many ex-students have gone on to bigger and better things and credited their success in part to the college. And if my career gives the impression that I'm someone who's achieved in this life, then couldn't it be argued that I, too, owe something of that to the place myself?

Maybe, but what haunts me is this. There are many points in our lives where decisions take us down one road and not another. Many of them are minor detours in regard to the overall journey. Others are of the huge, no-turning-back-now variety. If I'm angry about Upholland – which I think you'll have already guessed I am by now – it's because I firmly believe that my life splintered into two completely alternative outcomes as a result of my time there. And it was because of a decision I was too young to make – a commitment I was too naive to grasp.

My brain is always determined to question every outcome (admittedly, it will usually dwell on the worst possible ones), except for Upholland. That is one of the few occasions where my head, my heart, my intuition and my soul are in perfect agreement. Like the dancing dog on *Britain's Got Talent*, this eventuality galvanises all the judges.

I have so much to be grateful for sitting here writing this. I know that. Had I not gone to that place I might not now be viewed as anything special, any kind of success. There would probably be no publisher interested in printing the details of my life story. But – and this is a huge 'but' – I have no doubt whatsoever that I would be a far happier, far more emotionally balanced adult. It can't be proven, but it's what I believe and it makes me so very sad some days. For now, though, I'll pour myself another large vodka and do my best to get back to the one aspect of this story I can talk about with absolute certainty; i.e. what actually happened.

So these two lads seemed to have a rare free pass to come and go as they pleased from Frenchy's room. As I've said, with the exception of cake-face, we were all pals in Low figs, but we all had our own mini cliques within the year. And all I had to do was ingratiate myself into theirs for just long enough to become a regular *chez* Frenchy. (I didn't realise at the time but there's a name for someone like me: 'Stalker'!)

I set about casually enquiring what the boys were up to during our precious bits of free time over the weekend. Turns out they planned to gather holly, berries, twigs and pine cones for real Christmas wreaths, as gifts for family and friends (oh dear!) and listen to carols (I've made a HUGE mistake!) whilst building them in Miss Frenchy's room. (You big gay fucking beauties! ... I should add at this point that one of these boys was happily married the last I heard, while the other stuck with his vocation and now runs a retreat centre for priests too used to helping themselves to altar wine, so sorry for the, 'You big gay fucking beauties' assumption, lads.) I clapped at the prospect like an effeminate seal and was duly invited to join in the 'fun'.

After our hunter-gathering expedition, I was in! Her quarters were of exactly the same modest dimensions as Father Tower's from Underlow. In the tiny living-room there was a Vatican-issue chair and dining-table for one and a tatty high-backed sitting chair she'd personalised with a couple of tiny side cushions and some exotic-looking lace thrown over the back, probably bought in the course of her many international travels. Or in Nottingham. But its origin wasn't relevant. Either way, it was womanly and dangerously different.

As well as an angle-poise lamp, there were lots of books, and a portable TV that she never switched on. Plus a radio that didn't play anything vaguely recognisable from the charts, just some low exotic version of what I'd later come to know as muzak, thanks to the posh lifts in big hotels that JOHNNY would one day take me to. Jazz, she called it.

Madame had real class. Sexy class! Just the way she said, 'It's jaaahzzzzz. Do you like it?' made it sound illicit, like she was coming on to me in code.

In my quiet teen obsessive way, I'd actually done a good job of convincing myself that it was she who felt awkward over her unhealthy obsession with me. Which was denial in overdrive as the fact was, back in the real world, Frenchy hadn't really warmed to me at all. I think she'd sussed my ulterior motives early on and was doing her best to accommodate Gilbert and George's new associate.

The two other boys had no problem talking to her. They chatted away like they were shelling peas with Nanna in an episode of *The Waltons*; I'd chip in with all the casual aplomb of Hannibal Lecter interrogating Agent Starling. I envied how at ease with her they were. Every time I opened my mouth, there was a distinctive hesitation with even the simplest of responses. I couldn't trust myself with words because my balls constantly wanted to translate on behalf of my brain:

'Michael, would you like a glass of water?'

'Yes, I'd really like to see your breasts!'

'Are you sure you wouldn't like a biscuit?'

'Well, because of the lack of visual definition that your fanny has in direct sunlight, I haven't really obsessed over it in the same way I have your breasts, so I'll pass for now, thanks. I wouldn't say no to a squeeze of your arse, though.'

Even the room smelt like a come-on. Nothing especially perfumed or 'tarty', just fresh, feminine and therefore incredibly seductive. It was nothing like the hundred or so exact same rooms in that place. Her presence eliminated the musty odour of regret like a defiant Magic Tree air-freshener hanging in a morgue.

Most intriguing of all was the tiny bedroom just through the next door, which she sensibly kept closed the majority of the time we were there. Oh God, you can't know how much I wanted access to that off-limits inner sanctum, how badly I needed to see where the object of all my illicit desires slept.

I would picture her lying there with her hair down, resting across a crisp white pillow with flimsy bits of underwear strewn across the floor, or better still carelessly hanging off the end of a decorative brass bed-frame where she'd undressed before slipping naked under her duvet, despite the freezing temperatures. No hospital-folded starchy sheets and itchy blankets, her boudoir also having exemption from all the harsh realities I'd normally associate with that place.

I'd done my research into lingerie by accidental courtesy of the Grattan home shopping catalogue whilst flicking through it for the umpteenth time refining my Christmas gift list, so I had enough to sketch out these further additions to my fantasy landscape. But I craved actual first-hand confirmation of the colour and amount of lace transparency of her underwear.

I had considered carefully removing a couple of pages from the catalogue on a Saturday afternoon visit back home and bringing them back to Upholland with me. That way, once I'd managed to sneak a peek at her delicates, I would have a visual menu with which I could make comparisons. But I knew that at some point in the pages' removal process I'd have been bound to leave a telltale tear or obvious chink in the catalogue's otherwise smooth bind. And even if I managed a flawless extraction, I was sure Dad did a page count on sections that contained anything potentially salacious.

Plus where would I hide these pages once I'd returned to the seminary? Not in my bunk, bedside cabinet, tuck box or washbag, that was for damn sure! The building was huge and yet everywhere I imagined stashing them, I then imagined a perfectly plausible reason why they would be found and ultimately traced back to me. The only sensible option I could settle on was the hatch over our dormitory toilets that accessed the tower where Betty Eccles had once hung herself and now inhabited in ghostly form. Who else but a teenage sexual obsessive with knowledge of its seedy contents would ever dare to venture up there?

Common sense once again prevailed, though. For one, there was no ladder with which to access the hatch. For a split second, I thought of constructing one bit by bit with materials lifted from the art room as I'd seen in all those great prisoner-of-war escape movies. But then if I was having trouble hiding two or three folded bits of paper from the brassière section, where the fuck would I hide a ladder?

I'd have carried on seeking a solution to this problem if the mother of all 'what if?' fears hadn't struck home: what if, after building my ladder, and finding somewhere to keep it secret, and safely managing to stash my research, I climbed up there one night? If I opened the hatch, grabbed the pages, but was then attacked by Betty Eccles, really angry at my having turned her spiritual resting place into a cat house, which then caused me to fall, break my neck and die whilst still clutching pages 375–377? That would bring more shame than my poor relatives deserved, and make for a bloody awkward funeral.

As much as I was at odds with the Catholic Church at that time, I wouldn't wish that eulogy on anyone. So I returned to Upholland empty-handed and continued to develop my relationship with Frenchy based on first-hand intelligence gathering and imagination alone.

I did my best to feign interest in our ongoing Christmas gifts projects, but my efforts obviously lacked conviction. I just couldn't stop staring at her.

Crossing my legs to save us all embarrassment, I sat there desperately taking in every detail of her and the surroundings, hoping it would help embellish the fantasies I'd already designed for us from guesswork. I'd count the minutes till the sun would creep across her shoulder as she read so I might catch even the slightest outline of her bra strap. As subtle as I tried to be with my ogling, I'm sure the poor woman could feel my eyes on her. I was a tragic peeping Tom without a hedge to hide behind, nor a decent Christmas wreath to show for my efforts.

At night I would lie in bed and think of us together as I learnt to take my time and enjoy my trouser torment. Gone were the furiously fast wanks of Underlow, the clumsy spurts and sudden self-consciousness at the loudness of my breathing once the deed was done. Thanks to Frenchy, I had matured towards a more tantric nocturnal existence. I'd almost forget I was playing with myself as I dreamt of lost afternoons lying on her bed making what I thought was love and drinking sugarless tea without a single care for the world outside her door.

I was her Winston Smith and she my Julia. We defied the regime and laughed to ourselves about the state of all the other slaves to convention. I'd have had a lit cigarette and offered her a post coital-ish drag on it if she hadn't made it perfectly clear that she loathed the smell of smoke during one of the festive craft sessions. That was a shame seeing as I was so suave and witty in my imaginings, despite the fact that I still hadn't managed to construct a practical knowledgeable explanation of what had happened between her undressing, my orgasm, her smiles, and the kettle going on.

A shared Benson & Hedges would have definitely eased my quiet concern that what had just happened was both normal and just as ecstatic for her. I started to fantasise about our lazy chats every bit as much as I did about her pulling off her crocheted jumper so my hand could wander between skin and the delicate fibres that held her breasts in place, maybe because I needed it to be more real than the average pubescent fantasy: a genuine escape from the priesthood that was rooted as deeply in made-up fact as I could plant it, a tunnel out of there that led blissfully back to my crappy, lonely bed every time the lights went out.

10.

A SLOW-ACTING POISON WHOSE SYMPTOMS WON'T DILUTE

Once again I had found a survival technique – my way of getting through the dreary days of the autumn term. It was not one I was particularly proud of. I hadn't knuckled down and focused on my studies, or found an outdoor pursuit or sport that might fill my time and help burn off some of the extra energy my raging hormones had afforded me, as well as the excess inches my jam-butty diet had dumped on me.

Quietly I knew it was straying far from the path my Christian mentors thought they were leading me down, and I hadn't even asked for forgiveness from God, indirectly through Confession or directly through silent prayer. It wasn't wholesome in any way, shape or form, but it made me feel good. I had replaced my books with Frenchy, and the lack of a reading lamp would never keep us apart. The days could try their best to take their toll, but George Benson and I were singing from the same hymn sheet … Just gimme the night!

There we were, Frenchy and I, together alone. She was

fascinated to hear my opinions on Darth Vader's shock revelation that he was actually Luke Skywalker's dad as I assessed the moral implications and his inevitable torn loyalties between family and duty to the rebellion. She was a good listener.

She had to be, as quietly I had little comprehension of – or interest in – jazz or French.

Late one night, I was just about to share my thoughts with her on the comparison between men of the cloth and Jedi Knights, the similarities in code of conduct and dress sense, and the gaping differences in terms of apathy and action, turning the other cheek and slicing some villain's arm off to defend your principals, whilst simultaneously holding my own light-sabre snugly under the covers, when Frenchy's presence felt suddenly all too real.

My imagination had come on in leaps and bounds since our night-time affair had begun – it had had to – but this time I could actually feel something that wasn't bed linen brushing against my foot. For a brief moment, I wondered if sleep had finally called my number and a vivid dream was about to take over from where my fantasy would trail off. Lying there, I actually considered succumbing to the reality of this very distinct sensation, but even for a dream this felt all too real, too soon.

There it went again. Something had definitely brushed against my foot. Eyes closed and torn between escapism and actuality, I quietly came to an unthinkable conclusion. What if it was Betty Eccles? Oh shit. Oh shit, oh shit, oh shit, oh shit, oh shit! It wasn't the night on which legend said she'd stalk the dorm (or else I'd have been wearing my rosary beads and brandishing a crucifix instead of my genitals), plus I'd once again been lucky enough to be allocated a cubicle with a window and not one of the horse-boxes she was supposed to frequent. But there was definitely something at the end of my bed, and with the noticeable absence of a, 'Sssshhhh, Penno, are you awake?' I knew it wasn't one of my sleepless classmates looking for someone to share in a bit of nocturnal misconduct.

Hence I didn't flinch or dare to open my eyes. I tried my best to control my breathing and fake the appearance of deep sleep, but I couldn't stop with the shakes. I started to pray in my head, even though my hands were locked in fear around my giblets; I didn't dare move them in case the mystery apparition suspected I was awake.

'Oh God oh God oh God please let her pass on and torment someone more deserving of her wrath than me! I'd only half-planned to stash those catalogue pages in her tower, and in the end I didn't, so why me, Lord? Nobody told me she was psychic as well as tormented! Please, please make her go away!'

Just like in bad dreams, my body felt heavy and my muscles incapable of exertion. Even if I'd wanted to try and make a run for it or fight back somehow, the adrenaline had drained me of the ability to do anything but lie there and tremble.

'Are you all right?'

I won't write the quick-fire combination of expletives and ecclesiastical titles that burst into my brain at hearing something speak to me. It would only read as sacrilegious and I think this book is going to be hard enough going for my parents as it is, without getting myself excommunicated in the process. I have my issues with the Church but I ain't no Sinead O'Connor or Madonna. I'm trying to be honest, not actively goad the Pope into a gloves-off, pay-per-view public slanging match. But at that moment in time, I had instantly acquired the inner vocabulary of a Glaswegian docker who'd smacked his thumb with a hammer whilst reading out the bidding prayers.

'Are you okay there?'

All I could do was scrunch up my eyes even tighter and for some bizarre reason nod my head instead of shaking it. My petrified mind took a while processing what I'd heard, but eventually I came to the conclusion that it was a man's voice and not that of a murderous grey lady.

'Are you sure? You don't look all right.'

Yes, it was definitely a male voice, one with a tone that seemed genuinely concerned and not the least bit menacing. And so I finally dared to open my eyes and see for myself who exactly it belonged to. Now, imagine the same self-censored internal outburst from the previous paragraph but this time accompanied by church bells ringing and hosts and choirs of broad-minded angels singing 'HALLELUJAH!' because the shadowy figure at the end of my bed was none other than the bloody sixth-form dormitory monitor making his rounds before turning in for the evening.

Oh, thank the Lord! I quickly gathered my wits and decided on a more suitable tone of gratitude to offer up to the heavens. Thank you, God, and your son, the Lord Jesus Christ, for delivering me from evil and unto your faithful servant! Or something like that.

'I'm okay' I said, genuinely meaning it.

Fuck, what a scare he'd given me! And although a run-in with the dorm monitor usually meant a clip round the ear or, worse still, a report followed by a visit to Father Sammy's office the next day, I was so bloody pleased to see him.

Seeing how relieved I was, he ventured beyond the little privacy curtain and sat on the far corner of the bed, smiling and putting a single finger to his mouth making the 'Ssssh' gesture, followed by a thumb point to the dorm outside and then a sleeping mime.

I smiled, nodded and whispered, 'Sorry.'

'That's okay' he said, just as quietly. 'So what's wrong?'

'Nothing.'

I realised as I said this that I'd had my bloody hands down my pyjama bottoms for the entire time since he'd first spoken to me. Like a gunslinger standing down to a sheriff, I started to retreat them to a safe distance, easing them to a more dignified area as slowly and casually as possible so as not to draw attention to this embarrassing fact.

'So, why aren't you asleep like everyone else?'

'Erm …' I waited until they were resting across my tummy before continuing, 'I just have trouble getting to sleep. That's all!' I shrugged and pulled as casual a smile as I could manage considering the circumstances.

'Is there anything worrying you?'

And with this he kind of patted my foot again above the covers, but left his hand resting there this time. 'Well?' Giving my ankle a friendly, playful squeeze like a parent might do as he smiled.

'No, not really. Just not tired.'

I was hardly going to divulge the details of my night-time fantasy visits to Frenchy's room to him. The fact that he'd made it to sixth form might mean he was one of the really pious ones that intended to go on into a career in the priesthood. Besides, that was the best part of my day. My premature insomnia was somehow finally managing to pay some sort of dividend in that place.

As relieved as I was that he was not some zombified dead woman, and despite the fact that he had shown more compassion towards my sleepless disposition than anyone else since my time there, I hoped the conversation would end on my parting comment: 'Goodnight, God bless!'

I pulled up the covers and turned on my side to gesture that I was ready to go to sleep now. But his hand didn't move from where it had come to rest on my foot. In fact, he gave it another gentle squeeze and started to rub the lower half of my calf as he spoke.

'There must be something stopping you from getting to sleep. Something bothering you?'

He continued rubbing my leg in a way that I can only describe as completely alien to how anybody had ever touched me before. It wasn't how a parent held and comforted you. It wasn't how my mum had rocked me to sleep following a nightmare or during a sickly fever. It was nothing like the hug or innocuous kiss on the forehead from a tipsy dad. Something deep inside me felt invaded and immediately vulnerable because of what he was doing. He kept rubbing – stroking – the bottom half of my leg as he spoke, and the way he was doing it felt innately wrong and horribly fucking intrusive.

'If you want to talk about it, somewhere where you won't wake anybody up, somewhere safe, we could talk in my Dormer ...'

I raised my head slightly off the pillow and looked at him, hoping that a shake of my head would make him stop. But it didn't.

This is not the moment in my life I want to be defined by. It's not the hesitation I want to hear in someone's voice when they discuss this book. It's not the guessed conversation I want my imagination running away with when I see folk nudging each other, pointing, and talking in hushed tones when I'm standing on the concourse at Euston station.

Like a slow-acting poison whose symptoms won't dilute whatever you throw down your neck, this memory didn't rush the job and simply kill me; it just played its part in quietly defining me for the worst. I remember looking up at that fucker and seeing the difference between a sympathetic adult wishing to comfort a child, and the soulless, two-faced desperation of somebody who wants to interfere with you.

Even if I didn't have the words to explain my misgivings at the time, I'll never forget his subtle desperation, like he was the needier of the two of us.

His words were devoid of adult conviction. There was something about what he was suggesting that implied we might both be taking some unspoken risk, but with no innocent childish pay-off. There was something acutely wrong with the way he was touching me and the way he was looking at me, all the while whispering words of comfort, but somehow dead behind the eyes. There was no authority, no real sense of moral conviction from this grown-up who was in charge.

Sixth-formers never whispered! They didn't worry about who was sleeping and who might wake up. They wanted the whole dorm to know who was in charge and when somebody was in trouble. They never took you to their private room at the end of the dorm, because discipline was discharged in public for every kid to see or hear. We didn't dare go near that room, vacant in daylight or occupied at night-time, and as bold as we were at times when flaunting the rules, we never messed with that room for some reason. So why, why, why should he be so determined that I go there with him now?

'It's hard not being able to sleep ...'

And he moved that fucking hand again up and down my leg with less sincerity and more urgency, squeezing it in another fake compassionate way, but higher up this time. It made me want to crawl out of my own skin and disappear under the bed. I didn't know what he was doing; I just knew how wrong it felt.

Years earlier in junior school, the only thing I loathed about our weekly swimming lesson was the rush to get changed back into our school clothes and get back onto the bus. There was something about putting dry clothes on over wet skin that went through me. Like the touch of velvet to some, or the squeaking of polystyrene to others. Or an unwanted hand on your leg in the night that makes your soul shiver.

'Especially here. Isn't it?'

I didn't respond, not even with a headshake or nod. I just lay there rigid, not with fear, but rather some unfamiliar sort of contempt. Oh God, I just wanted him to go away and leave me be. Although my eyes were focused straight ahead on some silly detail of my bedside cabinet, I could sense that his were firmly fixed on me. I could feel myself wanting to cry but not understanding why. Worse still, somehow I knew that if I cried then that would give him the perfect excuse to continue with his insincere interrogation.

But that's the awful thing when emotion overwhelms me, as it began to then. Even to this day, when the deep sense of emotional injustice swells within, the deep growls I swallow in my determination to keep my tears at bay only serve to multiply them until they rise up and are spluttered out against my will and I'm left blubbering like a childish wreck. Booze eases the passage of emotions and helps numb us from the awkward shame of having let our feelings out. But, sober, unstoppable tears are a weakness I have always loathed in myself.

'Just come with me and we can have a little talk about what's bothering you.'

He was almost pulling on my leg. Not quite tugging it, but holding it with a greater sense of physical urgency.

I turned and stared at him. 'I'm ready to go to sleep now!'

I yanked my leg away from him and curled up into as tight a ball as I could manage. The words came out much louder and more determined than I'd anticipated, possibly because I was on the verge of tears, but at least it had the desired effect. He stood up from my bed looking slightly startled for a moment by the volume and tone of my reaction, then he regained his composure and the mock sympathetic tone was back.

'Well, as long as you're all right then. Goodnight.'

But he took his time leaving. And I could tell he stayed standing just outside my cubicle for quite a while. I didn't close my eyes or do a very convincing job with my breathing for somebody supposedly about to go to sleep. There wasn't much point. I just lay there, knees up to my chest, staring at that seemingly hypnotic detail on the cabinet, swallowing tears, and praying that he wouldn't come back.

II.

BENEDICTION HAD LONG FINISHED

On the (very) rare occasions when I have recounted this tale before now, and always after too much to drink, I've invariably felt the need to throw some bravado into the telling of it. How I kicked out rather than rolled up, and challenged the sixth-former with promises to get my brother to go down there and twat him. But we all know now that I didn't do any of those things. I just retreated into myself and tried to come to terms with what had happened that evening.

Perhaps because I didn't do the heroic job of fighting back that I'd subsequently boast about, or maybe – as I thought to myself over and over again at that time – because I'd been so bold in my rejection of Upholland's teachings, God no longer had any interest in hearing my prayers, but most likely because I didn't dare tell anybody at the time, especially my brother, that the dorm monitor did come back. Time and time again.

He never touched me again, though. On the nights he patrolled our dorm, I made sure to keep as much of myself as far up the top end of the bed as possible, well away from the privacy curtain and his horrible touchy-feely gestures. But that didn't stop him putting his head through and posing the usual questions:

'Still not sleeping?'

'Wide awake, again?'

'Bad dreams?'

'If you need to talk about anything, then you know where I am.'

But I never answered. Over time, his façade faded as the tone of his questions became less sympathetic and more sarcastic: pure mocking as opposed to mock empathy. And, dear God, how I prayed I'd be asleep before he'd start his rounds. Even if it left me more vulnerable, I prayed and prayed and prayed for sleep to take me before his taunting would begin.

I never thought to ask my dorm mates if they'd experienced what I had, and I'm fearful to this day of tainting other people's past with my own ordeal.

In years to come even JOHNNY wouldn't dare go near this shite with a ten-foot barge-pole. He knew I'd fucking kill HIM stone-dead if he ever dared!

There had always been weak whispers amongst the older students of who to watch out for amongst the staff, but these stories were never told from personal experience, always from the perspective of some student long gone. I tried paying more attention, to pick up more detail of those rumours after the near initiation into one myself. I wanted to try and make some sense of this horrible new obstacle the regime had put in my way. But younger students weren't really privy to conversations held by the older boys. I'd also hoped to hear of consequences for these actions – perverts ousted and punishments imposed, but there were none. Those incomprehensible acts were camouflaged by innuendo and laughed off as best they could be.

I know I wasn't actually physically sexually abused. I appreciate in a great many ways how fortunate I was. Obviously, I don't consider what I went through anywhere near as painful as what some people have suffered in their lifetimes, and I sure as hell don't consider any public profile a mitigating factor when trying to surmount my own personal demons. I know I had already turned my back on much of what Upholland represented. I know I had sinned and constructed my own blueprint for morality, throwing some of God's teachings back in His face in the process. And I'd learnt to justify this behaviour as a means of surviving that place. As a result, I thought I'd get through any guilt-ridden institutionalised double standard bullshit that they might throw in my path. But I was wrong, because this had beaten me.

I may have been at odds with Upholland up until that point, but now my very presence there sickened me. The whole college felt like some huge self-perpetuating conspiracy of silence, and by keeping my mouth shut and going about my business, I was enabling it to continue. I was the new generation of co-conspirator, and for the very first time there – despite all my shortcomings as a trainee priest and a Christian in general – I felt completely and utterly ashamed of myself.

I spent each day drifting, like the victim of some ongoing out-of-body experience, and yet I felt trapped in myself the moment lights went out at night. I dreaded the nights. I never thought of Frenchy again after lights out, even when the predatory prefect wasn't assigned to our dorm. I dreaded the idea that it might've been my nocturnal fantasies that had caused the whole awful mess in the first place. What if he'd seen me one night when I was in the middle of meddling with myself? How many times might he have watched me and thought that what he had tried to initiate was something I would willingly participate in? What if all those fucking fantasies – the details, the perving and leching over her, the fucking quest for intimate details of a grown woman – had led to this? Everything I'd devoted my quiet moments to embellishing now made me feel physically ill. I'd wanted to know what actual sex was like, so maybe I'd got exactly what was coming to me.

It was a self-loathing that I couldn't rebel against, because it came from within. And just like my very first few weeks at that awful fucking institution the previous year, I spent every night quietly crying myself to sleep and repeating to myself over and over again, 'I want to go home.'

When I finally did get home that holiday, I spent every waking moment wondering how and when I would tell my parents I had no intention of going back. I didn't want to spoil Christmas for anybody, or destroy the career that so many good and virtuous people seemed determined I should enter into, but every day I delayed, the fear grew in me that I might chicken out or back down into going back to the hell expected of me.

I argued the case for my defence with myself morning, noon and night. Christmas Day, Boxing Day, New Year's Eve and New Year's Day came and went but offered no distraction from the bombshell I was so desperate to drop. I shouldn't go back and I was determined I wasn't going back, but I couldn't translate the inner mantra into a coherent and decisive sentence.

So I kept my mouth shut. My mum packed my gear, and my dad packed the car. The only thing left to do was attend Benediction at the local parish church before we left. That way everyone could wish me luck and shake my hand and offer their blessings before going back to their own homes to sleep soundly at night without fear of someone molesting them.

I knelt in church and prayed to God for the courage to back up my convictions. Nothing.

I told Him that it wasn't fair to expect me to go back there knowing what we knew. Nothing.

I promised to serve Him more faithfully as a lay person if He'd only let me stay home. Nothing.

I begged Him to forgive me for wasting His time and that of the parish and all the decent priests and staff at Upholland. Nothing.

I threatened Him that I would not keep quiet about that fucking bastard sixth-former if He refused to aid me in my genuine hour of need. Nothing.

I apologised for threatening Him and promised to keep my mouth shut for ever if I didn't have to leave. Nothing.

Benediction had long finished and I don't know how much time had passed whilst I'd knelt there, hands folded tight in prayer, making bargain after bargain with my silent God. I hadn't realised how awkward the situation had become for my parents who were gently trying to usher me up off my knees and out of the pew. I just remember the sobbing starting. Big, loud, awful, snotty sobs disrupted only by my half-coherent pleading: 'I don't want to go back there. Please, please don't make me go back. I'm so sorry. I'm sorry, I'm sorry, I'm sorry. I hate it there, I hate it. Please, please don't take me back, Dad, please.'

I don't know how long that went on, either. My parents said nothing. They just led me out of the church, still crying. It should've been a huge relief, but I was such a mess. The fact that I had finally, and in such a spectacularly undignified way, trashed the dreams of my entire parish was clearly brought home by the silence and slack jaws of the remaining congregation who'd waited afterwards to see me off.

There was no coercion on Mum and Dad's part regarding my return to Upholland following that scene. We went home, a phone call was made, and my dad said we were to go and collect the rest of my belongings. If there was any regret at my decision, they hid it well. There was hardly anything in the way of conversation as we drove back there. I guess I'd said all that had needed to be said back in church.

I left my dad, who had to go and talk to the head of the college and explain things, and went to my dorm for the last time. I collected the rest of my belongings without speaking a word to anyone. In the hustle and bustle of unpacking for the next term, none of my classmates had realised that I was packing to leave for good.

We got back into the car without my saying a single goodbye to any student or member of staff, and drove away. I never attempted to speak or write to a single member of Low figs after I left. Not even my very best friend, Simon, who I miss to this day. I had no intention of visiting the place again, or sending news of my progress since sneaking away.

I didn't write to Lynne again, either, even though we were now at liberty to kiss in public and even maybe one day marry as I'd naively dreamt of so often. The source of my happiest memories there, tainted through no fault of her own, was dumped unceremoniously along with all the rest.

The truth was I was ashamed at having abandoned my fellow pupils there to their own fates. At not having said something to try and convince them to leave too, and come with me. I know how arrogant that sounds. I was no leader of boys, no inspirational figure amongst my peers. I was a coward and a cop-out, but I knew I'd learn to live with that if it meant my going home.

I just wasn't to know how long and hard I'd have to work at keeping all the memories of that place buried, along with all my shame at helping keep its secrets from the outside world I was now free to enjoy.

PART III
JOHNNY GERMINATES

12.

THE BLUE BLAZER

The dust quickly settled for the most part after leaving my vocation behind. It's frightening how quickly I filed the whole thing away, somewhere 'safe'. Nobody spoke about it, and I had no wish to dwell on the chunk of my childhood squandered.

I was determined to make up for lost time and, in comparison to Upholland, even school seemed like an exciting opportunity for normal mischief. All my mates from the juniors had gone on to Eddy Camp (Edward Campion High School) and although my two brothers, Rob and Mark, had already left, I reckoned they'd left behind enough of a name for themselves to ease my acceptance as 'new kid' amongst the older ranks.

So I did my best to join in the joke when Mum and Dad suggested that I go and take a look at West Park School instead.

'Why not buy me a briefcase, bowler hat and pipe while you're at it? Tootle pip!'

West Park's very name screamed 'Posh!' in Thatto Heath, an elitist throwback to the golden age of grammar schools. It was more an institution for bright kids and rugger-buggers than a school, and a million miles away from the *Grange Hill*-style camaraderie I had dreamt of at Eddy Camp.

After realising my parents were serious, I agreed to take the tour, but with all the enthusiasm of a skilled cobbler visiting a Nike sweatshop, making it perfectly clear to my folks that I had no intention of going there.

On the day itself, Dad went off to meet the headmaster and I was invited to sit in and sample a typical class there. Which I did, smugly, knowing I'd be home and watching daytime telly before they knew what had hit them.

The bell rang and without waiting to be dismissed along with everyone else, I got up to leave.

'Where do you think you're going?'

'Home. I only came here to have a look around.'

'Well, look from your desk!'

'But my dad's waiting for—'

'Sit down! The rest of you take out your text books.'

All the other kids were laughing as I retook my seat. I went salmon-pink with awkwardness but consoled myself with the fact that this guy was going to owe me a big apology once he'd realised his mistake. I sat through another lesson, but a different subject, taught by the same teacher.

He was one of those gym teachers who couldn't hide the fact that he found academia every bit as tedious as the majority of the pupils he was teaching. Men weren't built in the classroom, they were built out there, on the rugby field. Having the shit kicked out of you left a bruise, a badge of purple honour.

I paid as little attention to learning as he did as I looked for my dad's face to appear in the narrow rectangle of wired safety-glass set into the door. He'd tap his watch and I wouldn't stop walking this time. I'd seen enough.

The bell rang, but no Dad. I was escorted to my next class despite my heartfelt protests, and the next teacher knew my name.

My induction to West Park was short, simple and no nonsense.

'Michael Pennington. I understand this is your first day, but from here on in you will be expected to wear the appropriate uniform. Now take a seat.'

I walked home after the last bell having had to get directions, as I didn't even know the exact location of the school in relation to our house. And I was absolutely fucking fuming. The sly git had enrolled me and just buggered off without saying a bloody word!

I stamped through Taylor Park like a young Basil Fawlty, throwing fists at a tall, invisible protagonist and swearing revenge through a jaw clenched tight with rage. When I finally got home, what followed was more of a domestic than a tantrum.

Along with a childhood, Upholland had stripped me of the automatic acceptance that grown-ups always knew best. I threw everything at my parents from my moral high ground, plus some carefully crafted emotional blackmail for good measure.

'Just because you've lost your little priest to show off round the parish, you get back at me by this?'

That upset my mum, and it was wrong of me to say it. Deep down, even I knew it wasn't the case, especially where she was concerned. I had never resented them for Upholland. The fact is, I'd only ever blamed and hated myself in equal measure for ending up there. The parish had felt let down by my leaving, but I knew it was a huge relief to my mum, and simply a chapter that I reckoned had closed as far as my dad was concerned. But I'd have said anything at that time to ensure this West Park press-ganging ended there and then.

The fact that West Park would never have accepted me had I not been a former seminary student was just the ironic icing on destiny's shit-filled cake. The school was run by a religious order known as the brothers of the De La Salle. They were hardcore – the *Boyz in the Hood* of vocational hoodlums – and my mum's basic argument for entrusting my future to them was that my brothers had turned into arrogant thugs and this was somehow Eddy Camp's fault. She and Dad had decided I stood a better chance of making something of myself in high school if I went elsewhere. But that made it even worse! The fact that I was being thrown to a new set of lions for my brothers' crimes incensed me.

Mum tried to reason with me but Dad quickly lost his usual appetite for debate and told me in no uncertain terms that West Park was decided, done and dusted, simple as.

The odd bit of impending teenage rebelliousness aside, this was one of the rare moments in my life when I felt genuine resentment towards him. He'd never been the villain of the piece before, and it shocked me. The whole 'good cop, bad cop' scenario had been turned on its head, and I couldn't accept the reason why.

My response wasn't a mere sulk that would pass in time. Back there and then, I was morally winded by this sucker punch, and once again felt powerless to negotiate on my own terms against an overwhelming sense of injustice.

Years later, Dad let slip that Upholland had said I may well change my mind and want to return a week or two after term had started. As I sit here now, finding pieces of the puzzle under the rug of fate I'd previously taken for granted, it stuns me to think that, despite everything, they apparently regarded me as a promising asset to their institution and had offered to keep a place open for me should I come to my senses and wish to reconvene with my vocation.

For the sake of the father–son bond, I doubt I'll ever dare ask Dad if West Park was a calculated risk on his part to nudge me back into the seminary fold.

Whilst there, I'd grown used to hours on end of distraction-free debate with myself within the closeted walls of the seminary. I had learned to question my elders, my 'superiors', and saw the world with wearier eyes than most kids my age. So now my needs didn't feel like the simple, foot-stamping tantrums of a kid who simply wanted something but couldn't offer a full and valid explanation as to why. Like a body-swap movie, but even lighter on the laughs, I somehow felt like I'd accelerated towards the headspace of a thirty-something whilst trapped in the podgy body of a 13-year-old child with less fight in him than a gym sock. Protesting was useless, and all my rage turned in on itself, eventually decomposing into a mound of steaming, bitter futility.

I gave up. But somewhere, some place deep down in the empty space ignored by the heart and conscious mind alike, I suspect JOHNNY was taking notes and preparing a solid case for the defence (or should that be the prosecution?). Tapping away on HIS cognitive typewriter, poor Dad's card was clearly marked with an X.

So, with a blazer donated by the Ford family (West Park's being dark navy instead of the St Helens standard school black – a dangerous novelty that rendered all our domestic hand-me-downs useless at a stroke), I was inked in on the school's register. That blue blazer would catch the light perfectly as I tried to pass Grange Park School unnoticed as part of my long walk home along Broadway; the last quarter mile would become a mad dash to our garden gate whenever a pack of GP hyenas spotted the endangered blue-backed pot-bellied pig sneaking by.

I had no option but to give up my dreams of a reunion with the old gang from St Austin's, even despite the following obvious factors:

Fact: West Park scared me.

Fact: Nobody knew me; nobody immediately liked me.

I was a new kid. Nobody likes new kids in a real school. I was bottom of the food chain and nobody rushes to befriend a new kid with no discernible benefits other than geekiness by association.

Fact: They were everything I'd wished for without the back catalogue of junior school goodwill. They were normal kids. Normal kids who weren't missing home. Normal kids who thought homesickness was a cissy virus. Normal kids who didn't like school, but got through their version of the working day by pushing, shoving, piss-taking and squaring up. Normal kids, some of whom could shut you up with a glance, or a punch if the glance wasn't enough. Normal kids who didn't give a flying fuck about my emotional development as a result of, what, my training for the priesthood? A mere red rag to any normal young bull.

Diary 84 February

Upholland is now my past and have enroled with West Park High School. Unfortunately my friends from younger days do not attend but just to be home compensates for this....

The public uproar of my leaving Upholland hasn't really surfaced and I realise that the people I was so scared of dissapointing were never really concerned. Coming back to Earth with a bang brings with it the realisation of how unimportant my decisions are to the masses. Makes things much easier, for the moment.

I relish the feeling of insignificance, life outside the public spotlight is great, well for now anyway.....

Theres this fraction of nostalgia I feel for Upholland, not only for the good friends I left behind, but also because now it seems that all my bridges are burnt. No longer is there a choice in my life, this is the bed I've made and so in it I must lie. Decisions in my life now seem so insignificant, as do many of the issues so urgently undertaken by my new found schoolyard associates, but to involve myself means treating minor problems with the same zest as my allies, a digression towards the simple times before Upholland....

Friends and an active social life (due I suppose to the community in wich I am lucky enough to grow up in) impress constantly the need to balance myself in my new surroundings.

Now, don't get me wrong: I wasn't singled out by any particular bully. Apart from a few minor incidents, West Park had a very democratic sense of fairness when it came to sharing out the threats and insults. In fact, the first lad who'd tried to put me in my place, Spottiswood (you never forget a name so wanky), was a godsend. A posh, well-spoken prick, probably dropped off at school every day in a Bentley (or, at least, so the trainee class warrior in me insisted). He had all the intimidation skills of an asthmatic whelk with a sick-note from 'Mummy', and would've been a great boost for me had he shown up for our scheduled fight after the last bell.

I guess he thought he'd spotted an opportunity with a new kid quite visibly out of his depth. The fact that he considered himself able to pose a threat perfectly illustrates how far I'd slid down the league table of physical intimidation.

I bare-facedly chickened out of my next potential scrap though, and, to make matters worse, I tried implying that I was taking some sort of religious stand against violence. Truth was, I just didn't fancy my chances, and panicked with my retaliatory response.

'I'm gonna have you, come home time!'

'Well, I'm going to pray for you!'

Even my dad couldn't hide his disappointment at that comeback. I told him, hoping he would commend me on my faux-Christian bravery in turning the other cheek. He just shook his head and said, 'You should've thumped him!'

Thanks.

13.

CAT'S ARSE-KISSER AND DESMOND TUTU

Now, having said all that, some hope did lie in one of the neighbouring Ford clan. Fordy was in the fifth form, wasn't one to be messed with, and although he didn't take me under his wing as such, there was some fun to be had courtesy of him and his mates.

You needed to have a special pass to leave the school at lunchtime. These were meant for those who lived close enough to go home for lunch, and a gang of them would go to a house just up the street and hang out smoking, eating toast and playing Chucky Egg on the Spectrum.

Unable to get a pass, I would wear my gym kit under my uniform, sweat the morning out and claim I'd forgotten it. West Park was a school dedicated to sport and nobody was exempt – sick-notes were scrutinised like Diamonique in a pawn-brokers. I'd be sent home to retrieve it, and as they thought I was wasting my lunch hour time trekking all the way there and back, I'd be kicking back on a sofa waiting for 'savers' on a Benson & Hedges and my turn on Q*bert.

I wasn't strictly pals with them. I was more a tagalong, an apprentice reprobate who provided light relief through my eagerness to share in the bad habits of older lads. I'd walk home with them most days and save my bus money for 'loosies' (cigarettes sold separately).

One day, the whole of Fordy's fifth-form rugby team tried to kidnap me and take me to a match as their mascot. They threw me in the minibus and pinned me to the floor as Mr Murphy, the head of PE, willingly drove out of the car park. And I would've gone with them for the *craic* had I not had Mr Higgins for history straight after lunch.

Mr Higgins had a mean, no-nonsense look to him with a personality to match. His permanent five o'clock shadow called time on a rumpled face topped with hair that birds could've actually lived in. Had one of *The Wacky Races*' Ant Hill Mob fallen on hard times, it would be him.

He still employed corporal punishment as a teaching method, despite the ban, although I would later realise this was more a clever bit of psychology than straight-forward aggression. He would slipper you at the back of the class and dare anyone to turn and watch, suggesting themselves for a 'slippering' if they did so. I often fell victim to this and soon learned it made a great noise but barely registered on the pain scale. Still, the threat of it ensured Mr Higgins maintained a tighter ship than most in his classes.

Anyhow, after much pleading and dropping of Mr Higgins' name, the rugby team threw me out at Windle Island. I ran all the way back to school, managed to dodge the gate monitors and was just five minutes late for class, only to be rewarded with the obligatory slipper in the absence of a decent excuse.

As had happened with the sixth-formers at Upholland, this incident cemented my reputation with the other lads for being someone who could take a joke without squealing to those in charge. But in what seems like a blink of an eye now, Fordy and his mates left at the end of their fifth form, and suddenly I was a wannabe wild one without a patron.

I think I'd taken the protection afforded me by my casual association with him and his mates for granted. As a consequence, I hadn't really bonded with my actual classmates, and back there in my third year, I suddenly felt the pang of isolation – more a lonely arse than a smart one.

School and the continued academic success it promised meant little to me; it was just something I figured I'd have to endure as best as I could. The trick to fitting in was to not excel at anything in particular, and I enjoyed the initial dumbing-down by doing just enough to scrape by. Perhaps I was subconsciously punishing my folks for their underhand methods, but my immediate concern was to slide under the radar by deconstructing everyone's expectations of me and coasting in the slipstream of schoolyard social acceptance.

I made friends and got with the program: most of them seemed as keen as me on the minimum amount of social exposure. In the classroom, we only answered questions when pressed to, and at break time we'd find the quietest corners of the playground in which to congregate, and never joined in the communal game of 20 or even 30-a-side football.

Fights could start over nothing, so they were best left to it. For all my whining about Upholland, being out in the 'yard' at West Park felt like I'd moved from an open prison to a maximum-security wing. I was a blue-collar criminal doing hard time amongst Britain's most wanted.

Now, I understand how OTT that sounds, but I realised that the structure I had fought so hard against had also allowed me an odd sort of freedom to develop a false confidence – a misguided ego that thought I was somehow something quite unique. Here there was no time to ponder your place in the world, no us against them. It was us against us, them and everything!

I longed to sit on the fence and merely observe the differences between the past and my now chaotic present. I wanted to be the editor back in the safety of his office; not the reporter in the field, out there living the story. I had gone from self-styled hero to undeniable coward.

The simplest way to lie low was hanging out in the library at lunchtime. A limited number of pupils were allowed in strictly for study purposes, but once you'd gained access, the prefects rarely fussed over what you did. There was little chance of anything more confrontational than a tug-of-war on the same book from opposing sides of the shelf.

Academic indifference led to endless sketches and doodles. I would fall foul of one particular prefect from time to time, but only because his colleagues would coerce me into drawing cruel sketches of him carrying his stomach around in a wheelbarrow, which caused him much obvious anguish but could guarantee me entry to the library depending on whoever else was manning the door. I'd rediscovered my love of drawing since returning home from Upholland, and would idle away hours and hours of what should have been my education building on the characters and stories that transfixed me in *2000 AD* in a series of exercise books.

What I lacked in wit I could more than compensate for with a cutting illustration. My pen might not have been necessarily mightier than the sword, but it was definitely funnier.

One advantage of not regularly sneaking out at lunchtime any more was the fact that school dinners were fucking brilliant. There was a wide variety of deep-fried stuff, chips came with everything, and veg was optional! I had no qualms queuing up for my 'free meal' ticket. Some kids there seemed embarrassed by the stigma of their folks being on state benefits. Me? I was just happy getting the school-dinner equivalent of a McDonald's. The nicknames 'Pugsley' (*The Addams Family*), 'Roland' (*Grange Hill*), 'Aubrey' (fat cartoon character), 'Playtex' (bra advert – kids would dance around me singing 'Playtex has a bra for the way you are') and others less memorable had been awarded to me early on, so watching my figure felt like a lost cause as I tucked in like a starved, self-fulfilling prophecy each day.

At West Park, it was rare that anyone's real name was used away from the school register. Everyone below the cocks and their goons had nicknames based on either obvious physical short-comings, unfortunate information regarding their home life that had leaked into public awareness, or downright ridiculous, made-up crap.

My best mate (whom I'll get to in a wee while) was known as 'Cat's arse-kisser' after supposedly – obviously – kissing a cat's arse at a party for a dare. I knew it was rubbish, but still I revelled in throwing it back at him every time he made an issue of my man-boobs. We also had a 'Tree-fucker', again for the obvious reasons, 'Squid' (a lad who'd damaged an eye after an unfortunate accident with some scissors), 'Stig of the Dump' (a lad whose dad had recently been made redundant), 'Desmond Tutu' (a lad who was black), 'Spoon-head', 'Captain Beaky' … the list went on and on, and no potentially hurtful verbal stone was left unturned.

My appetite for alternate realities was re-ignited during this period of constant kow-towing to personal insults. Between my idle sketches and distancing concern to learn, my mind busied itself with fantasised confrontations – what I might say next time, what I should've said that time.

The drawings I did for public approval were all comically tailored, but my private cartoons all seemed inspired by violence and an unnatural bloodlust. The movies call it 'comic strip', but this was more than flirting with the notion of inflicting pain; this was a real, cold, joyless quest for retribution.

At Upholland, my escape route had been through a fantastical love affair with Frenchy, until Satan's touchy-feely accomplice turned up, but now I had an undeniable craving for confrontation. Not real face-to-face conflict, but unrealistic, imagined crossings of verbal swords where I always won the battles I was shying away from on a daily basis.

It's hard to write this because I'm not sure if it is the most common of traits and therefore unremarkable and unworthy of a mention, or if it is a distinct and clear-cut acknowledgement of mental health problems, but I know it matters a lot to me either way. It was around about this time my idle fantasies forged an inner monologue that would become a dangerous yet trusted mentor.

I believe it's the first time I ever heard **HiM** speak to me. Or try and shout out through me had I have been reckless enough to let **HiM** negotiate the schoolyard on my behalf. It should have sounded alarm bells, but I was a lonely individual who felt the only person who knew me and still believed in me was **HiM**.

He didn't yet have a name. **He** never formally introduced **HiM-SeLF**, but I felt like I'd known **HiM** all my life, and I knew I'd need never explain myself to **HiM**.

He got me. **He** was aware of why I went to such dark places, and **He** never dissuaded me from going there. In fact, I reckon **He** would wait for me there. But **He** never revelled in the dangerous solace I was seeking. Like a life-coach who understood the need for tough love, **He**'d drill me on the uselessness of introspection and tell me in no uncertain terms how **we** needed to take the fight to them.

It's bloody hard sitting here and admitting to myself in public that I lacked the normal coping mechanisms of a teenager and therefore constructed this alternative reality. And then I get defensive and cross and even now **He** wants to butt in and start ranting on my behalf. No, I didn't construct **HiM**. I never had a blueprint or plan for something like **HiM**.

It's pathetic that an adolescent should react to life in such an infantile way by embracing an imaginary friend. But whatever **He** was back then, **we** were all I had because it felt like nobody else gave a shit.

It's odd how subsequent success can obscure other people's memories of who you were and how you conducted yourself. Hence the number of ex-West Park pupils I'll bump into now who've rewritten my history as one of class clown and general all-round funny guy. I'm not being bitter, it's just that this simply ain't true.

I had one party-piece that won me a bit of short-lived notoriety. This involved an unwitting kid, normally from a year below us, being forced to approach me and ask, 'How's your sister's ballet lessons going?'

At that point I would turn to them, completely crestfallen, and start crying right there on the spot (a gift I can't actually remember discovering, but vital to the believability of the gag).

'I suppose you think you're funny, don't you?' I'd sob. Then I'd run off to a corner, bawling, whilst lads in my year would feign sympathy and run after me, apart from one who'd inform the prank victim of his mistake.

'You tight git. You know his sister got run over by a bus and had to have both her legs cut off! The headmaster said the next kid who makes fun of him is gonna get expelled!'

The poor kid would run over almost in tears himself, pleading ignorance and begging me not to tell the head, but he'd be ushered away, as I turned up the false sobs, with a curt, 'Leave him alone, will yer!' or 'Haven't you done enough?'

It was the kind of cruel comedy that went down well at West Park, and I can't deny some of the reactions were bloody funny. At least, they were until one lad decided to run straight to Brother Victor's office and throw himself on his mercy in a genuine flood of tears.

Trying to explain that my sister had not actually been in any sort of accident, and was in fact successfully holding down a Saturday job at Argos whilst studying art at the local Gamble Institute, was a struggle with Old Victor.

'No, she's never danced professionally, Brother.'

Trying to deconstruct the gag in order to explain the nature of the prank I was owning up to was like instructing the occupants of a nursing home on the differences in game play between Space Invaders and Galaxians, without the benefit of visual aids. There was a genuine relief when that malicious old bastard eventually decided to play it safe, response-wise, with a painful bit of corporal punishment, as it meant the real ordeal was over.

But back to my point. Apart from an unnatural ability to convincingly cry at will, I was not a 'funny' person. In fact, I reckon you've pretty much sussed by now that I took many aspects of life far too seriously for a kid my age. I wasn't anti-social, but I felt an undeniable distance between myself and the normality of others. This situation was a conundrum I could never quite crack. Did I envy them their sense of belonging, or resent everything it represented? Probably a bit of both.

Although **J**o**HNN**y would eventually go on to make a virtue of this overwhelming sense of alienation, I am, as Michael Pennington, ashamed to admit that I ceased for a time to share in my school community's fundamental enjoyment of life. And that is why I never went home and thought of funny stuff to do in school next day to win everybody over.

Everyone took it in turns to pose in front of the Ford's family car. Ours was up on bricks in the back garden and didn't quite scream the cool moody teen boy racer look I was going for.

There were none of the daft routines so many people presume an eventual comic would've desperately practised over and over again in front of a mirror. I was discontented and far too naïve to realise the comedy riches waiting to be mined from those dark, dank shafts of self-doubt and loathing. There are comics who are born needy opportunists, and they're the ones who per-petuated that kind of behaviour, but it was never my ambition. Neither, as things would transpire, was it **H**i**S**. **H**e never coveted a single thing they longed and trained for. **H**e saw it for the fool's gold that it is. **H**e would never simply argue the case for my social acceptance, because he wanted to prove to both them and me that they never deserved **U**s in the first place.

So, apart from the silly drawings, there was no wise-cracking on my part. The voice within was always waving **H**i**S** arms like a partner in a tag-team wrestling match, desperate to prove **H**i**M**S**e**L**F** and vocalise a weakness **H**e'd spotted in the other team, but I controlled **H**i**M** back then, and I knew if **H**e went shooting **H**i**S** mouth off that I'd have to deal with the physical fallout. My motto was, 'Why clown when you can cower?'

And so, far from them being water off of a duck's back, I absorbed the insults flung around, like an economy pack of triple-ply kitchen towels. I found the constant barrage discon-certing but, as I've said, only a small minority were immune from the communal taunting. And although the fact that the fake-sister-with-the-missing-legs routine worked on the prem-ise of guilt suggested a shared ethical framework, there didn't seem to be any moral line in the sand that the verbal cruelty of the masses there wouldn't cross.

Hence my high levels of apprehension in advance of parents' night. In denial about my weight gain, but suddenly conscious of my dad's solid build and my mum's limited height, I dreaded them coming into school. I had a pre-imagined list of names my exquisitely sadistic classmates might come up with. Stuff like, 'I see your dad has brought Orville along.' Although my parents had been responsible for dumping me at West Park, I knew nei-ther of u**S** would be able to ignore or laugh off an insult directed at them, and that would lead to the kind of conflict I was des-perate to avoid.

My folks mistook my unease for fear of imminent disclosure of deteriorating grades, which I actually didn't give two tits about. In the end, I faked illness on the night itself so my parents could attend anonymously, on their own. The report came back perfect as far as my ambitions were concerned: 'Average slipstream. Could try harder here and room for improvement there but, overall, treading water comfortably.'

There were no outstanding behavioural issues either, so my mum and dad seemed content enough with my 'progress'.

But there's always one, isn't there? Somebody who saw beyond the charade and wouldn't let go of the potential I had been so successfully dispersing around the school, like a PoW spreading dirt around the exercise yard in *The Great Escape* ...

14.

ROWENA VS IAN

She was a nemesis I would learn to love and admire. She had seen it all, taught the best and the worst, and never resigned herself to just instructing a class to open their text books at page I-just-want-my-pension-then-I'm-out-of-here and quietly read. She never 'just' taught: she jousted. She worked the room like a truly seasoned stand-up. Often funny, direct and uncomfortable when necessary, and passionately knowledgeable about the chosen subject matter, she was a lazy brain's idea of hell, but Mrs Rowena Rowlands proved herself the guardian angel of much that I now hold dear with regard to the English language and its literature.

Around the time she began taking a special interest in my academic underachievement, I became really good friends with a kid called Ian.

He was a funny lad who knew how to throw caution to the wind with a carefree shrug of his shoulders that I admired. He also had a quick wit and an almost Tourette's-like inability to resist giving lip back to harder lads. When confronted, he would pull a sarcastic 'Who, me?' face and somehow always avoid what should've been an inevitable kicking. Yet I could see he was quietly ready to go a few rounds if backed too far into a corner. And he was the only lad who could commonly refer to me as 'Fatty' without a trace of malice – it didn't sting, somehow, when he said it.

As we became better mates, I went from cowering amongst my disillusioned associates to walking just that little bit taller and finding things to laugh about throughout the days. And the more time we hung out together, the less time I had to listen to H'M. I think He took it pretty well, but to be honest with you, I couldn't be sure, simply because for the first time in a long time, I'd stopped listening and started living.

So, all in all, life was picking up, school-wise. I had a teacher I admired and respected, with a huge intellectual crush thrown in for good measure, and I had a mate to mentor me in normal teen rebellion kind of stuff.

I believe Mrs Rowlands was integral to defining what I would look for in a woman later in life, once the savage hormones had been tamed. She would teach a whole class but reach out with a wit that made me smile to myself, arrogantly thinking I was the only one in on the joke. Physical attraction alone would never be enough now in the long term. Rowena had spoiled me for the better, and my previous fantasy of one day sporting that trophy wife who'd turn the envious heads of past oppressors was redirected to wanting someone just as smart and funny as she.

She was bohemian in appearance and wore her hair wild and slightly unkempt. And I mean that as a compliment. She didn't seem to fuss over how she looked, like most women you were supposed to fancy, but she had a confidence that held more sex appeal than any amount of glamour painted on her contemporaries.

For some reason, I imagined her living on a barge, smoking high-tar cigarettes, drinking red wine and marking papers by candlelight. She'd have marched in the sixties and probably wrote countless letters in aid of loads of causes. I never wasted time sketching when I was in her class, because she wanted to know what you actually thought, not how much unconsidered information your brain could retain. And she never shied away from telling it as it was.

'Right, you're bored, and I'm too good at this to stand here wasting my time. But whilst you think you're the ones suffering here, let me point something out. You have all undergone some drastic physical developments of late, finding all manner of hairs breaking out in the process, no doubt. Unfortunately, you have yet to discover the men's toiletries section of your local Boots, hence you all stink to high heaven. All of you raise your arms. Come on, everyone! Now take a moment to appreciate the less than delightful aroma your armpits are emitting. Go on!'

And with that, the majority of the class, faces contorted with self-disgust, woke up and smelt the pungent pubescent roses.

'Not pretty is it? And a few open windows do little to ease the discomfort you've remained so blissfully unaware of 'til today. Now, if I must be made to suffer so, I think the least you could all do is sit up and focus for the remainder of the lesson, agreed?'

A class full of awkward, shame-faced lads nodded, and Rowena proceeded to impress upon us the deteriorating state of Macbeth's sanity. She was class through and through.

In Ian, I was rediscovering the kind of unruly spirit Upholland had hoped to stamp out. We'd wag it from school at lunchtimes and sod off smoking somewhere. Or we'd try and jump the drainage ditch – effectively it was a protective moat – that separated West Park from the neighbouring girls' school, Notre Dame. I never made the jump, but still it was funny stamping back to class stinking to high heaven from the knees down.

We'd also wag it from PE by joining the cross-country team and hiding in the first bush we came to before returning straight back to the changing rooms, getting back into our school gear and sodding off to doss about somewhere (sometimes nicking beer towels off the washing line at the Seven Stars pub, purely because they were there).

I somehow didn't fear getting caught because I had a partner in crime, a Butch to my Sundance. Plus, Ian had a way of daring me that would make the thought of not doing it unthinkable, and the possible consequences of getting caught seem utterly inconsequential.

The only time I managed to stand firm in saying no to one of his dares was when he alone tried smoking some dry banana skin as he'd heard it could get you high. I laughed till I almost puked when he turned a pale colour of nausea no human should ever turn and retched the whole way along the all-weather pitch, back to class. But even he couldn't stop a grin at the expense of his own stupidity breaking out in between chunks of his lunch coming back up. Ian was shite at being serious, and when he tried now, that cracked me up all the more, which in turn set him off again.

'It's not funny, Fatty [smirking]. I might have food poisoning [violent hurling].'

I laughed like Upholland had never happened thanks to that lad. I laughed like a kid again, and for what felt like the first time in years, tears of pure, unadulterated joy rolling down my big, chubby cheeks.

Mrs Rowlands did not appear to share my appreciation of Ian, though. She had spotted what she saw as real potential in me, and was doing her very best to coax the academic achiever back out from his hiding place. And it was working; well, at least as far as English was concerned.

I read books with her enthusiasm still resonating in my head but with the intellectual freedom to interpret as I saw fit. I read dialogue and realised the difference between passion and manipulation. I rallied to her cause every time she dared to raise dead passages to life. She was a beautifully demented Frankenstein and I was her Igor.

I even risked a kicking when the curriculum forced each of us to read aloud a section of literature chosen by ourselves. After an impassioned section of John Wyndham's *The Chrysalids*, Rowena actually stood up and applauded me:

'Now that, class, is how you read a book!'

I had to dig deep to cover up that inner burst of pride. Here was my beautiful mentor publicly acknowledging her appreciation of me, and it felt great. My dramatic reading had been the best way I could come up with of letting her know that her methods worked and were genuinely appreciated, and it had paid off. I felt like Babe as she winked at me as if to say, 'That'll do, pig, that'll do.'

I soon realised that I was a porker to the slaughter, though, as loads of the lads mimed the time-honoured wanker/slit throat/ blowjob gestures, or pointed to the classroom clock then buried a fist into the palm of their hand. But it was worth it, and although there were no physical consequences to my showing off – just a week of 'Teacher's pet' and 'Arse-licker' – I loved her all the more for dropping me in it. It had confirmed what I'd quietly come to believe: Rowena got me.

So I couldn't understand why she failed to see how important my friendship with Ian was. Or why she seemed so determined to split us up as pals. Yes, there was more than a bit of the old Bart Simpson to him, but there was no malevolence. He wasn't one of those kids with bare-faced cheek and two fingers stuck up at pensioners passing by on a bus. He wasn't hell-bent on badness or acting out in consequence of any deeper psychological traumas.

His folks were decent people, like mine. He wasn't the one who went round breaking all the rules; he just left a few dents and scratches on them along the way – nothing that future responsibilities wouldn't panel-beat back into shape. Basically, he was just better at being a kid than me.

We'd go into town on Saturdays where he taught me how to shoplift. Nothing major. Well, not to start with. Mainly stationery, 'cos it was small and easy to slip into your pocket. Telling my parents that Ian's dad managed a stationery company helped explain why I'd come home with pocket-loads of the stuff. Oh, and tins and tins of Silly String, for some reason. But we'd dispense of that evidence with one big fight that would leave us both caked in the stuff (it was a kind of *Tiswas*-inspired ambition that ordinary pocket-money would never realistically stretch to).

Woolworth's and Martin's were our two main targets. Simply because they were always busy, security was lax, and they both faced the fountain from either side of Tontine Square, which was always handy if someone had put washing-up liquid in the fountain and a bubble fight broke out, because that attracted lots and lots of girls. And if we knew that was a no-go by late afternoon, we'd buy at least a dozen eggs and go and throw them at folk from the top of the Tontine car park.

It's odd because I was doing stuff that, had I been caught, I'd have been temporarily ashamed of once my parents found out. Yet having experienced the attempted manipulation of unnecessary shame at Upholland and the very worst of sins, which had gone ignored, simple, straightforward, wrong misbehaviour felt right, if that makes sense. Like butter instead of margarine, or sugar instead of sickly sweeteners, Ian's influence was proper butcher's mince, and I was a fresh-faced puppy fed for far too long on Quorn.

At least the fact that wrong was now recognisably wrong left a faint hope that right might also be right. I'm not fully condoning our actions, but there seemed to be far bigger evils in the world that people found it all too easy to ignore by focusing on their obsession with trivial misdemeanours.

Hypocrisy was not monopolised by Upholland. It was a trait that I couldn't help questioning, and that **He** had loathed even before I'd begun contemplating it.

But Rowena didn't see any of this empowerment within the friendship I had with Ian. She just saw a scally ne'er-do-well who would distract me from achieving all that she believed me capable of. She didn't know my back-story, so all of her concerns lay in my future, without understanding my need to claw back a past childhood. Everything she did came from a sincere place, a good heart, but she mistook a determination to enjoy all of life – in books, in art, but also in all its new-found potential for daft abandon and petty lawlessness – as my simply being led astray.

She'd find silly excuses for giving me mini detentions at break times and, in private, make no bones about the fact that it was to deter me from hanging round with Ian. That might sound harsh, but she was actually quite sweet in her misguidedness. She'd bring me a hot drink and give me books to read outside the set curriculum. I have her to thank for my introduction to *A Kestrel for a Knave*, the book that turned into the film, *Kes*, which is possibly my favourite of all time. (I can't say for sure, and I know it's a pale tribute, but I think it was seeing *Kes* that inspired me to start keeping budgies. And Dad accidentally killing one after he fell on it following a disastrous rescue attempt from the kitchen curtain-rail would certainly be grist to JOHNNY's mill.)

Even Mrs Rowlands's school reports had a streak of comedic flair. 'Michael needs to keep quiet if I am to preserve my sanity. He can talk to any person, at any given or ungiven time, willing or not to listen. Please teach him to shut up!'

Any other kid would've been mortified taking home a comment like that, but I appreciated her wit and knew it was done with a healthy dose of knowing sarcasm. My dad laughed out loud.

She'd talk to me with a tone and an honesty that matched my own self-assessment of precocious intellectual maturity – something I'd always felt was unnatural for someone my age (and was why Ian's youthfully mischievous influence seemed such a godsend after the meddling of the God Squad). But as much as I adored her – and I really did, as a teacher and as a warm and thoroughly decent human being – my fear of being dictated to was still too raw to be nudged in any direction, however well-intentioned, and so I threw myself into more and more outlandish behaviour with Ian whenever an opportunity presented itself.

I'd blagged a job in the school tuck shop. It was run by the teachers responsible for Physical Education to raise money for school athletics equipment, yet ironically sold nothing that could remotely be considered one of your five a day. Hot pies, pasties, sausage rolls, crisps and chocolate were the wares on offer. It opened at morning break and took a bundle.

Although I'd given up on all athletic endeavours, Mr Murphy still seemed to have time for me. He'd encouraged me to try out for the school's second or third rugby squad, but that meant training on Saturday mornings and coming into more contact with the really committed rugger-buggers than I could be arsed with. No offence, lads.

Just as kitchen positions are always sought-after in prison, there was a long list of pupils with their name down for jobs within the tuck shop, because while it paid only a very basic wage at the end of the week, that was still money earned whilst being stuck in school. For some reason, the most likely being my seminary background and the trustworthiness it promised (however fallaciously in this case) – although Mr Murphy's inexplicable belief in me as someone who might eventually return to the fold athletics-wise might also have played a part, despite the fact I was piling on the pounds week by week – I was allowed to jump the queue.

I was given the obligatory talk on the responsibility and trust that came with such a prized position before being put to work, and I felt momentarily good about myself and the faith they had shown in me. In the months that followed I would, however – assisted by my good friend, Ian – proceed to rob them blind.

We had a system. He would take huge numbers of food orders from years 1 to 3 under the guise of jumping the line for them (the school pecking order ensured that most of the hot pies and pasties were gone once the older boys had finished feeding their faces). He'd place the orders whilst pocketing the cash, and I'd give the pasties to him for free, after exchanging a bundle of small change so as not to arouse suspicion. He'd also order food for us, which meant we ate a free lunch and could throw our dinner money into the pot.

Dad was back in gainful employment by this point with a company that specialised in fixing up old churches by putting lads to work as an alternative to prison sentences, hence I was off the free school meals system. It was a dream position for him, working on houses of God whilst supervising the social and spiritual salvation of society's downcast. And yet all the while he toiled, under his very nose back home, his golden child was getting his own hands dirty with the spoils of ill-gotten gains.

My new job also spelled the end of my mid-morning book club and life chats with Mrs Rowlands. I used to tell myself later in life that most regrets are society's attempt to compete with the pull of Catholic guilt, that life is so random and fast at times that you mustn't resent yourself for decisions taken in the heat of the moment, or out of naïvety. But that theory emerged out of drinking and mastering the art of denial.

I never managed to drown out the regret of pulling away from Rowena and all the faith, knowledge and common decency she shared with me. I reckon she sensed at the time that I'd made my choice of mentor, and although she never gave up on me as such, she never again took me aside to remind me of all the potential I was wasting through my other, less commendable exploits. She had pointed me towards the light, but I was too preoccupied with stumbling about in the dark, and so she got on with the earnest task of teaching and gave up trying to second-guess if her words were sinking in or not.

There was that beautiful advert a few years ago centred round the phrase, 'You never forget a good teacher.' That's true. The worst thing is, though, you never forgive yourself for turning your back on them, either. In fact, I'm still ashamed of it.

Back there and then, Ian and I were loaded, and yet we kept on going into town and stealing stuff we could afford anyway. Bigger, more ambitious items became our targets. One year, I'd stolen every single Christmas gift I sat and watched my family open on the big day.

'Oh, thank you. But you shouldn't have ...'

'You got that right!'

All the natural guilt that should've tainted our activities somehow didn't seem to materialise. I was a teenage lad with day-to-day priorities of my own that demanded cash flow, and a conscience that was more interested in financial recompense than moral salvation.

'Had an accident at work? Believe you deserve compensation but don't know who to turn to?'

'No, but I broke my soul tripping over life, how much is that worth?'

By that time, I'd even given up going to church. I'd reached an age, along with my brothers, where we were trusted to attend

Sunday afternoon Mass instead of mornings, as a family, and treat ourselves to a lie in. But, instead, we borrowed a ball and played football in the empty playground of St Matthew's School.

Each week, one of us would take our turn to nip in the back of St Austin's Church and gather the general gist of that week's sermon along with a parish newsletter, this being proof enough for Dad that we were in attendance.

The guilt of lying about this was sadly minimal, and because we were all complicit in the deceit it meant that for one hour a week, although denying myself Holy Communion and the good grace and spiritual protection of God's love as a result, I was treated almost as an equal by my two older brothers. Or, at least, I wasn't picked on, and that felt a decent enough trade-off against life eternal for someone who so desperately wanted to feel accepted by two of his own.

My and Ian's Saturday afternoon crime-sprees came to an abrupt end one afternoon whilst sitting on the fountain in the town centre eyeing up girls. A big bloke approached us and pointed at Ian. 'You, come with me.'

I pulled my, 'What's his problem?' face at Ian, but realised from his expression that something was wrong.

'What d'you mean?' He said quizzically, but there was guilt written all over his face.

I was genuinely confused because the guy was wearing a Boots staff badge, and so far we'd only targeted Woolies and Helena House.

'You know what I mean. Get up, empty your pockets.'

'Listen, mate ...'

'Get 'em emptied!'

He said it with all the impatience of the, 'Get in the back of the van!' copper from *Withnail & I*, but looked a lot more intimidating.

Ian stood up and turned out his pockets, but nothing fell out except loose change, gum and a bus ticket.

For one stupid moment, I thought we were in the clear, but then the guard unzipped Ian's tracksuit top and out fell everything he'd nicked that day. There was a lot of stuff – rubbish mainly, things we didn't need but took anyway because we could.

To be honest, I'd started dumping some of the things we'd lifted on the way home because I couldn't explain from where I'd got them. But almost as embarrassing as getting nicked was the fact that the incriminating bit of evidence the security guard was looking for was a Hawkwind cassette.

Hawkwind? I hadn't even heard of them before that day. Turned out they were some hippy hangover band Ian's brother was into that he'd snatched from Boots while I'd gone off getting a corned beef pasty and an apple turnover from Gregg's.

I just sat there, gob wide open in fear and disbelief, until the bloke turned to me.

'And what about your mate here?'

'Wha–?'

Despite all the *craic* we'd shared together, I was ready to dump Ian with all the good grace of St Peter prior to the cockerel crowing thrice. I'd already angled my body away from the unfolding drama, but stupidly I couldn't stop gawping.

'You, what's in the bag?'

'Wha–?'

I couldn't form words, so I just stupidly made to open the plastic bag between my knees.

'Hope you've got a receipt for whatever's in there?'

'Wha–?' I managed to nod but without an ounce of conviction.

Now, to this day, I'll never know why he didn't bother looking in that bag. Maybe because he hadn't seen me in the shop with Ian, or perhaps it was the fact that I looked so surprised at the mention of the Hawkwind tape, maybe just because I had a carrier bag and therefore must've actually bought something from a shop (some bloodworms and a feeder from Jean's Aquarium for my fish – as adept as we'd become at shoplifting, water-stored larvae were beyond even our talents. Plus I liked Jean, so felt better using dirty tuck shop profits than having her be out of pocket).

But whatever his reason, my interrogation ended there. He took my phone number and then, like a scene from *Angels with Dirty Faces*, Ian was escorted away and I was left sitting there mid-panic attack wondering what the implications were, now that we'd finally been busted.

I raced home, but someone from Boots had already called the house. Fortunately, Mark had answered and probably knew it was just a routine call giving the family a heads-up on my recent activity, denying me the day in court I'd fretted over all the way home on the 10a bus.

Mark knew the difference between a caution and intent to prosecute, this being the lad who'd super-glued a 'Support The Miners' poster on a neighbouring policeman's front window. Still, that didn't stop him torturing me with the valuable information that'd fallen into his lap. By the time he'd finished, the trial was over and I was preparing for a ten-year stretch breaking rocks in a bloody chain gang. I didn't dare ring Ian's house, so I spent a weekend lying low around the house, sick with nerves and barely able to string a sentence together.

At school on Monday, he told me how they'd dragged his parents in and read him the riot act, but he didn't seem too bothered by the shame of it all and, more importantly, he hadn't implicated me.

I tried to act equally nonchalant but I reckon he knew how selfishly relieved I was that only his name had been dragged through the dirt. Not long after that, though, even when we'd slowed down operations and taken what you could call quite a considerable pay cut, I was quietly let go from the school tuck shop.

There were no official accusations, no kangaroo court, but the manner and tone with which Mr Murphy ended my employment reeked of disappointment, and it was quite telling that I never bothered to ask him why.

'I think it's best we give someone else a go behind here for a bit, don't you?'

'Mmm.'

I'd got the life I'd thought I yearned for. After leaving Uphol-land, I'd managed to disappoint a whole parish, but with a conviction that was wholly justifiable to myself. Now, though, I was abusing the trust and kindness of all the people I actually liked and respected.

I don't know if it was just an extended period of letting off steam, a two fingers to the very notion of respectability, or just normal teenage rebellion with petty theft thrown in for good measure. If it was normal, then once again it seemed normality fitted me just as badly as my Farah slacks, and if it wasn't, then whatever I was doing to get back at life certainly wasn't giving me the satisfaction I'd hoped it would.

15.

THE CATHOLIC MEN'S SOCIETY NEWSLETTER

Ian and Mrs Rowlands might have been fighting over my soul, but that didn't mean the old tug-of-war between Dad's Catholicism and my own ever-burgeoning adolescent sexuality was over. My brothers were no strangers to bridging the gap between fantasy and reality with a copy of *Penthouse* or *Knave*, and my dad had an almost sixth sense when it came to finding their un-Christian stashes of reading material. He would conduct regular searches in their absence and dispose of the contraband by means of a mini bonfire in the backyard.

He never raised a face-to-face fuss over what he found. I'd like to think, despite his core Christian beliefs, that he remembered the frustrations endured by boys their age. Perhaps he was just too embarrassed to confront them personally with the evidence of their wicked deeds? Still, we all got the message when he sent those legs-akimbo witches back to hell, Salem style.

My brothers were persistent, though, and the war of porn versus pious abstinence became one of attrition. As Dad torched his way through countless issues of men's mags, they got ever more inventive with their hiding places, which is probably why he opted for a change of tack that would eventually leave me scarred by the conflict.

I once discovered a well-thumbed (if that is the appropriate digit) copy of *Razzle* that had been deliberately slid down in-between the side of the bath and the false panel in front of it. I'd over-filled the bath again and flooded the bathroom floor; desperate not to wind up my mum, I had mopped up all that I could with a towel, but realised that most of the water had run underneath the panel and would find its way down to the kitchen through a light fitting if I didn't get to it first. That was when, lying on my back with my left arm wedged into that narrow gap, I struck gold.

Amongst the readers' wives straining to look provocative and exotic despite holding mugs of tea while posing in front of tumble-dryers as their husbands struggled with the flash (giving them red eye in the process, and making them look like something you might well go to hell for fantasising over), there was a sweet-looking lady, loosely masquerading as a police woman, who I took a particular shine to.

I'd hazard a guess that she was a professional glamour model as she seemed a lot more relaxed as she stripped in the name of law and order. Plus they had devoted four full pages to her exploits, as opposed to one or two badly lit Polaroids, which helped me create more of a story-line as I prepared to come clean.

As demoralising as life got when pleasuring yourself over a cheap top-shelf job, I had never lost my knack for over-embellishing a simple fantasy; perhaps because of what I'd learned from my time obsessing about Frenchy, but more likely because I'd always needed to justify to my own low self-esteem just how I might manage to take a relationship on from friendship to something more physical (even when the friend in question had staples through her and was obviously lying about what it was she did for a living).

Thanks to the advent of PC Sure Thing, my baths became more frequent as I made time for our date nights. Sharing a bedroom with two brothers, and a strict house rule that there were to be no locks on that bedroom door, meant that the bathroom was the only place where any of us got any quality alone time.

I'm now sure my dad had caught on to this fact and, unbeknown to me, had gone on one of his crafty paper witch-hunts.

I had thought it business as usual as I ran the taps on low for a slow, 15-minute fill of the bath. This meant I had noise cover whilst I retrieved my off-duty sweetheart and could open up at the appropriate point.

With hindsight, this was another dead giveaway to Pops that I was following in my brothers' depraved footsteps. The nagging guilt, combined with the inferior paper that those magazines were printed on and the less-than-perfect storage solutions, always made the turning of a page sound like the creaking of a great oak door that hadn't budged for centuries: 'WWWAAAA-AAAANNNNK!' was the deafening screech that seemed to echo through the house every time I opened it. Running water was my only means of stifling the sound, but the fact that our bath was not a huge one and my growing waistline caused a higher level of water displacement than an average teen my age, meant that the clock was ticking.

That's why I'd skipped the formalities of my fantasy copper cautioning me for, appropriately enough, stealing a men's magazine from a newsagents. After my explaining that it was curiosity and loneliness that had driven me to a life of crime, she'd already taken pity on me, asked how far I'd been with a girl, taken more pity on me when she'd heard the answer, unbuttoned her blouse, taken off her bra, raised her skirt, spread herself, and insisted that a climax was my only way of avoiding a future prison sentence.

I liked twisting this masturbational scenario into a morality tale where I was the victim. It made me feel less sordid. So I was already naked from the waist down and halfway through choosing freedom with one hand when I knelt down and reached for my photo finish with the other.

To my eternal shame, it was then that I found I had already been saved from a life of swapping imaginary sexual favours for liberty by my bloody dad. Because, just as the point of no return was close to being reached, I pulled out what I had every moral right to expect would be a pornographer's vision of fantasy law-enforcement and the ultimate solution for prison overcrowding. What I got instead was a copy of the Catholic Men's Society monthly newsletter, with a large image of Our Lady printed on the cover.

The cunning sod had pulled a switch that left me almost retching with remorse. My cock did a rapid impression of one of those torpedo-shaped balloons with a failed knot at the end: it both shrank and retreated from my hand almost immediately, leaving me with a flaccid, guilt-ridden sorry excuse for a pardon. I went foetal with my own awkwardness and shame.

He knew! He fucking knew what I was up here doing! He knew I wanked! He knew I looked at those kinds of pictures and took sexual gratification from them! He knew why I took my baths and why they took so long! He knew that every time I turned on the immersion heater and ran up the gas bill heating some more hot water that it was a sham! A costly, steamy veneer for my selfish, base, wanton sexual urges!

Oh God. He knew, even before I did, that I was objectifying women and concerning myself with fannies and tits and arses and stockings and different-sized tits and naked policewomen and compromising positions. Especially compromising positions where you could also see their biff and their arse, and possibly some side boob because they were bent over on their knees, smiling back at you! He knew that I wanted the kind of women that wanted me to betray my Christian upbringing by wanking over them. HE KNEW WHAT I WAS, AND WHAT IT WAS THAT GAVE ME GRATIFICATION!

I had hot flushes of shame as the guilt raised my blood pressure to a point where I could hear my blood pumping in my ears. The illustration of the Holy Mother was staring up at me, but the tortured yet kind expression that artists had always bestowed upon her over the centuries was now completely devoid of the compassion that I'd always associated with her. She didn't appear annoyed or disgusted with me, just disappointed, and a little bit awkward.

That was something my dad had twigged was a trigger point with me way back in my youth. Being told that I had somehow let him down or diminished his belief in me because of some serious bit of bad behaviour had always struck a painful chord with me far worse than the smacked arse that most of the kids my age I knew might receive. The minor discomfort of a slap was fleeting; even the stinging thwack of the cane wore off by the time you'd return to your classroom. (I knew this because corporal punishment was still allowed and had been actively practised by a small number of the staff in my junior school.) But falling short of my father's expectations was a painful consequence that always lingered long after the lecture had ended.

Don't get me wrong; I equally dreaded my mum's telling-offs. She could get herself into a right state once we'd pushed her too far. She struggled to keep a lid on her frustrations as calmly as Dad did, but then she was responsible for looking after us a good 90 per cent of the time, and my brothers and my behaviour rarely reflected the stable, loving Christian upbringing afforded us.

In time I'd grow to realise that my mum had a lot more emotional baggage than my dad, and seemingly none of the whimsical, 'We were poor but happy' childhood stories to recount that Dad always relished telling. On a literary scale, if Dad was *The Railway Children*, Mum was more *The Boy* (or girl, in this case) *in the Striped Pyjamas*. She'd had a hard upbringing and, I believe, had buried many unsavoury memories as best she could.

There was nobody more loving than my mum whatever pain she'd endured, and I reckon she was determined that the cycle of bitterness would be broken when it came to raising her own family. But through no fault of her own, she had a short fuse, and a temper that seemed more punishing to herself than to her children she was scolding.

Every time the dust had settled, I imagine Mum regretfully reviewing the sign in her head, much like those ones in factories stating how many days had passed between injury or incident, and wearily rubbing off the number and replacing it with a zero. Thanks to us kids, Dad's irrepressible cheeriness, or the constant worry of running a household on a budget as flimsy and uncertain as a bird man on the edge of Brighton Pier, she would rarely, if ever, have made it up to double figures.

As unpleasant as it was being on the receiving end – I guess that's the whole point of a bollocking – poor Mum seemed to completely embody the phrase so often abused by tyrannical headmasters when they raised that cane above their head and took aim at a guilty kid's backside: 'This is going to hurt me far more than it is going to hurt you!'

Like they say with all good portraits, but especially religious ones, the eyes of the Blessed Virgin Mary seemed to catch me wherever I sat, rocking, in our bathroom. Her sadness at my skydive from grace seemed omnipresent, so back behind the false panelling she had to go.

I washed my face and dried my hands first (we both knew where they'd been), picked up the newsletter and tried my best to replace it exactly how I had found it.

I then went through the motions and did my best to fake a bath. In fact, I probably went a bit OTT between the over-sloshing of water and humming of innocent-sounding bathing songs. TUNES TO BATHE TO WHILST AVOIDING ETERNAL DAMNATION AND THE FIERY TORTURES OF HELL, Volume I! No discernible tune or lyrics, just a general hum. A 'lah-de-duhm' melody composed around the theme of 'Listen to me, innocently taking a bath and definitely NOT WANKING!'

I tried to take the same amount of time as usual so as not to raise suspicion, but seeing as all my tub-time lately had been post-coital and carefree, I wasn't sure how long a soak was long enough. Who knew how long I'd already spent reeling on the floor while silently begging for forgiveness?

Eventually, I had to let the water out, but didn't move until the bath was empty. I just sat there feeling dirtier than when I'd got in, despite having worked the soap down from a standard bar to credit-card dimensions. When I finally got out of the shamemobile, I remembered to flush the loo – despite it having no telltale paper floating in it – still desperate to give the impression that it had been bathtime as normal and I was sticking to my usual, supposedly innocent, regime.

I got dressed and faked a happy-go-lucky rhythm to my step as I went downstairs. Thank God I couldn't whistle, or my family might've mistaken me for a young Tommy 'Half a sixpence!' Steele when I entered the living room.

To my unbelievable relief nothing was said. I made a cup of tea and dared believe that all was well and nothing had changed between Dad and me. It would simply remain a most unfortunate misunderstanding between Mary and myself. After all, it was my brothers who were responsible for stashing naked tarts around the house – Dad probably wouldn't have even dreamt that I'd have gained access to such filth. It was them he was hoping to catch out; I wasn't even on his redemption radar, so what was I worrying about?

For the first time in an hour or so since I'd exposed myself to you know who, my heartbeat settled back into a normal pattern. I even got my appetite back, which definitely meant all would be well, and so treated myself to a biscuit.

Chomping away, I went to sit down on the floor to watch telly with everyone else. I gave my sister a big smile with my mouth full of Digestive. She had a natural dislike for how I ate my food and loved grassing me up to Mum on matters of manners, but I was feeling unusually cocky. I had beaten the rap, and as hungry as I was after my adrenaline rush, I was determined to make a real meal of it. I widened my grin to show more crumb and raised my eyebrows in a 'Is something bothering you?' style. She was just about to snap when Dad broke the silence.

'Have you finished with the bathroom?'

'Huh?' I mumbled, sending bits of crumb flying, his question catching me completely off guard.

Dad didn't take his eyes off the telly, but repeated the question with a slow, measured clarity and an emphasis on just one word.

'I said, have you FINISHED with the bathroom?'

I swallowed everything down hard and croaked, 'Yes' thinking, 'Hold your nerve, he suspects nothing!'

'I hope you left it just as you found it?'

The biscuit jumped straight back up my gullet and sat in my mouth like a wheaty turd. 'Busted!' All I could do was nod as my face went red from the neck up, like a cartoon thermometer.

'Good,' he said. 'Because you know what they say, don't you?'

I wanted to answer but I couldn't swallow the sickly mixture of gluten and bile in my mouth, so I just shook my head.

My dad then looked at me for the first time. It was a poker face that only I could read.

'Cleanliness is next to godliness.'

And with that seemingly innocuous pearl of theological wisdom, I knew how much I'd disappointed him. Swallowing the partially digested biscuit no longer posed that big a problem for me. All I could taste now was remorse.

I didn't turn away from the TV for the rest of the evening for dread of catching his eye. That was the longest fucking episode of *Juliet Bravo* I would ever sit through!

I'd love to say that Dad's unorthodox approach proved a permanent cure for my lusting over smutty visual stimulation, but unfortunately the combination of teen hormones and teen female indifference would eventually send me back to scouring the house looking for my brothers' new hiding places. But one thing stuck.

No matter how provocative, how well-lit, how absent the evidence of domestic appliances, how uncompromising their positions or how convincing their uniforms and back-story, I could never again get off to a glamour model if they were wearing any jewellery that included religious iconography. In fact, on particularly pious days, I would avoid the photos altogether and limit myself purely to the written word on the dirty confessions pages (an unfortunate title, considering my circumstances).

I'd like to think that it was a conscious moral decision on my part. My way of trying to strike a deal with the man, and more importantly his mother, upstairs, that retained some allowances for my weakness of the flesh without courting all-out blasphemy. But, in the end, I think I'd have to admit it was mainly down to deep-rooted remorse surrounding that day – a permanent association between porn and shame that extends beyond the normal sociological boundaries regarding the objectification of women.

I doubt if publishers like Paul Raymond or Larry Flynt ever found themselves in a similarly uncompromising position with a copy of the Catholic Men's Society newsletter (I imagine they were beaten around the house with a rolled-up copy of *Broads Illustrated*). But, as inhibited as it might've left me, I'll always have a begrudging respect for the 'softly, softly, catchee monkey' technique that Dad employed so well.

16.

NUTGROVE'S HERE

I loved my parents, I truly did, and nobody respected them more than me for the morals – both religious and in terms of basic social awareness – which they had striven to instil in us. But since Upholland, and then my time at West Park, there was a widening divide between what was expected of me, and how little I had come to expect from myself.

Everyone seemed to think they knew what was best for me, but none of them had really taken into account what it was like to be me. And that wasn't just the normal teen angst crap of, 'I didn't ask to be born. You've ruined my life. Nobody understands me but Morrissey!' For a start, every well-to-do prick who arrived at school every day in a flash car felt that Morrissey 'got them', and their angst turned me off him straight away. Morrissey might not have been the confidante I was looking for, but **He** understood me perfectly.

I was a fat, godless coward who compensated for the self-loathing by stealing or eating and could only confess my sins to **HiM**! **He** never told me to do these things; **He** just understood my need to do them. And **He** never fucking whined like Morrissey, **He** just promised **HiMSeLF** that things would get better.

We both had to believe that!

I had one pair of Farah slacks I'd begged Mum to get me as school trousers. We'd gone to the stall on Tontine Market where three coats unzipped on hangers acted as curtains. (A gang of classmates happened to be passing that Saturday as the woman running the stall announced like a town fucking crier: 'A 36-inch waist is the biggest we stock! My, he is big around the midriff, isn't he?') Mum had relented and bought them, despite the fact they had all the fit and comfort of a gastric band. They squeezed my inner thighs together so tightly that I'd suffer almost unbearable friction when I walked, which in turn caused the material to bobble and eventually come away so that if I opened my legs I looked like I was wearing something from Ann Summers. I couldn't bend down in them because the arse would split, so anything dropped in school stayed lost.

I had one trendy T-shirt, a Fila BJ I'd bought second-hand and refused to sell on – even though the badge alone was worth three times what I'd paid for it – despite the fact that I could barely pull it over my big, ugly, awkward, shapeless mass of a body. I bought a Slazenger tank top and stretched it to tearing point with two broom handles through each arm-hole so it would have a bit of slack and not highlight every single ounce of slovenly imperfection. I'd lie on my bed, feet on one handle and hands on the other, pulling away at it like some homemade Bullworker work-out programme, whilst desperately trying to avoid my own reflection in the small dressing-table mirror because I disgusted myself.

Yet I still desperately wanted girls to like me. Not just like me like me, I mean *like* me like me.

And then, out of the blue, a letter came from Lynne, the girl I'd met on that hostelling trip during my time at Upholland. Far from saving my emotional bacon as it might have done, this unexpected bounty merely served to bring into still sharper focus all the disdainful looks thrown my way by the girls I walked past on a day-to-day basis – looks I'd learned to somehow blinker out in a sad and desperate attempt to further the

A letter from Lynne following my departure from Upholland.
Like all memories of the place she was unfortunately filed under
'No longer known at this address'

myth that it's what's on the inside that counts. And that is a lot of denial when you consider that as much of a disgrace as I looked on the outside, an even messier fucking entity had taken up residency on the inside.

Let's say someone miraculously saw beyond the shuffling 12 stone of social surrender that was my outward aspect ... what would be the fallout once they'd peeked inside and seen HIM shouting back at them?

It wasn't Lynne's fault. She'd only written to touch base again, having been so unceremoniously dumped along with everything else that was associated with Upholland. At first, she once again proved to be that little bit of light at the end of the tunnel, somebody who knew me and still seemed to like me like me. But then she started posting photos of herself and asked me to do the same.

I looked through all the recent pictures of me and hated them, absolutely detested what I'd become. So I posted old photos, pictures back from when she knew me, images of how I wanted her to remember me until I could get my shit together at this end. She was as complimentary as any 15-year-old girl can be when they receive a photo of a pen-pal, dressed up all smart and slim, at his first Holy Communion.

I wanted this to work – oh God, I wanted it so badly. So I kept putting off her requests for more recent pictures whilst poring over the contents of the biscuit-tin full of family photos and trying to decide on the latest possible cut-off point. What could I dare risk sending her? It had to be something that could be laughed off as pre-teen puppy fat but not look like full-blown 'Why don't you write to me any more?' obesity.

Eventually, the fear of her looking me up, down and all around with the same air of disgust as other girls my age proved too great and, once again, I ignored her sweet, funny correspondences until she finally got the message and gave up. It was another major blow to my confidence.

I'd already fallen far behind the majority of lads my age as far as carnal knowledge was concerned. I'd been painfully aware of this ever since my cousin had returned from a heavy petting session over the Clegg and asked me to, 'Smell that finger – that's the smell of a woman enjoying herself, that is.' Whilst everyone was busy getting to first, second or whatever base, I was still sitting on the team bus sticking my finger in a belly button I hadn't washed for days in a doomed attempt to recreate the same exotic aroma.

Opportunities for new romantic entanglements were not legion at the Grange Park Youth Club, which I attended most evenings as it was just around the corner from our house. Some genuinely rough lads went there, and there were no field trips as we were barred outright from every other local authority venue.

Glue (and sometimes gas if you were going up-market) sniffing was a favourite jolly of a good percentage of its members, and although this practice technically meant an automatic ban, the pastime merely shuffled deliriously out back by the fire exit. There were nights in there when it looked more like a junior rehab centre than a council-run defence mechanism against kids 'running amok'. A lad once told me that after a giant dragon had crept behind him all the way home, he'd decided that he was, 'Never gonna snuff outside again! Only somewhere with fucking doors and curtains, you know?'

When they weren't off their tits on Bostik, we'd play a bloody barbaric version of Murder-ball that resembled those historic drawings of early football matches between villages, their inhabitants enjoying a good, old-fashioned bit of biting, kicking and gouging. But however rough things got, we were never singled out from the mayhem for special attention. We were never picked on.

I say 'we', because my brothers also went to this youth club. Whereas West Park had softened me up to the social consistency of a wall-flower, Eddy Camp had toughened them up into lads who rarely backed down from any confrontation, even with each other. In fact, they would go at each other just as aggressively, if not more so, than with anyone else.

There were far harder lads in the club, but there was a kind of unspoken code amongst them: a pack instinct, if you like. They played rough but never really went to town on anyone once you were accepted. The real violence was reserved for those from rival gangs, other youth clubs or different boroughs within the town.

I'll never forget the day a mob gathered against the railings on St Austin's field at the far end of our street. It was early tea time, and I was heading home from a half-hearted game of football on Rock Street when I clocked them.

It was a curious gathering, because you didn't often see more than a couple of kids at a time, or the odd adult, using the field out of school hours. It was a convenient shortcut from Nutgrove, and even Rainhill, into the top end of Thatto Heath, if you didn't mind the drop off a six-foot wall. But this lot had stopped on the 'border', and just seemed to be staring down our street. I damn near filled my pants when they started shaking the wire fence and chanting, 'Penno! Penno! Penno!'

I ran to our house and did my best to casually usher my brother Mark outside, whilst feeling absolute terror rising within. It was

my gut instinct that he was the Pennington they were shouting
after since he'd recently taken up a hobby which involved picking fights with the cocks of some nearby gangs, but in a vigilante
style of tracking them down alone and then squaring up to them,
so I thought it best to let him assess the situation before involv-
ing the grown-ups.

'Mark, I've gotta show you something.'

'Sod off, I'm having me butty.'

Our Mark's 'butty' consisted of cutting up a single Pimblett's
steak pie (legendary pie-makers in the town) into 16 (yes, 16)
individual squares and then spreading each measly portion
over half of a half of a slice of bread - 'The secret's in squashing
every piece out thin and into the corners but not drowning 'em
in marge.'

By the time he was done and had them all piled up, his plate
looked like a Wigan wedding buffet (had you also torn open a bag
of crisps and laid it out beside them). It was a time-consuming
process considering there was a crowd – a full-grown, angry
fucking mob of about twenty-five, maybe thirty lads – at the end
of our street baying for blood like a scene from *The Wanderers*,
and which would now probably have to wait.

I have to say that this is not a story where the numbers
involved or the sense of danger have been exaggerated over
time. Amateur rough and tumble had somehow turned pro.
Real violence – like the footage you saw at a safe distance on
your TV in some inner city miles away – was definitely on the
agenda.

Eventually Mark followed me out into the street. He stopped
when he spotted the crowd I was desperately pointing at, but
didn't flinch. A lad called Jamie McGann strolled over. He'd
taken Mark under his wing as a bit of a tearaway protégé. Then
our Rob popped his head around the front door – probably
hoping to see me get what was coming to me – saw what we
were all staring at, and decided he'd stretch his legs a bit.

Mark turned to me. 'Nip down the club. Tell 'em Nutgrove's
here. Go on!'

I tore down there and in through the doors, rambling loads of desperate nonsense that nobody really paid much attention to till Masters stopped me and asked, 'What the fuck are you going on about?'

I took a deep breath and began to try and explain, but didn't get beyond, 'Nutgrovers!'

'Where?'

'Austin's field.'

Masters only shouted out those two bits of information and the male members of the club immediately emptied outside and tore arse up Sunbury Street. There were only six or seven of them because it was still early evening and the club hadn't really started to fill up yet, but that didn't seem to matter. An opportunity for a fight was an opportunity not to be wasted, however ridiculous the odds.

We got to the wall and I thought I might be spared the carnage as my weight meant I was no longer able to scale it with the same ease as the rest of them, but some bugger offered me a pog up.

The gang from Nutgrove backed off and formed a semi-circle entered by our group, with me furthest at the back and closest to the exit route. I couldn't climb, but I'd drop like a sack of spuds thrown from a ship onto a quayside once this turned nasty.

Masters walked up nose-to-nose with the lad who looked like the ring-leader.

'Right then, what's the bother?'

You could see in the Nutgrove leader's eyes that he hadn't counted on certain members of our youth club attending that evening's mayhem, but he did his best to go about his business.

'It's now't to do with you. It's him we're after!'

He pointed to our Mark, who stepped forward looking like a dog bred purely for fighting and desperate to get off its leash and tear into its opponent.

Masters moved forward slightly and dug his forehead into the space just above the bridge of the nose of this lad, a move just like any other in the animal kingdom that tested the determination of the challenging male to fight, it being the perfect technique for lining up a head butt.

'Woah, woah, woah,' Masters said. 'This has got every fucking thing to do with me. You go with him, you go with us.' He dug another half inch or so into the other lad's face so bone could feel bone.

As he did so, the lad leaned back to ease the pressure, until eventually he took a full step back, signalling that he was backing down to the dominant male.

I couldn't believe it. We were at least three-to-one outnumbered, more so when you included me – the gang mascot no more capable of inflicting injury than a drummer boy on the field of battle amongst heavy artillery. But with their leader backing down, it seemed the bloodlust was leaking out from the rest of the mob.

'He jumped Jez, him and a mate. Fucking hit him with a wrench!'

Even I couldn't deny this warranted some form of retribution, but it didn't matter now because there was no authority to this lad's tone. It was more a plea for justice than a call to arms.

'I don't fucking care what he did. You want it out with him yourself then now's yer chance. Anyone else wants a fucking go, we all go.'

I can feel my relief even to this day, right here and now as I'm writing this, that there was nobody willing to take Masters up on the offer. The lad was already backing away, still trying to save some face with a parting shot: 'Yer bang out of order, Penno. You won't always have your fucking mates with ya – we'll catch you then!'

But it had no impact on the few of us still standing there, and especially our Mark: 'Go fuck yourselves, gobshites!'

That's when I realised what kind of reputation the lads from Grange Park Youth Club had, the kind of lads that we mucked around with on a daily basis. The lads on whom us Penningtons – the God squadders who dressed smart for Mass

on Sundays and who had never had a visit from the social services – could count on as allies.

Masters patted me on the back as we wandered back down
Hayes Street. I had a slight limp (turned out I fell just as lousily
as I climbed).

'Enjoy that, young 'un?'

'Yeah, just wish they hadn't bottled it,' I answered, with all
the conviction of a Tory MP announcing their continued commitment to the NHS, not knowing for sure if anyone had noticed
that I'd pissed my pants.

'Don't worry, plenty more where that came from. You'll get
your chance!'

I said a silent prayer there and then that I wouldn't; a 'right
to the point' short and simple offering to Him upstairs: 'Dear
Christ, I hope not!'

And with that we all went back to the youth club and celebrated with a simple game of Tick, but with a pool ball, and a
strict policy of no throwing at anybody's head (which wasn't
really all that strictly enforced).

Years later, as we all settled down and life took us off on our
different paths, I'd still bump into lads from there down around
the Lane. Masters, sorry, *Paul*, never failed to let on to me. Last
time I saw him, I was trying to shoot a low-budget pilot based
in St Helens and we were filming at the bottom of Sunbury
Street, just past our old youth club, which the council had run
us out of years before. He was leaning off his council flat's
balcony, a bit worse for wear but with no malice, shouting,
'Hey, Mike, put me in your film, will ya?'

Despite the aggravation he was causing the director and crew,
he made me laugh.

I'd inherited the slack he and the others cut me at Grange
Park rather than earning it myself, but at an odd price. As one
of my brothers once said to me, 'If you get any grief, tell me.
Nobody is allowed to hit you, except me.'

And he meant it. I hero-worshipped my older brothers for a
time, Mark especially. I'd sit, watching him getting ready to go

out for a night of violence, throwing on his Mod parka, wishing I'd inherited his aggressive fearlessness. But I would learn over time that the blessing in disguise his 'protection' offered was more like a smack on the head from a poisoned chalice.

There were only three years separating myself from Mark, and four from Rob, but it was a chasm as far as they were concerned, and my reluctance to want to prove myself in their alpha pecking order only made it wider. Although we are as close as brothers can be now – with much water under the bridge – at the time, and especially with the introduction of alcohol into their adolescence, the line between natural goading and the testing of each other's brotherly patience blurred, and actual physical and psychological bullying was the result.

Rob was pure physical and really heavy handed with his poundings – they lacked panache – whereas Mark was more controlled, more psychological, only ever hitting me with an open hand and belittling me further in the process by reducing me to the rank of a domestically abused housewife from the 1950s. He'd always been a master of it and wanted to provoke a response because, I reckon, knowing my reluctance to fight plus the fact that I didn't stand a chance against him if I did, meant he couldn't bring himself to hit me properly unless I went for him first. So he would goad me until I did.

I always preferred an honest-to-goodness beating off our Robert than 12 rounds of psychoanalysis from our Mark. Bruises fade, shit sticks.

Years earlier, he had managed to convince me that I was adopted. The methods of persuasion were really well thought out and actually quite brilliant, and his performance itself was definitely worthy of a BAFTA nod.

It started with a casual, matter-of-fact, 'You do know by now that you're adopted, don't you?'

I gave him the sarcastic 'Nice try' smile and continued trying to read my comic.

'You just have to look at you to see that.'

This was really amateur stuff by his standards and so

far-fetched that it didn't even warrant a verbal response as far as I was concerned.

'I mean, look at us lot, and look at you. There's no other chubbies in the family, is there? Just you.'

I was going to get up and leave, as I wasn't in the mood for fatty references, when he baited the hook a little more and let it dangle. 'Haven't you ever noticed how there's hardly any photos of you when you were younger?'

Now, the odd thing was that I *had* noticed this. Not realising that the novelty of taking pictures tends to lessen with each new addition to the family, I had often wondered why I featured so little in the biscuit tin of family memories. (It's probably why I asked for a camera at quite a young age and became the unofficial family photographer. And, later on, why I would find it so exciting seeing JOHNNY's face on posters, flyers, reviews and magazine articles.)

'And the baby pictures, well, they could just be anybody a bit like you.'

At this point I did the stupidest thing ever. I bit. I took the bait and responded with a well-considered, 'Shut up!'

That's when he knew he had me. Sitting down beside me and giving a sigh like a parent might before discussing a matter of a delicate nature with their child, he changed his tone to a mixture of sincerity and slight remorse. 'That's why we never have proper birthday parties.'

Which we didn't! Well, not in the traditional invitation-to-friends-to-come-and-play-Pass-the-Parcel kind of way. We'd have a tea party, and Mum would put on a spread a bit like a buffet with all sorts of treats, but it was kept within the immediate family.

Now, thinking straight, I'd have put this down to the simple fact that money was tight and my folks were celebrating the best they knew how on what little they had. And, come to think of it, I had never, ever bothered to raise a fuss about having a more traditional birthday party, so why wouldn't they presume that I was happy to celebrate it in this way?

Still, our Mark had got into my head by now and had set unfamiliar cogs turning.

'It's because they don't exactly know what date your birthday is. They just chose a random date out of thin air. You know, so you wouldn't feel left out.'

For some stupid reason it started to make complete sense: invisible pieces of a puzzle I'd been ignorant of until his mischief had brought it to my attention seemed to slot into place. By now I was listening, because he'd got me believing it completely.

'I mean, you must've asked yourself why we've never been abroad before, eh? Why we always went to Butlin's?'

I shook my head, my bottom lip quivering and my eyes welling up.

'No. Why?' I nearly choked on the question.

'Well, they've no birth certificate for you, so they can't get you a passport, see? And they couldn't just take us abroad without giving the game away, could they?'

I shook my head, determined not to cry but really struggling to contain the fact that I had found the recent disclosure that a huge chunk of my upbringing had been a lie, a conspiracy that the whole family was in on apart from me, more than just a little bit upsetting.

And then Mark did a most unusual thing that was a stroke of despicable genius: he put his arm around me and side-hugged me.

If I'd had a shred of doubt before that what he was saying wasn't true, then that gesture, alien to normal brotherly inter-actions, quashed it.

'I'm sorry, I thought you knew.' And then he got conspira-torial on my ass. 'Tell you what. I'll break into Dad's bureau, if you want? Let you take a look for yourself, but I bet you won't find anything.'

That was the final nail in my Pennington DNA coffin. Dad's little writing desk had a lock on it and was where he stored all and any important paperwork: bank statements, marriage, birth and death certificates, plus his favourite clippings from the *Catholic Pictorial* (a newspaper dedicated entirely to how great the Church was and how everyone not directly connected to it was going to hell in a handcart) – all items of extreme importance. None of us in our right mind would ever dream of snooping around in there, not even at Christmas when the hunt for stashed presents hit fever pitch. It was sacrosanct and we all, every single one of us, knew that, including Mum.

In fact, she went on strike one year when Dad refused her access to look at the details of the deeds to the house. He'd been seriously ill months previously and she had realised that he had always taken responsibility for the financial running of the house as far as the mortgage and utility bills were concerned.

It was a sensible request in case he relapsed, but Dad, in a boldly chauvinistic move, refused Mum access to the information contained within his walnut-veneered sanctum. So she went on a laundry strike, for six weeks.

Now, before they went completely electronic, I'd seen my dad take apart and teach himself how to repair a washing machine. He has a slow, methodical patience with inanimate objects and how they work (which he didn't pass down to me through the gene pool – I once kicked the bejeezus out of my ten-gear racer after taking the back wheel off to repair a puncture and only then realising I couldn't fit it back on. I mean, I went completely Ike Turner on the poor thing). So I knew Dad could mend the washer, but he hadn't a bloody clue how to operate it. He resigned himself to buying fresh underwear from Tontine Market and simply storing the rest in copious amounts of bin bags, whilst his day-to-day clothes took to whiffing like Johnny Wellies' (so called because he only ever wore Wellington boots), St Helens' most notorious practitioner of shouting randomly at shoppers or mumbling nonsense happily to himself for the unintended entertainment of kids and town drunks alike – an obvious victim of institutions and falling through the system's cracks.

We all tried to play our part in the peace negotiations as the smell became the source of much disgust and social awkwardness, but neither Mum nor Dad would relent. Eventually, a compromise was reached and she was allowed to inspect certain documents under his close supervision. And he got his washing done.

Now, if Mum – his wife of all those years – didn't dare break into this bureau, you can imagine how convinced I was of Mark's sincerity by his offering to pick the lock and risk the wrath of Dad by allowing me to take part in my homegrown version of *Who Do You Think You Are?*

I think his intention was for me to lash out in anger. See it for the cruel joke that it was and throw a punch that would justify a full-on confrontation. What he didn't expect was for me to tear off in tears looking for direct answers from my adoptive mum and dad, because our brains, although born of the same biological parents, simply didn't work alike.

Instead, Mark caught me and, muzzling me with one hand and both restraining and lifting me with the other, carried me to a safe distance, over at Hankey's Well, all the while me kicking and screaming inaudibly.

He set me down, making it quite clear that he'd sit on me if I tried to run, and waited impatiently for my crying to stop.

'Of course you're one of us, ya soft, fat tart!'

'I'm still telling Mum!' I said, but I didn't. He bought my silence with seven Benson & Hedges and savers on the cig he'd already lit.

I struggled to comprehend why siblings would want to come to blows with each other – having no more or less regard for the pain or injuries they might inflict than if they were fighting some random lad from Nutgrove – while my brothers couldn't comprehend what it was that I struggled with.

They tried to beat the question out of me, or cloud my judgment with mind games designed to scar on the inside and elicit a more manly response, but it was more than just a simple acceptance of their obvious physical superiority over me that stopped me hitting back. It was a genuine sadness that these feeling of antagonism could exist in the first place, and even **He**, who ordinarily had an answer for every bit of emotional garbage I threw H!S way, even He was perplexed by this particular quirk of human behaviour.

'Never let them steal your peace,' was something Dad used to say, and I often wondered if my apparent 'peace' – or social apathy as I'd have called it – antagonised them. If only they could have heard H!M inside me trashing my head like a young Roger Daltrey let loose in a penthouse hotel suite, then perhaps they'd have cut me the same kind of slack the lads at the youth club had? I don't know, because as a teenager they didn't.

What I do know is that He either felt the same way, or realised my physical limitations and opted for the old approach of 'I'm a lover, not a fighter!' as our survival technique. Because despite H!S appetite for confrontation, and my private obsession with cartoon fantasy violence, He knew instinctively that by making us the victim, we could do the bully's job for them – and hopefully avoid a beating in the process. For all that H!S power over me might increase, He still understood one simple, symbiotic fact: if I went down, He went with me. And so self-preservation took priority over self-respect.

But I know that JoHNNy remained secretly embarrassed by my limited physical capacity, and I know now why He never spoke of my siblings when out on stage. In fact, to hear him in full-on, anti-*Waltons* flow, you'd be well within your rights to think him an only child.

He was ashamed of stepping back from the head butt, of turning the other cheek. Perhaps I should've joined a boxing gym or taken up karate, given H!M a fighting chance against my brothers, or anyone else for that matter, but I didn't. It just wasn't in me. Rather than wail against the injustices of brotherly love, He chose to quietly airbrush them out of the VegaS family portrait instead.

Two young people, a male and female, were jailed for a total of 14 years in 2007, charged in connection with the untimely demise of Paul Masters, who was beaten to death in his own flat. I hope I haven't misrepresented him in any way with this recollection because, believe me, he was a bloody nice lad.

17.

A NEW VOICE

As grim as Paul Masters's fate was to be, by my mid-teens my future wasn't feeling much brighter. I'd lost sight of who I was and had no ambition beyond getting out of school; despite the fact that I couldn't care less what I did once I was free of the place.

I started faking illnesses even though it was obvious there was nothing wrong with me. It became a stupid game between the school secretary and me after my crying wolf way too often. I'd claim to feel sick and so get sent down to the school office. Over time, the school secretary began to make a point of refusing to ring my parents and have me sit outside instead till I felt 'better'. It was a dull punishment, but one I'd see through with quiet determination, glaring at her through the frosted glass of the sliding window.

I can't say I blame her. My symptoms got more and more vague and the pantomime got duller and duller for both of us, until eventually I'd just slide the glass, show my face and assume my regular position on the chair, hoping someone would be sent down for the strap to break up the monotony.

For some stupid reason I once even tried faking it at home, by rubbing a few drops of Olbas Oil around my eyes. My mum packed me off to school looking like a technician who'd neglected to put on his protective goggles at a nuclear testing site. Bloody hell, it burned! (Just a little 'Don't try this at home' disclaimer for you there.)

At least I had time in my own head, where I was at my happiest. No, not exactly at my happiest – I just found life more manageable as a fantasist, strolling around in the shadowy recesses of my own brain for hours and hours on end with no particular interest in reality. Life had so far spectacularly failed to live up to my expectations, even after I had lowered them so spectacularly myself.

I used to think I was a happy-go-lucky kind of soul when I was younger, but this bloody book doesn't half beg to differ – it's turned up so much despondency I'd previously filed under 'Irrelevant'. Ordinarily, we have so little time in our days to reminisce on the past – I suppose that's why we merely highlight landmark emotional moments for quick reference or anecdotal purposes. So much is glossed over and possibly rewritten over the years, but the unfortunate luxury a project like this buys you, especially when you're as slow a writer as I am, is the time to relive past events in slow and painfully honest detail; like stepping away from a slide show featuring preconceptions of simple childhood charm and entering an IMAX cinema running your life back exactly as it happened, not as we've learned to believe it has.

Life was good in so many ways, but I managed to ignore that fact. I was unhappy as a child, and it hurts revisiting that which we learn to veneer over as me, as myself, because, before starting this book, I preferred the abridged version, and I can't manufacture it into something salvageable like He can.

It kills me not to carry a torch for that working-class ideal that I've gone to great pains to sell as my salvation; the notion being that honest-to-goodness folk find a way of turning misery into humour as a fundamental survival strategy, and that hurt merely cascades off us like water off the proverbial duck's back.

Folk laugh off misery in public because it's the done thing, but, in private, away from social expectations, they're soaked to the marrow with quiet fear and regret. Thanks to this book, I'm right back to being embarrassed for being me. I want to give the whole thing over to HiM right now and let him belittle my shame for public approval. But, like I said at the start, it wasn't always HiS story, so He can wait HiS fucking turn.

There's a podgy young lad my son and I pass on the mornings I do the school run. He looks so down on himself and always walks alone with his awkward blue duffel coat buttoned all the way up, most days with the hood up too, come rain or shine, as if he's trying to shut the world out because it only brings with it disappointment or disdain. I want to stop him and tell him that his story has a long way to go yet and that things do eventually work out okay, that this isn't the be all and end all. But I don't, because that would make me a weirdo.

I wonder if he has his own version of VegaS simmering away behind that downcast, browbeaten expression. And if so, will that boy's life be better or worse for having HiM there?

I certainly needed a helping hand at his age. I had lost interest in school, in faith, in bettering myself, or even fitting into childhood clothes. The only thing I still obsessed over was the fairer sex, but they had made it quite clear they had no interest in me. Oh, and my fish, but they're the only animals that enjoyed staring into space whilst saying nothing more than I did. Perhaps that's why I was so fond of them.

I lacked perspective because all I tended to do was look within. What was the point? There was so little in my day-to-day existence that felt worthy of celebration. It was hopeless; I was hopeless. And it didn't matter for a while what He thought, because He didn't live in the real world like I had to do. You can aspire to anything in your head because anything's possible, safe away from practicality in there.

What I needed was a good kick up the arse – something real, something palpable – so I could start appreciating life again in all its wonder and teenage glory.

When this kick up the arse finally arrived, it came from an unexpectedly sombre source.

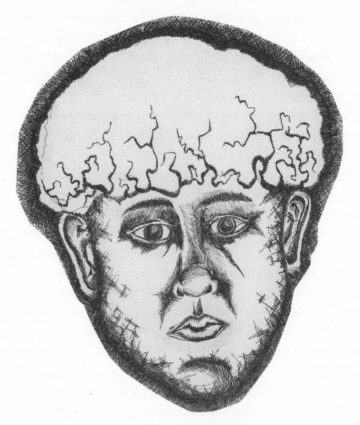

My not so subtle attempts at suggesting I was dying of a brain haemorrhage after striking a deal with **DEATH**. **'You can draw it, but if you say it out loud it will happen, you will die!'**

I remember so distinctly, even now, the first morning I woke up convinced that death was coming for me. I can remember it like a switch going on, but lighting a black bulb that flooded the emptiness inside with a new gloom. Only this wasn't some theoretical form of teen self-pity, no, no: this was an absolute fact of life that I knew affected us all eventually, just some unfortunate buggers sooner than others.

It was mad, because despite the fact that throughout my entire life – and especially during my time at Upholland – I'd had the promise of eternal life dangled in front of me like a golden carrot, I'd never really given more than a moment's thought to the actual prospect of dying – you know, the actual crossing over from this life to the next. And this wasn't because I had any smugness with regard to some notion of automatic acceptance at the Pearly Gates, either (quite the reverse, in my shoplifting phase).

The explanation was most likely the simple fact that kids don't think about death because theoretically it's something way, way off in the distance – along with plastic hips and a fondness for *Murder, She Wrote*. But, that morning, when I woke up and went to put on my socks like I'd done every day for the last ten years or so, I found myself examining my left foot.

'What the fuck is that?'

I'd found a lump in my foot. A lump I could've sworn wasn't there when I took my socks off the night before (despite the fact that I hadn't bothered to check then). It felt horrible and alien and I almost had to dare myself to touch it again as I didn't want to believe it was real.

'Ooh, fucking hell.'

There it was again. In line with my big toe in the middle of my foot was a definite abnormality, although the only word that kept repeating in my head at the time was 'lump'. There was a lump, there was no denying it – it was there every time I ran my finger over the top of my foot. And every time I did it, I shuddered.

Mum was shouting for me downstairs, but before I could shout back, a dark and inescapable explanation came over me:

'It's cancer!'

It wasn't.

'Maybe it's cancer?'

It was.

'IT'S CANCER!'

Something in my head had popped like an aneurism of medical certainty that did not feel the need to seek a second opinion and had no desire to concur with any other possible explanation for the presence of the lump that might contradict the fact that it was cancer and it would kill me.

Any problem/medical query was always offered up to the general consensus of parents or nosy siblings, rather than our local GP.

This was only a lump …

'A lump, a cancerous lump!'

Sorry, a lump, a lump in my foot!

Anything could've caused it. There were possibly a hundred explanations, diagnoses and treatments at the very least. But it wasn't a rational part of my mind that was functioning any more, and this is what is so important about the day I woke up as a hypochondriac that I have to explain to you properly, so you can understand the bits of my history and my sad, mad mind that I'm striving to share with you right now.

The first certainty I'd felt in years, the only belief system that had replaced the absolutism of Catholicism and Upholland's crap attempt at enforcing it, was a definite and quite final realisation that death was upon me. It was as if a more determined part of my head had bought majority shares in all other growing concerns and shut them down so the entire noggin could focus on that season's crazy investment.

I felt a sickness and sadness all at once that's so hard to do justice to, even with all the words in my vocabulary. Within a heartbeat, I was overwhelmed with fear and a terrible remorse at a life wasted through selfishness and apathy; I actually started crying, it felt so definite. I didn't even think to check the other foot for a matching tarsometatarsal joint (as it turned out to be) – there was no point, the hypochondria had already decided.

Even **He** shit his pants.

'It's cancer.'

'**Fucking Hell, I think you're right.**'

'Really?'

'**It's a lump, isn't it?**'

'Yeah.'

'**Then I reckon it's Fucking cancer.**'

'Of course it's cancer. It's a lump, therefore it's cancer. Malignant and untreatable

cancer. Perhaps you knocked your foot, like that local lad who got kicked in the shin playing football and got cancer of the leg. It's definitely cancer and you're definitely dying.'

'Oh, shit!'

'Hang on a minute —'

'Time you left, Mr—?'

'Fucking hell, no, no, no ...'

'Never mind what my name is ...'

And with that, He was ushered out of my consciousness. Just like Ian from West Park, Simon and all my other mates from Upholland, He was gone. But, in my defence, the new bloke wasn't much of a one for democratic discussion.

'I'm not ready.'

'Nobody is. You're going to be dead soon because you have cancer.'

'So what do I do?'

'There's nothing you can do. YOU HAVE CANCER AND YOU ARE GOING TO DIE, SOON.'

He was nowhere near as much fun or as supportive as the other guy, but he spoke with an authority that made His ordinarily irrefutable logic sound like a nursery rhyme.

'And then you'll be dead.'

'Shut up!'

I started crying again. Luckily this was one of those rare moments when I had the bedroom I shared with my two brothers to myself. Regret fell on me like a fat man with cataracts tripping off the end of an escalator.

I didn't default to God like I tended to do during the million or so other minor crises I'd had – I just had this overwhelming sadness at having blown my short time on this earth as my new-found lust for life suddenly made me realise all the potential I'd been wasting in feeling sorry for myself.

18.

SAVED BY THE WHEEL

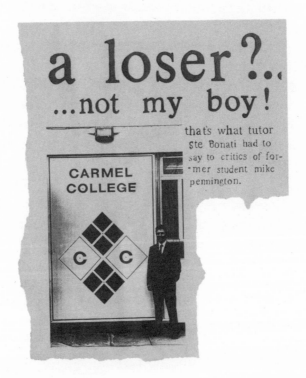

a loser?..
...not my boy!

that's what tutor Ste Bonati had to say to critics of former student mike pennington.

CARMEL COLLEGE

If apathy is ruining your day, step into a busy road for a second where you know cars have no intention of stopping, and dice with death. If you survive your day, you will be bursting with potential, I guarantee.

My mum called me down for breakfast, but the grief was overwhelming at the thought of telling them my awful news.

'No parent should ever have to bury their child,' my dad would sometimes say following bad news on the TV, so how the hell would they react to this bombshell?

I closed my eyes and dared to touch the lump once more.

'Definitely cancer.'

I cried again – into my fists this time, to muffle the sound, desperately trying to pull myself together. I went into the bathroom to splash some water on my face and get rid of the redness. Mum called up again but with the tone of someone losing their patience. I wanted to call back, but knew that any response I attempted would turn into a sob.

Eventually I had to go downstairs and face the family. I walked into the kitchen/living room and the chaos of breakfast was suddenly beautiful and nostalgic. Everything had a wonderful, rose-tinted glow to it, despite the domestic drudgery of fighting for toaster access and moaning over who'd taken the last of the milk. The scene that greeted me was reminiscent of a Bisto ad, but with the addition of the Grim Reaper slouched on the couch, checking his watch.

God, I was going to miss all this! Once again, I had to fight back the unbearable urge to cry. I'd not been this consumed with emotion since that first attack of homesickness all those years ago at Upholland.

'What's got into you?'

'Cancer.'

'Nothing, Mum. I'm fine.'

'No you're not, you have cancer.'

'Shut up!'

'There's toast there, but best get a move on or you'll miss that bus.'

'Never mind the bus, you're dying, you have cancer.'

'Mum?'

'What?'

'He has cancer.'

'Nothing.'

'Cancer, cancer, cancer, cancer!'

I grabbed my toast and left, bursting into tears again as I got out of the front door. Ironically for one facing this particular health scare, my response was to grab my 10-pack stash of Benson & Hedges from behind the little privet hedge in our front garden and run to Hankey's Well to spark up.

My bloody hands were trembling, trying to light the thing, and all the while this new voice inside my head just wouldn't shut the fuck up.

'I wonder if it will spread to your leg and then all the other major organs?'

'Well, maybe I can get it amputated and just have a false leg?'

'No point, it's cancer. You're dying.'

I stopped on the field and took my shoe off to check my foot again. God it went through me, touching it.

'See, it's massive. It's cancer.'

And only then did I have the bright idea of checking my other foot for a comparison.

Standing in damp grass in just my socks, rubbing both bits of my feet, I thought I'd felt something.

'Just there, feel it? I'm sure there's one on this foot, too?'

'Cancer in both feet? Don't be so stupid. That on the right is a bone, the one on the left is a lump. It's cancer.'

'Shit, you're right. Well, what do I do? Go and see the doctor?'

'Just so he can tell you for definite that it's cancer? Yer a braver man than I am. What'll happen when he tells everyone else you've got it, eh? How are people gonna treat you then, eh? Once they all know that you're dying because you have cancer?'

And that was the sly genius behind this new torment. I wanted to pray that all of it was just in my imagination, or that I was over-reacting to some other straightforward medical dilemma, but to do that I would have to go and see the doctor and that might only serve to confirm my worst nightmare. And this voice seemed so sure of **himself**. **He** had cunningly secured **himself** the position of my new personal physician, and **his** infallible logic guaranteed that the majority of **his** diagnoses would remain our little secret.

I don't think it was **his** intention to torment me quite so much but good God in heaven, **he** seemed to feel the need to remind me of whatever false condition I truly believed in my heart of hearts I was suffering from 24/7. **He** was relentless! **He** wasn't someone I could turn to in times of stress, not like (whispering) **HiM**, because **he** was the primary source of all my worries.

In the days, I would wander around like a preoccupied zombie. I drifted out of West Park and into Carmel Sixth Form College with four O-levels in English Literature, English Language, History and RE, after failing a common-sense aptitude test for the last few remaining apprenticeship posts with the local council.

I'd thought I was going to be a joiner, just like my dad and my brothers, but the results said otherwise. My brother Mark knew I'd failed before I'd even opened the envelope.

'You've ballsed that up!'

'How do you know?'

'Second-class stamp.'

And he was right.

I should probably make it clear here that this happened during the introduction of 'Youth Opportunity Schemes' and the phasing out of proper apprenticeships. Most of the town's main employers had surrendered to the notion of slave labour, along with a certificate at the end of two years' 'training' (instead of the traditional four), which wasn't worth wiping your arse on as far as most building sites were concerned – it was just a dodgy attempt at juggling unemployment figures whilst paying next to nothing in the process.

Fortunately, my dad was on to them, as was I, and thanks to my sister Catharine paving the way by being the first Pennington ever in our immediate family to enter into further education, I opted for sixth-form college as opposed to the blatant manipulation of a locally despised Tory government.

Dad didn't seem too hurt that I hadn't followed on in the family working-class tradition of becoming a tradesman. In fact, during the interview process for entry into the newly opened Carmel College, he intervened on my behalf when a hesitant Steve Bonati, the art teacher there, pointed out that it was highly

irregular for somebody who hadn't done O-level Art to undertake an A-level in the subject.

'He may not have the qualifications, but the lad is always
drawing, always. He's got books and books full of these doodles
and sketches that he does, and all of them off his own back.
I don't honestly know if any of 'em are any good – it's all just
scribbles to me if truth be told – but you've got to acknowledge
the lad's keenness. And as my father used to say, one volunteer is
worth ten pressed men.'

God bless you, Dad, for that, because your sincerity and
honesty swung it for me and, as a result, I fell under the tutelage
of another incredibly gifted and dedicated teacher. A man who,
thanks to his perseverance and patience, would go on to steer
me out of trouble and into a career choice that has never stopped
rewarding me with creative dividends. A man I owe a massive
debt to and who, I am proud to say, remains a dear friend of
mine to this day.

One benefit of having **Doctor Death** talking on and on and on and
on in my head every day was that I had learned to appreciate
people and moments all over again.

Whatever grudges I'd consciously or subconsciously harboured
over my time at Upholland or West Park were temporarily forgotten about, and the acceptance that my time on this earth was
dwindling away rapidly meant the slate was wiped clean. I was
in a headspace that meant I was desperate to cherish my entire
family again. I was secretly in love with life because (as **he** was
so fond of reminding me), it could end any time soon.

The nights were the worst. There was no distraction from **his**
constant reminders of my latest terminal illness (and it always
had to be terminal!). I'd watch anything on TV that could help
keep my mind distracted; well, anything other than health-
related shows: if any medical condition was described in a factual documentary, or a character in a drama fell ill, then I would
inevitably develop the same symptoms.

So what happened if the family was watching something and
I couldn't switch over? I'd have to leave the room immediately

or cover my ears, close my eyes and hum really loudly like a lunatic so as to block out the information.

In those days there was no overnight TV, and we were way, way off being able to afford a video recorder. Oh God, what I wouldn't have given for one of those: 24-hour distraction with movies or shows of my own choice! I used to sleep over at the Fords' house all the time as their mum, Joan, didn't have a problem with my sitting up in their living room watching the same movie over and over again to drown out **him** and **his** constant updates on the imminence of my death. But, back at home, I would dread that time when all the family would turn in and Dad dictated that the TV went off. It was like someone pulling the plug on my life-support when that screen went blank and silence descended on the house. Well, silence for everyone but me. Each night I'd pray that someone would stay up just that little bit later, but with no programmes to watch, why would they?

To this day I still can't sleep without a television on, or a radio at the very least. And a light on, ALWAYS a light on! I'm an insomniac, which has served me well in some respects, and frustrated the hell out of me in others. It's the reason that once booze came into my life I could drink beyond the night and through into the day, long after all the pill-heads' potions had worn off. I've never needed speed to keep me going, just the fears that bounce around inside my head.

The minute I'd get into bed **he** would start on me.

'You've got lockjaw.'

'No, no, I haven't.'

'You have. You've got lockjaw and you're going to die from it. Can't you feel your jaw seizing up? That's tetanus, that is. It starts in the jaw, that's why they call it lockjaw.'

My jaw did feel achy, and it would seem I couldn't open my mouth as wide as I used to be able to. What the irrationality of my hypochondria chose to ignore though, was the fact that I had lain awake for four nights solid, moving my jaw constantly to stop it from locking (as well as when it wasn't too noticeable in the daytime), so therefore it was bound to be aching. Plus, never

in my life had I measured how wide my mouth opened before –
why the hell would I?

'You mustn't have had a tetanus injection.'

'I might've.'

'Well, obviously you didn't, because you'd remember.'

'Well, maybe I did and I forgot? Oh, fuck, oh no, please, please
remember. Please don't let me die from this!'

'Too late for that now. Check your jaw again.'

'I have, it's still numb. Oh God!'

'And can you open your jaw as wide as you normally do?'

'No! No, I fucking can't! You know that!'

'Then it's lockjaw and you're going to die.'

And I would go into the bathroom, sit on the floor rocking
backwards and forwards and cry whilst our conversation
started again like a malicious broken record. Eventually at 4, 5,
or even 6 a.m. I would fall asleep through sheer nervous anxious
exhaustion. Other nights I didn't sleep at all, even after – in a
move that surprised me more than anyone else – I inherited my
sister Catharine's room once she'd left for college.

With no brothers to disturb, I could switch a light on for the
entire night (blocking out the evidence with a towel across the
bottom of the door) whilst I contemplated death until alarms
went off throughout the house and I could fake the process of
rising from my non slumber.

Then, hallelujah! Some time in the mid-1980s, Channel 4
started showing late movies. Black-and-white French movies
mainly, some incredibly dull and up their own arse, some with
the odd flash of nudity, which was always a welcome bonus.
And although I might have found myself having the occasional
tug to one or two of them, I can honestly say (hand on heart, not
penis) that my prime objective for watching these was the desperate distraction they provided from **him**. It gave me just
another hour or so of respite from the fear.

Now, I don't know if it was the adult content of these films, or
simply the fact that I was breaking curfew by sneaking out of
bed to watch them, but my dad took great exception to my solo

midnight movie club. So much so that he started taking the plug off the TV at night time. I nearly bloody killed myself trying to stick the bare wires into the sockets one night in a desperate bid to see if it would work. In the end, though, I went out and bought a bunch of plugs (OK then, I'll come clean, I actually stole some off electrical equipment left idle at Carmel College). At night, Dad would take the plug off, but then later on I'd sneak down with one from my own stash and attach it. Some nights he was so shattered from work that he would sleep right through, others he would come down and without saying a word unplug the TV and simply cut the cable with pliers.

He wasn't one for losing his temper, but I could see the frustration and disappointment in his eyes at my constant disobedience.

I wanted to explain why this was such a vital lifeline for me, and that I wouldn't ordinarily dare keep ignoring his requests to go to bed and stay there. I so desperately wanted to tell him that his youngest son was dying, but then **he**'d remind me: '**If you do, then you'll make it real and he will take you to a doctor and they'll confirm it and you will die! By the way, that asbestos from the garage roofs you all used to throw onto fires to see it explode—**'

'Yes?'

'**Tiny particles of it is in your lungs now and you have asbestosis and you are going to die.**'

As I've said, **he** was with me all day and all night, and the only key to surviving was distractions. In college by day, and although only a **voice** and not a fully formed apparition, **his** interventions were quite like what happens to Russell Crowe's character Professor Nash in *A Beautiful Mind*.

I couldn't stop **him** talking, but there was enough to busy myself with so that I could refrain from getting drawn into any actual discussions. As a result, apart from the odd panic attack that I'd manage with a multiple fag break in the college quad, I was happy at Carmel.

There was another side effect to my absolute belief that death was soon coming for me: I wanted to die well liked; I wanted to be remembered as a nice guy. I'd often run my own funeral scenario in my head – in an odd kind of way, it was a comfort for me, in between the bouts of fear – imagining everyone gathering together outside St Austin's and talking about how untimely my death was, and from a stroke of all things ...

After leaving Upholland, in the light of the ensuing sense of having let down so many people and especially on realising how little regard my brothers had for me during my teen years, **He** had taught me to ignore other people's opinions of **Us**, or at least allow **HiM** to process them. But since **He**'d been bullied out of the picture by **him**, I desperately craved the acceptance of my peers, and in going out of my way to be popular amongst them I became a bit of a doormat, a social walkover.

Sixth form wasn't like school. There were hardly any fights, and the majority of disputes were settled by debate. But I didn't really grasp the opportunity to stand up for myself within that comfort zone, because I was too busy hoping I'd say the right thing to gain popularity instead of what I thought and believed. Although I hadn't heard from **HiM** in a long while, I know this must've been killing **HiM**.

On the upside, I'd found a new mentor in Steve Bonati. He was so laidback, and yet encouraged more work out of me than any other teacher since Rowena Rowlands. I loved the fact that such a big chunk of my timetable was devoted to art, and the real clincher was we were free to come and go as we pleased as long as we finished our coursework. As a result, you couldn't get me out of there.

By being handed the responsibility to manage my own time, rather than being told when and where to sit and what it was I had to learn, Steve converted me to the religion of art by basically teaching us to teach ourselves through experimentation, and that suited me down to the ground. I thrived on the belief he placed in me by treating us all as creative equals, not empty heads that needed filling with his own ideas.

My other studies may have suffered as a result of my dedication to A-level Art (well, that and something else I'll get on to in a wee while), but I felt like I had stumbled across

something beyond a career. I believed I had found my vocation. In fact, the teachers of my other subjects: GCSE Maths
(a career back-up in case I ever wanted to go into teaching);
GCSE Business Studies (another career back-up, in case I
decided to apply for middle management with Argos where
my sister, Catharine, had helped secure me a Saturday job);
A-level Craft Design Technology (Steve Milton, our tutor, was
a great guy who once commented on an essay I'd written: 'This
would've been a brilliant essay if Andy Warhol had actually
invented the angle-poise lamp. Less bull, more facts'); and
A-level English Literature, all politely invited me to exit their
courses eventually.

Miss Cannon was just how I liked my English teachers –
strangely foxy for a woman with a West Country accent, sarcastic
and tousled of hair – which made the coolness of her final dismissal all the more devastating.

'I get the feeling your heart's not in this class.'

'It's not that, it's just ...'

'STOMACH CANCER!'

'Go, go on, be free. The knowledge that you crave does not lie
within these four walls.'

I had no beef with any of them; they were great tutors, and
patient with me almost to a fault. But if I could cue up Lionel
Richie's 'Hello' right now as you read, and remove the awful
stalker hangover from the video and just focus on the craft element, then it might just help you understand how no one else
could hope to get a look in from the moment Steve Bonati first
introduced me to pottery.

19.

MY TRUE VOCATION

I'm dead serious when I say that I thought I'd found my true vocation in pottery. Despite my being an enthusiastic doodler, I struggled getting to grips with the technical aspects of drawing and painting; but with ceramics, I just loved the process of building something in three-dimensional form, something that would be fired and have a real, solid presence.

Now don't get me wrong, my stuff was terrible – most sixth-form ceramics are – but at the time it didn't matter. I felt like an artist, and I realise now that I thrived on the excitement of doing well at something: years of apathy were parted like the Red Sea as Steve Bonati led us students to the Promised Land.

Building scaled-up reproductions of everyday household objects was par for the course, although painting them in gouache because I was too impatient to wait for the finished results of a glaze was pretty unforgivable. But I was happy in my work, and that's all that mattered. I should say at this point that it still kills me that to this day Steve insists on displaying the ceramic shoe I'd go on to make for my interview for a foundation course in art and design. The brief was to think of a job and create an item of footwear based on that chosen career.

6th form art at its best/
worst. Look out Converse,
there's a new kid in town.

Name	M. Pennington	Subject	Art(A)
Subject Tutor	S. Bonati	Group Tutor	J. Hall
T.G. 11	Year 1	Date	December 1987
Attendance	Good	Work submission	35%
Punctuality	Poor	Exam. mark/grade	

Subject Tutor's Comments

Mike, you have shown ability in your craft option – Ceramics and you seem to have a wealth of ideas and imagination for compositions. this is fine in theory. The practice, however, is not so good. You are wasting too much time in lessons because you have not prepared work previously at home. You have some ability in this subject – do not waste it. SB

Steve Bonati coming down hard on me with some tough love!
We argued about this over pints in The Grange.

I opted for a hunter – a common skill no doubt in great demand down at the local job centre – and made a monstrously large shoe constructed from various bits of carcass from dead/hunted animals, only in clay. Ta dah! It was bloody awful. And when asked at my interview why I'd only opted to make one, instead of a complete pair as requested in the brief, I lied about the fact that one alone had simply taken too long and bullshitted a response along the lines of, 'Hasn't there been enough slaughter?' They nodded knowingly, accepted my excuse, and I learnt my first lesson in the potential for bluffing your way in the art world.

On the nights when Dad won out in the battle for late-night telly, I could still sit up in my room drawing or painting, eventually without the aid of a towel across the door. If Dad did get up in the night he would happily allow me to continue – mistaking, I reckon, the need for some relief from **him** for the same kind of dedication to my studies that my sister had shown.

But the best discovery I made during this time – the only true relief I got from my obsession with dying, and the only time the dark clouds truly parted, allowing me to feel the sunshine kiss my soul again – was how much better I felt when I drank.

It was sweet, funny, riotous relief: God in a glass with all the answers to all of life's questions. Not that I hadn't drunk before, of course. It was a culture growing up in Thatto Heath that we were all well indoctrinated in by our early teens. School discos, under 18s-discos at West Park, impromptu house parties, my sister Catharine's 18th birthday party when my dad had to walk me around the car park for over an hour after getting hammered minesweeping unwatched pints in the room, or just kicking back over Hankey's Well – we never missed an opportunity to well-oil the evening's proceedings with a bottle of Strongbow, cans of cheap Ace lager, sherry in a Barton's pop bottle bought on draft from Metcalf's, homebrew or mixed spirits lifted in unnoticeable amounts from each bottle of the family liquor cabinet. Anything would do, and we'd go to any lengths to get our hands on it. There was always some bloke down on his luck happy to go in to the offy and buy us booze – as long as there was a can in it for him – when we had the money. Or one of us ready to steal it, if we didn't.

My mum and dad didn't ever keep booze in the house, apart from a bottle of whiskey my mum would mix an occasional hot toddy from in the absence of the addictive sleeping pills her GP had kept her on for years. And my dad once made homebrew, but the stock was closely monitored.

He drank up at St Austin's Catholic Men's Society Club, religiously, every Friday night, and Saturday afternoons when he wasn't working on a side job or signing on and so money was too tight. And also around the Lane, the Vine, the Railway, the Springfield and occasionally the Elephant – but drinking at home just wasn't really practised by my folks.

I can't ever remember seeing my dad drunk like other blokes, who'd stumble out of pubs. He appreciated a drink, but never to my knowledge abused it. He was always up and at it work-wise after a night out or a family function. It was one of his few commandments that he strictly enforced with zero tolerance, especially now my brothers were both in gainful employment: 'If you're man enough to go out drinking, you're man enough to get up and go to work.'

So with zero supplies around the house, I had to fund my contributions to the Hayes Street Junior Jamboree in other ways. Regrets, I've had a few, as the great man once sang. Selling all my *2000 AD* comic collection to Andy Cave whilst at West Park for one, including my mint *Judge Death* book signed by Brian Bolland and Mike Collins, amongst others, after queuing up for hours outside the Forbidden Planet offices in London with my mate, Martin Hurley, a fellow fan. And all for a mere £3.50 with which to buy booze – a mistake that still haunts me to this day.

St Helens' forerunner of Cash Converters was a little shop called Magpie's Nest on North Road. I sold them so much stuff from our house that I reckoned no one would miss that their display window started looking like a miniature museum devoted to the Penningtons. I even sold my sister's goldfish after she left, despite the fact that she's had it for years and I'd promised to take care of it in her absence. I got 70p for it from Gene's Aquarium to put towards a bottle of cider.

After that lucrative transaction, Ian and I actually tried our hand at pond fish-rustling. This experiment ended in disaster with me sat soaked to the skin in about a foot and a half of water pulling a classic Oliver Hardy: 'Well, why don't you do something to help me?' frustrated expression and Ian setting off a security light as he staggered around the garden we were in, laughing.

These goldfishy misdemeanours were bad enough, but the most shameful error of judgment was stealing from the charity tubs we'd been shaking at the entrance to the cinema as volunteers representing Grange Park Youth Club during the holidays. We collected at the start of the early evening movie and got to stay and watch the film for free afterwards as a show of thanks.

Everyone had taken their turn at helping themselves to the collection and we'd gone to the Float each night afterwards, the only pub in St Helens where as 15-year-olds we were more or less guaranteed to get served in the empty lounge/snug with its tiny serving hatch, well hidden from the disapproving regulars who populated the bar. So, as much as I genuinely protested when it came to my turn to lighten the charity coffers, it was pointed out that I'd already drunk my share of guilt and therefore had to do it, if only to avoid the wrath of my fellow do-gooders.

One lad was supposed to keep watch as I tore open the plastic lid and emptied the contents onto the toilet cubicle floor to sort the silver and gold from the slummy.

'There must be about nine quid here, look at all them fifty pence pieces!'

But the smile soon drained from my face – along with any colour – when I looked up and realised that the person easing open the cubicle door was the cinema manager, and not my supposed lookout.

'I knew you lot were up to something! Go on, you thieving little git, get yer mates and bugger off!' And he grabbed me by the scruff of the neck, lifted me off the seat and threw me out of the toilets.

I prepared a weak excuse for the youth club that I'd put my bus fare in the box by mistake and was merely retrieving it but, oddly enough, the manager never grassed us up to them. We were just told that our services were no longer required.

Given the reputation of the youth club, I reckon the volunteers there had already guessed why and thought the least enquired about, the better. Looking back, it was embarrassing to have confirmed everyone's poor opinion of us but, thanks to our brazen thieving, I enjoyed some truly amateur nights hammered.

When I came staggering home, I'd try not to cause the same kind of bedlam I'd seen my brothers produce when they'd imbibed too freely of the grape or barley. This softly-softly approach usually involved claiming that whatever disco or party I'd been to was, 'Just the usual, a pop and crisps do', despite my having possibly spent two hours lying on the cool concrete of the disabled access ramp of Thatto Heath Park Library trying desperately to sober up so as not to give the game away to my folks; who'd obviously seen it all before, but possibly appreciated my making the effort to at least appear sober.

Around this time, I remember throwing up over the balcony at Peter Street Community Centre one night, not five minutes after getting there myself for the birthday party of some girl Ian knew, to the outrage of new arrivals below. I'd drunk two-thirds of a bottle of Croft Original and stashed the rest outside.

The police arrived to shut down the party due to the amount of booze that had been smuggled in, but the pissed young me thought I must be the reason for the 'raid', and responded by doing a runner with all the grace and purpose of one of those cowboys in a Western movie who've been tied to a horse and forced to walk behind it for three days straight. (Once at a safe distance, I found it easier to crawl to the bus stop than do my human pinball impression.)

Waking up to the rank smell of faeces and my head between my knees with my mouth full of boxer short elastic was another moment of teenage drunken infamy. When I'd finally got my bearings, I realised that I'd shat my pants, but either couldn't manage to get my trousers off, or simply couldn't be bothered in my drunken stupor, so I must have opted instead to divest myself of my underwear by attempting to chew through the waistband and tear the rest of it off. I was like a somewhat less heroic version of that guy in the Danny Boyle film who fell down a ravine and had to cut his own arm off to escape.

The last I remembered, a large bloke had been escorting me out of West Park's junior disco night for attempting to sit on a ghost chair and taking an all-too-real table with me as I collapsed to the floor. I can promise you now that, as the bouncer carried out his routine lift, carry and eject procedure, a dirty protest was the last thing on my mind.

I'm not trying to make any excuses for my disgraceful antics, but I do reckon the fallout might have had something to do with the fact that in my naïvety, I had also drunk the lion's share of the sediment from the bottom of a large bottle of homebrew after having heard somewhere that, 'That's what gets you really pissed. It's like the worm in tequila!'

None of these are the kind of highlights you'd like flashing before your eyes in your dying moments, I'll grant you, but then, these were fledgling attempts at getting to grips with drink. Thanks to school, an unsteady cash flow, the sometimes alien concoctions we were consuming and the irregularity of our get-togethers, there was no way to build up any kind of technique. We were the sight-impaired leading the sight-impaired, learning together through trial and error – without ever questioning the error of our ways.

I don't write these stories down with any bravado because I know that as a young bloke, I put myself in countless amounts of danger and/or endless degrading situations in a bid to act more grown up, but that was our culture, for better or worse. It's just what we did.

But once I'd got to the sixth form, everything changed. We were treated more like adults and we behaved more like adults, to an extent. I'm sure the tutor chaperones at the college discos would beg to differ, but to me the drinking that followed there felt like I was truly stepping into manhood in style.

My dad had taken me to one side at the age of 16 and simply said, 'I know you're gonna go trying getting served and supping in pubs now, and don't try telling me otherwise because there's better liars gone before you. But if I walk into any local of mine and see you threatening the licence of its landlord, I'll turf you out myself, got that?'

'Erm, yeah, but ...' I said, trying to sound bemused by the accusation, while quietly being chuffed to bits at this green light for go.

'Just do me and you a big favour, okay? Don't drink what doesn't agree with you and don't bring bother beyond this threshold. We all like drink; no one likes a drunk. A pint's there to be enjoyed.'

Growing up, I'd always thought our upbringing much stricter than that of other kids in our street, but the flipside of that was that I was treated as an adult at a far earlier age than many of my mates. There were no threats about what would happen if I dared go in a pub, just an honest acknowledgement that it would be expected of me to do so, and no sermons on the evil of booze (which might inadvertently lend it a more glamorous sheen); simply an earnest word of caution from one who had seen it all. And I respected Dad for that, I respected pub culture (until last orders) and I didn't just enjoy my pint, I bloody cherished it, each and every one of them!

When a pint was passed over the bar to me, it was like being awarded a trophy for greatness; like I was being honoured by a rowdy, vibrant and slightly rougher-round-the-edges local Round(ish) Table Association each and every time I raised a glass and poured the life-affirming contents down my grateful gullet. Everything made sense with a drink inside me. With every one, my fears and over-analytical predictions were diluted into manageable quantifications. The glass was half-full, whereas it had been half-empty for so, so long. I could stand up to fate, laugh in its face, howl at the moon of misgivings and show my arse in the Woolworth's window of what once was!

I had self-belief when tanked up. My opinions mattered. *I* mattered, goddamn it! Just as Mrs Rowlands's report had predicted, I could talk to any person at any given time – whether willing or, yes, on occasion, unwilling to listen – on any given or ungiven subject.

Here, finally, was the confidence I'd envied in others and so self-loathingly despised the lack of in myself. I hadn't lost it completely: it wasn't languishing in some dormitory in Uphol- land like a pair of old socks I'd forgotten to pack; it wasn't cow- ering in the library or dodging a stray football in the playground of West Park. Arthur Guinness, John Tetley, James Forshaw, Thomas Greenall, Samuel Whitbread and Co. had merely been holding it in trust for me until I'd come of age. And they had taken fine care of it in my absence.

My brain never ran hot on beer, it lay chilled out on a lilo that drifted sweetly across an infinity pool of positivity. I didn't rock myself to sleep praying for heavy eyes and **his** insidious medical insights to cease. Instead, my body was drawn to my bed like a lumberjack's chosen tree falling to the ground, heavy and immovable, knackered and incapable of fighting sleep even if I'd have wanted to.

So this was what pure tiredness felt like ... my God, it was beautiful. My head would sink into my pillow with a smile sloshed across my daft and happy, drunken face, finally able to extend my gratitude for this haven most folk took for granted. Life was, when inebriated, and for want of any better word, truly intoxicating.

Now, don't get me wrong: **he** was not at all happy with this, and so **his** efforts to remind me that the end was nigh intensified. Remember the old saying, 'Whatever doesn't kill you only makes you stronger'? Well, as much as booze managed to anesthetise **him** temporarily, **he** would come back at me harder and darker whenever there were insufficient amounts of alcohol in my bloodstream to piss on **his** chips.

I had days in the ceramic studio when I was suddenly gripped with the fear that I had been arguing with **him** out loud, under my breath, instead of in my head. My dedication to art and the process of working at my ceramics was a definite lifeline, but at best it was a mime, a sort of performance art show of defiance.

As far as **he** was concerned, this was nothing more than a silly bit of, 'La la la, I'm not listening to **YOU**!' It did little or nothing to deter **him** from **his** obsession, but at least it gave me a sense of accomplishment in the meantime.

As I write this now, a new realisation has just struck me. I cannot say for sure, and I hope this doesn't sound wanky, but I wonder if my attraction to ceramics went beyond a conscious enjoyment of it and a modicum of technical ability? I loved the impact of three-dimensional art and the physical ability to walk around it, appreciate it from different angles, perhaps even hold it in your hands as the artist once did. It is an added appreciation that's never left me and one that has stood me in great stead against the snobbery of fine artists who might dare view ceramics as a mere craft, a cottage industry with no place displaying itself in a gallery, and us potters simple night-school fanatics with ideas above our stations. (Fucking painters!) But I wonder now if the permanence of these structures appealed to me on a subconscious level, too. Maybe I was looking for something that would outlive me – like Easter Island or Stonehenge (albeit on a slightly smaller scale) – some grand statement that said for definite that I'd been here. Perhaps my work was unwittingly just an ornate set of headstones for me to be remembered by? They certainly spelt RIP when it came to my final A-level grade but, along with my desire to be well thought of after my death, I can't say for sure that my body of work wasn't also a far more desperate plea just to be remembered. (That's what a therapist might call a breakthrough. Or more likely nod and say, 'Yes, yes, you *are* being incredibly wanky.')

Now though, at long last, there was some guaranteed relief from **it** altogether awaiting me in the bottom of my next pint. **His** monopoly over my entire existence was fractured, and that would always be something worth celebrating. Especially when, first with a whisper through the cracks, and then with renewed confidence and all guns blazing, it meant that **He** could come back.

You have no idea just how much I'd missed **HiM**! I mean really, really missed **HiM**. And to think I'd thought myself fucked up when **He**'d been kicking around upstairs ...?

Death could wait **his** turn as far as **He** was concerned. Back then, I didn't understand **HiS** fear of the big sleep, or why **He**'d turned tail and run at the first sign of mortality, but I didn't think to ask because I was just too damned pleased to have someone fighting my corner again. And what was lovely was the fact that w**e** shared the same 'Fuck you!' attitude once the Dutch courage was upon u**S**. Even though **He** tended to sleep in late and leave me to deal with **you-know-who** by day; still, at least the night was o**Ur**S – 'Y**a**a**a**a**a**a**a**a**a**a**a**a**a**a**a**a**a**a**a**agh!!!! C**o**M**e** **a**nd g**e**t **U**s, **DEATH,** y**a** f**U**cK**er**!'

20.

ARGOS FUCK YOURSELF

GONE:
BUT TO A
BETTER
PLACE?

Jane Symme, manageress
at st.Helens 'ARGOS',
shares staff dismay at
Mikes decision to persue
a career in art instead of
retail management with

*Ah, the Argos years, or as I like to think of it, my tribute
to Bukowski's POST OFFICE.*

And so I drank my way through whatever nights I could, and worked at my A-level Art in between, everything else kind of slipping by the wayside. Apart from, that is, my Saturday job at Argos, that being my main source of income now for socialising after a string of disastrous dead-end, part-time jobs.

God, the hangovers I'd work through there on a Saturday, only to go out and happily do it all over again the following night. They kept me upstairs in the stockroom because initially there were no uniforms that fitted me, plus I doubt very much that I represented the slick 80s' image they thought they represented within the retail market place anyhow.

I continued giving them the wrong measurements as I hated their uniform, which was three different shades of brown: turd brown, old sofa brown and *The Mary Whitehouse Experience*'s 'Milky Milky' pervert sketch character beige brown, with a yellow trim through the V-neck of the pullover, and brown clip-on tie to really pull the whole outfit together.

As relentless as the work was upstairs, at least picking out the orders and sending them down the conveyor belt meant we didn't have to deal with angry members of the public face-to-face, especially mid-riot over a Christmas shortage of the Teenage Mutant Ninja Turtles.

Over time, I embedded myself to the point where I was more or less considered a porter rather than jobbing Saturday staff. That was a real badge of honour for me, because the full-time stockroom lads were like the cool reprobates of the place. They only dressed in civvies, and knew where stock that wouldn't fit the regular storage bins was kept, and could tut knowingly whilst leading the way when a newbie, or someone from front of shop temporarily drafted upstairs would understandably struggle to find the item we'd stashed away elsewhere. I felt like an old hand around the place, as opposed to someone too fat to successfully pull off the Argos triple brown combo.

When Christmas came around, I was drafted in for their three stock deliveries a day and, being classed as part-time Saturday staff on paper, that meant all those hours counted as overtime. Three deliveries – 6 a.m., 12 noon and 6 p.m. – three days a week, and always out for pints afterwards. Lots and lots of pints, but never a shift missed. I pulled my bloody weight in work-terms when I was there, just as Dad expected from us.

I was good at drinking; I was a good drinker. I never back-chatted my mum, I didn't piss in wardrobes, and I wouldn't come home looking to sort out my brothers or deep-fat-fry anything if not *compos mentis* enough to avoid starting a kitchen fire.

I did take our dog, Emma, for the occasional walk and lose
her but she always made it home before me, and made for an
excellent alternative to a duvet should I find myself crashing
on the couch rather than risking the stairs. I'd attempt to look
her square in the eye as I whispered a promise to try my best
not to die, and she would lick the sticky bits of beer off of my
chin in a bid to break up the awkwardness of the moment.
(They reckon now that dogs can smell cancer. Thank God I
didn't know that way back when, or else he'd have had me
convinced that a friendly hello from Emma meant testicular
cancer, for sure.)

I was pulling in so much money I bought scarves for all my
female relatives from the Avon catalogue and didn't flinch once
at the bill. Rolling tens off my stack of bills, I was pure pimp
daddy rock 'n' bloody roll, you'd better believe it!

I was also the man hammering the jukebox in the Grange that
year when 'Fairytale of New York' had just been released. So
long as I had any say in the matter, I made damn sure that The
Pogues and Kirsty MacColl played at least every third song.

If I play that song even now, We're right back there, in that
very pub, taunting the monotony of a sober existence. It was possibly oUr first experience of a sing-along outside a church choir,
and the passion and commitment with which this congregation
sang was quite telling by comparison. This was pure gospel but
with the accent on harmony.

That is one Christmas which is for ever branded on the bit of
my brain that stores happiness, despite the awkwardness of
waking up on Danny's couch and hearing his dad ask up the
stairs, 'Daniel, did you pee on the television again?' as his mum
gathered up empty bottles that had, the night before, held exotic
spirits gathered from their worldly travels that they had been
saving for a special occasion (my guess is that the arrival of an
unexpected teenage house guest wasn't exactly the kind of event
they'd had in mind).

Of course, there had to be a comedown, a morning after the
night before: a string of phlegm that couldn't merely be coughed

up after 8 or 9 pints and 30-odd Benson & Hedges. It had to be dragged out, like some gross 'flags of the world' magic trick, but utilising the oesophagus instead of the inner lining of a jacket sleeve.

'You're dying you're dying you're dying you're dying you're dying.'

'I think you might be right. Come on, or we'll miss the bus.'

'Tuberculosis is making a comeback! Didn't you see *Honkytonk Man*?'

'I ran out of the room, remember?'

'But you heard the cough. Check your phlegm for blood.'

'We'll have to do it on the way and I'll be late for work.'

And I'd climb on the bus with my fare in one hand and a sample of mucus in the other, which I'd keep tucked firmly inside my pocket until an empty double seat would allow a closer inspection, before arriving for work looking rough as arseholes. Then I'd work through the beer-sweats, before sitting idly through my dismal staff appraisal with the store manager, Clayton.

'And should you wish to peruse your chart here, then you'll see further confirmation that, given your ongoing stats, you are unlikely to progress beyond your current position within the company. 'What's that on your top?'

'Sayer's pastie. Cheese and onion, I think.'

'Can you cover this Friday?'

'Yes.'

What can I say? Bukowski had his post office, I had Argos.

I'd often have nosebleeds on the stock I sent downstairs, which didn't help. It might've been something to do with the dust in the room. Still I'd busy myself picking more stuff up before the bitching and moaning would drift upstairs:

'What the ruddy hell's that – blood? Here, I'm buying this as a gift!'

'A three-way mains adaptor you bought, did you, as a gift? Some lucky bastard you married!' And I'd shuffle off while wishing the strength-sapping fuzz that my head was emitting would finally cease, yet all the while dreaming of ironing my Burton's shirt later and hitting the town. It was not the career I wanted on my headstone, but it was a fun, 'I can't honestly be arsed' way of paying for my **mortality** ear plugs in the meantime.

21.

PROJECT GUTTENBERG

I had different drinking pals through different nights and different stages of Carmel College. Sadly, Ian and I never really saw anything of each other after West Park. I became a student, he went into work somewhere, and although there were no big bust-ups on Brighton Beach, it was a bit like Mods and Rockers in St Helens, as with a lot of places – especially big, polytechnic towns or university cities. The students drank in their little packs and associated safe pubs, and those with proper jobs likewise in theirs. There weren't any strict no-go areas – I drank everywhere and anywhere that would have me – but, in some pubs, trouble seemed to have no bother finding you.

I should know, as I had my head kicked in by two lads outside Jesters 'fun' pub and spent three long painful days in Whiston Hospital with a face like a trampled Happy Meal and a suspected hairline fracture to the front of my skull. Unprovoked, brutal, and only stopped from being beaten unconscious by a passing Samaritan, the attack left me fearful of town-centre pubs and unfamiliar faces for a long while afterwards.

66535

ST. HELENS AND KNOWSLEY HEALTH AUTHORITY

Patient's Copy

ST HELENS. HOSPITAL

CLOTHING AND OTHER PROPERTY

NAME OF PATIENT _MICHAEL PENNINGTON_ CASE SHEET NO.
(Surname first in block capitals)

ADDRESS

DATE OF ADMISSION/DEATH _12·11·88·_ WARD _A1E·_

1 PR SHOES.
1 PR SOCKS.
1" TROUSERS.   £1·13P·
1 TIE   1 KEY.
1 SHIRT
1 COAT.

J. Rickerby   S.E.N.   12·11·88
Signature of Staff member receiving above   Rank   Date

_____   ← PATIENT.
Signature of Witness   Rank

I verify that the above list is correct and I understand that any articles retained in my possession are held on my own responsibility.

JW / SN

Signature of Patient

Received in General Office by

on behalf of Sector Administrator   Date

ntative   Date
entative's name in BLOCK CAPITALS and relationship.

Hospitalised over £1.13 and a key! Had my mystery saviour not dragged them off there may well have been a need to tick date of **DEATH** _instead of admission._

One of many illustrations sketched from my hospital bed at Whiston Hospital. Who needs a police sketch artist with detailed pictures like that to work from?

The fact of the matter was, students seemed more intent on pure partying, without the added agenda of a brawl to make their night complete. So I sought security amongst them, and my friendship with Ian, who'd been such a necessary part of my surviving West Park, inevitably waned.

Everyone got on really well in the art class; it was like our own little youth club back there in the studio. But there was a gang of six of us who worked and played together: Ursula and Martin, the inseparable Posh and Becks of the gang; Malory, Mike, Jane and myself.

Every lunchtime, we'd pile down to Jane's house and ransack her poor dad's fridge and freezer for food (mainly pies – he kept bags and bags of Holland's frozen pies on tap). The place was a free-for-all and short of having a front door key of my own, I virtually took up residence there for a while.

She was an incredibly kind and extremely funny girl, was Jane, with a really laddish sense of humour. I never had to worry over how to act or what to say around her, and I loved the fact that I didn't need to be hammered to relax and enjoy her company.

I agonised over proposing the crazy notion of taking our friendship further, but when the Dutch courage was upon me we were always out in company while, sitting soberly in her house, the familiar fantasy of brushing the hair out of her eyes and holding her face for the inevitable kiss that followed on from, 'I guess you know how I feel about you, and how you feel about me? Let's stop kidding each other and just give in to it' was never realised.

'I know how you feel.'

'Do you?'

'Yeah. I'm still hungry myself, greedy mare! Another pie?'

'Yeah, go on, ta. Cheese and onion.'

I was teased mercilessly over my blatant, massive crush on her, which didn't help matters. And so, saving us both, no doubt, from a painfully awkward exchange, followed most likely by a swift and irreversible end to our friendship, once again I walked away with nothing but a slightly expanded waistline.

No, tell a lie, I also relieved Jane's dad of a 12-spool box of 18lb fishing line and a couple of Lee Trevino golf clubs that had been gathering dust in his garage, but ultimately found their way into the Magpie's Nest front window; albeit with Jane's full and generous permission, by the way.

But that was my love life for you: one long, disappointing line of consolation prize after consolation prize. Yes, I had confidence issues with the way I looked, and no, I didn't do myself any favours in the fashion department, but nobody deserved the catalogue of unmitigated disasters that was my sex life up until that point.

Relatives, friends, my wife! This isn't going to be pretty. And those of a sensitive disposition should really skip straight on now to the next chapter. Contained within the following pages are the truth, the whole truth, and nothing but the sorry truth. You know, the kind of stories you might tell down the pub when you've had a few too many and are opening up far too much. It's not easy committing them to the page like this, but I think it's important to understand how women and I became such mysteries to each other.

Where do I begin? With the girl in my street who shall remain nameless? I was 15 or thereabouts, and we'd both been at the sherry when I had my very first encounter with breasts, up against our back garden fence in the entry that ran behind the house. We were drunk, loud, and I was as clumsy and unsexy as you'd expect.

Unfortunately for me, my brother Mark was in the back garden at the time having a cigarette. He heard every bit of our conversation, and took great delight in mortifying me by repeating it back for weeks on end:

'Ooh, you've got beautiful tits, dead kissable.'

'Not so hard, you, you'll bruise 'em! Ha ha ha!'

He also told the girl's older brother, who was so furious he dragged my hand 10 yards or so along a wall, taking all the skin off the knuckles in the process, which ruined my plans for a week of celebratory tugs in honour of this milestone. My rhythmically challenged left hand – the understudy – put on a brave performance, but we were all quietly desperate for the star of the show to scab over and return to centre stage.

We never spoke about it afterwards and she never expressed any interest in us going out, or making our 'relationship' exclusive; she would just get drunk and initiate messy forays into uncharted physical territory. We were both massively inexperienced and I reckon I was her practice run, the next step up from necking with your hand – not that I was complaining about our non-negotiable arrangement.

Well, not until the night she, a friend and I did a litre of Strongbow each and went to see *Police Academy 2*. We sat near the back and, after she had launched on me with some heavy petting, she threw her coat over my lap, unzipped my fly and wrenched out my manhood like she was pulling up a carrot (which made me feel better about my own ineptitude in the tenderness department). She proceeded, for want of a better phrase, to 'wank me off'.

It was during the shampoo switch scene – I remember because I sat staring straight ahead filled with an overwhelming combination of elation and terror – that first incredible moment all teenage boys dream of: a hand on your cock that's not your own. A welcomed hand, a special moment, a rush of inexplicable pleasure to savour, a time to give in to desire and allow sweet nature to take its course (although what was going on under that coat bore more resemblance to Sylvester Stallone's arm wrestle epic *Over The Top* than *The Lovers' Guide*). Or, if you happen to be sitting in the Cannon Cinema in Bridge Street, St Helens, a time to try to calm the suspicions of the man seated two seats away from me via a sudden and disturbingly exaggerated appreciation for the comic timing of Steve Guttenberg and Lieutenant Mauser.

'Ha ha, glue, ha ha, not shampoo! Ha ha ha ha ha ha ha ha!'

If my covert attempt at coming of age hadn't attracted the unwanted attention of my fellow cinema-goers, then that little outburst sure as shit might have (to be fair, even Barry Norman would have struggled with his critique under similar circumstances). She, meanwhile, was doing a far better job of projecting an air of casual indifference as she never stopped bloody chatting to her mate throughout:

'It's not as good as the first one.'

'That gang leader's funny.'

'Ooh, his voice, though, it does my head in.'

'I wonder if he talks like that in real life?'

And, just as I approached the point of no return and all my worries dissolved into a rush of sweet surrender – 'I'm going, I'm bored.'

And she released her grip of iron, whipped off her coat and stumbled out.

I froze in a state of shock just long enough for the bloke nearby to spot my predicament and burst out laughing. Slipping off my chair and onto my knees, I crouched over, trying to right myself. But, just like a pop-up tent, erecting it's the easy bit, folding the bugger back down is a nightmare …

After much cursing and a damned good impression of an escape artist who'd hidden the key in his Y-fronts, I stood up, took a deep breath and attempted to edge past the highly amused bloke and his disgusted-looking partner with the last shred of dignity I could muster.

'Ha ha ha, thanks for that, pal!'

'Sorry?'

'Don't be. That were fucking funnier than this piece of shit.'

It took a while to come back from a confidence killer like that, and the girl obviously thought she'd learnt enough to go out and find herself a real man, because never again would I feel her vice-like grip through my imitation Levi's.

Still, I got back on that horse after getting chatting to two girls in Thatto Heath Park with my cousin, Simon. He was cocky, and something about his self-assured swagger told me he'd already pulled when they agreed to get some booze and meet us back there later by the swings.

Her mate was nice enough, but you could tell she was being dragged along to keep me occupied. The phrase, 'Don't fancy yours much' must've been on my birth certificate somewhere. But that is the beautiful thing about booze – the beer goggles, the ill-conceived lowering of standards that unfortunate-looking youths like myself depended on. And so it was that, hours later, we were round the back of Sutton Heath's small, wooden Baptist church after trying to get served with more cans at Metcalf's on the lane.

Our Dimon had vanished a while back around the other side of the hut with her pal, whilst we stood there suffering the all-too-familiar awkward silence that hangs like humidity when in earshot of other people 'getting it on'.

I never made the first moves, I never dared presume, but it was a huge relief when booze and boredom prompted her to take the initiative.

'You're proper shy, you, aren't you?'

'What do you mean?'

'Ow't left in that can?'

'Only dregs.'

'Pffffft. Oh, well, come here then.'

'What?'

'But, hey, it dun't mean I'm a slapper or anything like that.'

'Nah, course not.'

And with that she pulled me towards her, but in a really sweet gesture she hugged me first and kissed my neck before letting out a little beer burp, which just added to her cuteness. Here was the tenderness that I'd been searching for; here was the stuff of romantic movies.

She kissed me, open-mouthed, full tongue! I reciprocated, but as we chewed the face off each other I suddenly felt a third party in the equation. At first I thought, 'Shit, I've lost a tooth,' but when we eventually came up for air, I spat into my hand what turned out be a partially digested chip. It was only then that the stench of vomit hit me.

The only problem was there was no evidence of it on her, or the ground. By now, though, the wetness had worked its way through my shirt and I could feel it clinging to my back.

That's the downside of booze. It tends to have as much of an adverse effect on people's digestion as it does their judgment. As pretty as she was, and as lucky had I'd got, I couldn't bring myself to kiss her again, which was fortunate, as she'd started to gently slide into a slump on the ground.

'I'm just gonna sit down for a bit.'

'You do that.'

Then our Simon piped up from around the corner:

'How you getting on, kiddo?'

'I'm nipping home to change my top.'

'Yer what?'

'You'd best tell thingy to keep an eye on her mate, she isn't feeling too good.'

At this point, his friend chipped in with an inadvertently loud whisper: 'He's proper shy, isn't he?'

And with that I walked home and did my best to come up with a way of explaining to my mum how I'd managed to be sick down my own back.

I needed an older woman. Someone wise in the ways of love, with a strong constitution when it came to keeping her ale down.

First, though, a wee digression from the disaster theme, to properly allow me to set the scene. At sixth-form college, I belonged to another drinking gang, many of us who'd known each other since St Austin's and had begun to head out for some memorable, big, mid-week nights. Our ringleader was a guy called Kav who'd moved over from Zimbabwe in the last year of primary school, but it was only at Carmel that we started palling round together.

There was an emotional maturity to Kav – a thousand-yard stare from a life already well-lived with respect to women and wine; a knowledge he was more than willing to share without ever feeling the need to show off, and a coolness that I desperately wished would rub off on me. He was a big-built lad – not fat, but by no means Littlewoods catalogue material – but the difference was he carried it well. He had it all going on with his attitude, and never projected that apologetic aura that I had so pitifully perfected.

Even **He** sat up and took notice of Kav, although **He** never liked to admit it. I always seemed to be looking for role models outside my own head – people like Ian and Kav, folk who could teach me practical social survival skills out there in the real world. It was like an ongoing hangover of naïvety where I ticked all the boxes for some kind of care-in-the-community scheme, and I was constantly searching for a new social worker to take me shopping for life's basic necessities: booze and women.

There was certainly no finer hunter-gatherer than Kav: he was the Ray Mears of our wanton walkabouts. He had a car for starters – a Mini – and that set us free to travel to drinking holes even an all-zone travel card couldn't get you to – exotic, far-flung climes with nightclubs that helped rehabilitate my confidence and get over the fear of drinking in pubs outside my local Thatto Heath boundaries.

Kav, Danny, Tunny, Kep and I would take off to the Palace, Blackpool, on a college night and sleep in the car afterwards – four or five of us – then feast on cold kebab for breakfast before driving straight back to Carmel. The place had three, count 'em, *three* dance floors: one huge space downstairs for the really polished shakers and movers, and two more upstairs for those who couldn't dance, or were new to this mega meat factory and wanted easier prey to stalk – ideally, drunken hen-parties too plastered or too numerous to boogie with the downstairs Ace Faces; or those of a slightly more mature vintage who merely wanted to slouch in a corner and laugh at the young-uns' antics.

It was perfect for a young cub like myself kept too long in captivity. Those two upstairs squares of light, music and leg-lessness were shallow ends for the likes of me, who needed to learn how to tread water whilst hoping one day to take the plunge into the downstairs Olympic-sized pool.

After a lot of flailing, my perseverance finally paid off, and in a dark corner amongst a feisty bunch of hammered hens I pulled. No puking, no rough stuff, just civilized, tipsy kissing. Coming up for air, we headed towards the bar. On the way, she laughed and said, 'Ooh, hey, you'd think I'd know better at my age.'

'You know all I need to know' I thought, but, as I turned to respond, the brightness of the bar revealed a woman who I'd have felt safe guessing had already got a fair bit of mileage from her free state bus pass: there was no way she was under 60! (And I'm not exaggerating for the sake of a better story.)

'Still, you know what they say?'

I didn't, because my mind had blanked out all other things other than to double-check her voice matched the one of the mere cougar I thought I'd been kissing moments earlier.

'You're only as old as the fella yer holding!'

And she grabbed me and attempted to wiggle herself playfully.

Forget cougars, she was Bagpuss with suspected false hips if her wiggle was anything to go by. It had been dark over by the booth, but bloody hell! I'd wanted a woman with experience, someone who'd been around the block a little, so to speak, but her block was probably 'all just fields as far as the eye could see' when she were a lass.

If I was in any doubt about the dubiousness of my recent club conquest, it was quickly confirmed as she yanked me in for another smooch and I caught the four slack jaws of my mates looking on in abject horror. Despite the music volume and their distance from us, the 'Fuck me, look who Mike's got into!' was deafening.

Drink in hand, she led me back to her dark lair and proudly told me all about her darling grandkids before once again pulling my head towards hers and sucking my tongue into her mouth.

Despite her drunken keenness, this smooching lark had become a far more delicate operation for me now that I had to take her age into consideration. It felt like I was kissing crêpe paper due to the frailty of her skin, as if she might somehow tear at any moment. And the very real prospect of dislodging false teeth from their Dentugrip setting meant I engaged minimum tongue and maximum chat as I attempted to engage her on some favourite subjects. *Murder, She Wrote*? Bingo? Meals on wheels? Stannah bloody stairlifts? Anything to prolong the pauses between smooches!

We must have presented a sad state of affairs to onlookers – at least the ones who weren't my mates and doubled over, laughing. And it made sense now why all her mates had been so vigorous in their encouragement of us kissing earlier. I had briefly wondered why they were so keen to see their mate passed off on such a poor male specimen as myself, but had put it down to drunken hen high spirits. The fact of the matter was they were chuffed to see Nanna getting her teeth out for the boys.

In a sad kind of way, despite all the grief I'd get off the lads afterwards, a kiss was a kiss was a kiss as far as I was concerned, even when leading to such a warped form of notoriety. The continuation of my dreadful track record with women, the lack of stories I had to share with the group when young male bravado prompted such insensitive discussions; all this meant I was still quietly chuffed at having 'pulled' in front of them all in a nightclub.

I had become quietly suspicious that the jokes and jibes Mark had begun to make about my being gay had developed into genuine suspicion amongst the rest of my immediate family. They couldn't figure out why I'd never brought a girl home up to this point, and although the reason was never openly speculated upon, I feared they were misreading all the signs. And I dreaded those sorts of rumours taking root amongst my friends. Not because I was homophobic, just simply because it wasn't true, and the painful fact was that there seemed to be someone for everyone out there, except me. Girls didn't want to know me unless they were pissed, practising or past it. But, as far as my sexuality was concerned, I'd proven to my mates that I would readily grab a granny if that was the only opportunity presenting itself.

But it was just a Band Aid on a quietly festering wound of female indifference. He knew how much the endless rounds of rejection took its toll on my self-esteem, and if I didn't act soon then I genuinely believed I'd get left behind altogether. The carnal-knowledge gap between myself and the rest of my generation was widening to chasm-like proportions, and I didn't want to be left standing on the far side with the priests, trainspotters and *Star Trek* fans.

Around this time, my brother Rob made the noble decision to undertake a VSO (Voluntary Service Overseas) position over in Africa. That virtually made him a missionary in my folks' eyes and so they threw a wee going-away party for him at the house.

He'd recently met a girl and she duly attended, along with her best friend who, for her reputation's sake, we'll call Nell. Much like Jodie Foster's character in the film of the same name, she was a woman of few words. Almost out of nowhere, she and I somehow ended up in a drunken but extremely passionate embrace on an old deckchair outside in the back garden.

The romantic mood wasn't helped by revellers from the party popping out for cigarettes and laughing at our indiscreet attempts at joining the '6-inch-high club' (or possibly 2-inch, given the extra weight of us two star-crossed, Stella-sloshed lovers). Either way, it duly collapsed under the strain, with my right hand inside her bra and the less fortunate left crushed, as it remained clamped to her arse.

Plus we could hear my mum actually shouting from the kitchen: 'Will somebody get him away from that girl. She's a wrong 'un!' which seemed odd, considering the concerns surrounding my sexuality. Sure, it was hardly a scene straight from *South Pacific*, despite the now-destroyed seating arrangement, but surely our indiscretion was worth overlooking when you considered the fact that the way things were going with this girl, there seemed a real chance I might give Mum her first grandchild – the Holy Grail for all parents, and the surest way for me to step out of the rumour closet in true un-contraceptioned style, with everyone a winner.

Not that I was in any immediate rush to start a family; I was just desperate to shed the ongoing stigma of my virginity. Like a cherry tomato, it had remained preserved way beyond its natural 'best before' expiry date. It had outstayed its welcome on the chilly shelf of sensual yearning.

Although few words were spoken, something about Nell's hand down my pants told me she had the sexual appetite to devour it whole. Even we weren't drunk enough to continue with the backyard side show, though, and when Nell suggested we find, ' ... somewhere more private, where we won't be disturbed?' I suggested we go for a walk out in the woods.

We called it 'the woods', but there were probably no more than ten trees in total, and they were too widely spread out to provide any real privacy, but it sounded romantic enough to keep the amorous momentum going. Nell may just have planned on us heading upstairs, but that was never going to happen. Not on Dad's watch, not ever, and certainly not the way my mum was carrying on. Besides, the bedroom shared by my two brothers and I came with its own built-in consignment of passion-killing memories for me.

Lying there late one night, unable to sleep and suddenly aroused by an erotic event in my day (could've been anything really – it never took much to set me off, and it was always a welcomed, brief distraction from **him**), I decided to quietly bring myself relief whilst I had a rare bit of time on my own.

Being the quiet, considerate lover I was with myself, I used my free hand to raise the duvet to eliminate tug swoosh and kept my breathing slow and steady. (When you share a bedroom, and can't excuse the slow running of a bath at 2 a.m., you learn these tricks. I'm telling you, there'd be butterflies who'd wish they could masturbate as quietly as me.) I was just hitting my stride and about to climax when the magic moment was broken by an abrupt bit of advice from my brother, Mark.

'Oh, for fuck's sake, if you're gonna have a wank, then hurry up so's the rest of us can get some sleep. I've work in morning!'

Mortified just doesn't really do justice to my sudden state of awkwardness. I didn't respond, obviously, but chose to lie there holding my impatient member whilst pretending to be asleep and therefore oblivious to the false accusation. I even threw in a subtle bit of nasal strain for good measure.

'And fake snoring won't bloody help. Just hurry up and get it over with.' But there was no way I could 'get it over with' in those circumstances so, purely for my brother's benefit, I faked an orgasm with an extremely quick bit of heavy breathing and a grunt.

A definite low point, despite my elevated position in the top bunk.

So it was that Nell and I walked through the woods and ended up getting passionate behind a low wall in the grounds of St Matthew's, the local C of E church. Despite the moral religious implications (I couldn't really justify this against the fact they'd kept their railings), I was just desperate to get this over with, for real! Not even **Death** was gonna spoil this for us, even though **he** actually had a point this time:

'You've no protection. What about AIDS, or syphilis? That one'll drive you mad first, remember your history – King George? Then it'll kill you!'

'SHut UP!'

Luckily, I didn't have to worry about how to go about initiating anything, or saying the wrong thing, as Nell took the lead and hurriedly undressed both of us.

This was fortunate as, up to now, the majority of my information about how you did it was based on porn, rumour and that cousin who'd once got intimate with a girl and then had a gang of us sniff his finger.

Still, rolling around on the cold stone ground half-naked, I was desperately trying to think of what I might do to not come across as the complete novice that I was.

I put my hand down to her crotch and could feel a warm, wet sensation. 'This is good!' I remember thinking. 'This is a good sign that's she's enjoying herself. They always talk about getting "damp" in the dirty stories section.' Like a real Lothario, amidst the quiet grunts and groping, I made a sudden emboldened decision to kiss my way down towards the source of her obvious pleasure.

I did my best to leave no sensual stone unturned, but with the combined lack of light and knowledge, I doubt I did much to enhance her love-making pleasure. I knew nothing of the position of the clitoris, and while I don't want to turn stomachs with details, I imagine my approach had all the sensual aplomb of blanket bombing: the occasional tactical hit, but overall more of a widespread oral massacre.

'Come here, come on, do me, do it.' And with that, she pulled me up to a position that suggested she wanted me inside her.

'Fuck me, this is it, this is it!'

I couldn't believe I was finally about to cross that threshold into true manhood. It was all I'd ever wanted for as long as I could remember, so why then was my dick doing such a great impression of a cat being forced into a washing machine: resisting every attempt to achieve penetration?

The amount I'd drunk didn't help, but it felt like I was charging at a castle gate with an inflatable battering ram that just bent or gave way on impact. Eventually we got there, after some embarrassing assistance from Nell, and what followed was what I understand to be a pretty universal first time desperate rush to the finishing line.

There were no great stud-like thrusts or grinds as Nell was getting quite impatient with my falling out of her whenever things got too athletic. Like an *It's A Knockout* contestant trying to cross a greased pole, I clung on for dear life doing just enough to ensure the task reached a satisfactory conclusion. I say satisfactory, her reaction was less so: 'We should go somewhere with more light, so maybe then you can see what you're doing wrong.'

This was hardly the great romantic climax of our age. True, our interaction wasn't quite as much a chore from my perspective, but it was hardly the heavens parting and some fantastic new carnal insight imparted to me, either. Just a rush of lust, a sudden loss of urgency, a brief sense of relief that the shame of my enduring virginity had lifted, followed by the awkward realisation that I was certainly not a natural trailblazer when it came to the making of the beast with two backs.

Still, reading between the lines, I took that as an invitation to a second chance at not making this night memorable for all the wrong reasons.

'Well, then, can I walk you home?'

'No, but I've keys to my mate's place.'

With that we dressed, and I rushed home to pick up a coat, leaving her outside so as not to wind my mum up any further than necessary. Still, it was hard hiding the smug, contented grin of a man who'd left by the back as a boy and was now striding in through the front door a man: 'Just play it cool, nobody knows a thing—'

'Oh my God, what's happened to you?'

My mum was on me like a shot the second I walked into the hallway, and half scared the life out of me.

'What do you mean?'

'Don't you come that with me! You know what I mean, what's gone on?'

'Nothing's gone on!'

I kept on the move and made for the little cloak cupboard in the living room. Luckily everyone was too engrossed in party talk in the kitchen and out the back to notice the inquisition that was hot on my heels. How the fuck could she tell straight off like that – oh, please God, don't say she followed us up to the church?

I just needed to grab my jacket and get out.

'Where've you been?'

She hadn't followed us then, thank fuck!

'Nowhere! Just out walking.'

'You don't come back like that just from walking!'

Seriously, I mean, Mum and I were close, but this was scary. What the hell had I done to give myself away so easily? *She's bloody telepathic, she is! Wipe your mind, don't think about ...*

'Well, who's done that to you?'

Shit!

'Done what? I'm going back out, you're mental!'

I didn't know how but she knew, and I wasn't hanging around for her to come straight out and say it. I headed for the front door but risked a chance to check myself quickly in the hallway mirror.

And then I saw it, the source of Mum's sudden mystic powers of deduction. There was blood all around my mouth, chin, cheeks, nose and even smeared across my forehead. Fuck me, I was a mess. I looked like I'd just gone one round with Mike Tyson, like a vampire fresh from feasting, like a red dye-pack on money from a bank job had just gone off in my face. Nell hadn't been aroused, she wasn't taken with my foreplay 'technique'; there were no 50 shades of grey, just one big smear of crimson on my face and all over my hands.

'Oh my God,' I thought, 'I know I'm clumsy, but what the hell did I do to that poor girl?'

I ran out to the shrill yells of Mum, who obviously thought I'd been in a fight and was heading back out into the night to look for a re-match. Which of course I was in a way, with Nell waiting out there for me.

It was not the easiest of subjects to broach, the fact that I might have ruined her for all other future lovers – and certainly not in a good way.

'I, erm, I think I made a bit of a mess,' I said as I held my hands and face up towards a streetlight. I was waiting for a scream and trying desperately to think of a decent apology.

Now, I don't know if it was the drink that made her so indifferent, but while her response – 'Oh, right, I must've got it early. You can have a shower when we get there' – was a huge relief, it was also pretty puzzling.

'It ...?' What the hell was 'it'? And then the penny dropped. Although I was standing there looking like Hannibal Lecter, the fact that I wasn't going to be called up on an assault charge anytime soon was good enough for me and off we went. After all, it's not as if my self-esteem was in any real, strong position to object; in fact, if my track record building up to that ultimately un-monumental event was anything to go by, the evening had been a success of sorts. I just wish I'd quit whilst I was marginally ahead.

What followed was disastrous for very, even more, awkward, but perfectly lit reasons. We didn't really connect, physically, verbally or emotionally. Nell's attitude in bed left me thinking that perhaps during sex women were like cats and adverse to eye contact.

There was zero guidance or encouragement, and I reverted to putting on a sad kind of tribute to the sex montage scenes from the infamous *Confessions Of* ... movies. All we lacked was the sped-up plinky-plunk accompanying music as, desperate to impress, I abandoned the simple missionary position and attempted to contort myself into acrobatic shapes that did as much to enhance the evening's fornication as her pausing for crisps (which, if I'm honest, did me a favour as I, too, was peckish, plus I hadn't the athleticism to hold those poses for long without a bit more co-operation). To quote a famous line from *Top Gun*, my ego was writing cheques my body couldn't cash. And it, along with all my sexual aspirations for a good long while, simply crashed and burned.

He had nothing to say on the subject during the long walk of shame home, but I could sense **H**i**S** disappointment with both me and the lady who'd popped my cherry tomato. I was crushed, but I sensed **H**e was almost embittered. I wanted to put the whole sorry mess behind me and forget about settling down one day with that special someone. In fact, forget about a sex life, full stop.

But **H**e would hold on to these feelings until somehow, someday, **H**e could make this disaster work in o**U**r favour.

PART IV
JOHNNY TAKES ROOT

22.

LET'S GET A PERM

HE'S IN!

celebrates
the head of the
foundation course
in st.Helens this
week

Starting at the Gamble Institute for Art and Design in St Helens on a one-year foundation course was a huge social and psychological shift for me. Apart from my family, my best friend, Bryan, and those I'd always drunk with locally, it was a symbolic severing of links with a huge chunk of my past. Only two of my friends from Carmel had signed up for the same course and, deciding it wasn't for them, they both left in just over a week.

I was no longer just a student; I was an *art* student. I had become the lowest of the low, the single greatest drain on further educational resources and an unashamed walking waste of the hard-working tax-payer's money. I was a pariah, a joke openly shared by my brother and co down at the Springfield: 'Pottery? Well, go on then ... mek us an ashtray, ya dozy twat!'

My choice, of course, also posed a quandary to the older ladies and gents who drank at the St Austin's Catholic Men's Society club, where I'd got myself a bar job a few evenings a week.

'A good waste of a brain' was how one punter put it.

I'll always be grateful to my parents for the stick they must've taken for allowing me to pursue an ambition so openly misunderstood by folk around them.

Laura, who trained me as barman, though, was more understanding. She was well used to the uninformed conclusions of the locals, as she had a son, Tez, who was in a band that practised down at the Dead Fly recording studios by the old road into town.

Now, that was a no-go area as far as most parents around us were concerned: the 'types' that gathered there made us art students look like missionaries by comparison. You might as well come home with a purple robe, pentagram flag and a goat to offer up to Satan than be caught hanging around with God's rejects in that place.

They claimed to make music there, but it wasn't nice music with a proper chorus and melody you could sing along to. Oh no, they made rock music – loud 'DUM DUM DUM!' ear–bleeder music in there – that is, when they weren't summoning up Lucifer, or taking drugs, or most likely doing both at the same time.

There was a prevailing fear of the unknown, the untraditional, those who dared to tread the path less followed, that both amused and saddened me at times. I'm not mocking my beloved home town of St Helens, but there were times when I shared the character Frank Owen's frustrations in *The Ragged-Trousered Philanthropists* regarding people's fear of change, and their eagerness to belittle those who dared to dream of something different to that which the majority had convinced themselves was all there was to this life. As if ambition might prove infectious, shedding light on forgotten dreams and potential crushed by all those years of Tory tyranny.

I can't say for sure, but I reckon that's why our ex-mayor, Teddy, proved such an ally. He'd talk with gusto on the notion of broadening one's horizons and paid no mind to the danger of embarrassing yourself by trying. I wonder if he'd seen enough of 'what might have been' fall by the wayside through policy and failing belief in renewal. I guess he believed in people, but knew all too well the damage that had already been done to the majority of them.

I'm not trying to paint myself as some kind of *Ryan's Daughter* – no great mob hunted me through the streets before lopping off my hair and debagging me. But I sensed I'd become a bit of a cautionary tale, a daft lad who'd signed a death sentence as far as my future prospects were concerned by turning my back on any number of promising, proper, decent careers and enrolling in that Goth-riddled hideout for lazy, workshy, good-for-nothings.

I relished the notoriety that came with that myth. And do you know why? Because it signalled an end to the disappointment I'd felt with myself for feeling – and being – different, and the start of a slow drip-feed of pride in that very same reality.

I felt like I belonged in art school. I didn't feel a prick for not fitting in elsewhere, because now I was part of this gang of social misfits, amongst whom I had nothing to prove to anyone but myself. The secret to making the most of your time there was to stand out, be as individual as possible, and make your mark however best you saw fit. I no longer aspired to be cool, just original and honest with myself about who I was and what I wanted.

There was no great shaft of light, no immediate epiphany. They didn't take me down to Taylor Park lake and baptise me in its waters so I might be born anew. They simply placed a value on the thoughts and idiosyncrasies – be they dark or light – that made me, me. All of a sudden, what went on in my head was a cause for creative celebration, not mourning, and I could explore my oddness in public rather than bury it along with everything else.

Of course, **he** wasn't at all happy with this: my illustrating the torment that was meant to remain strictly our secret was tantamount to mocking **death**. In the end, we came to a compromise. I could express the fact that I knew I was dying in whatever medium I liked, but I would not discuss it openly with the tutors. I'd like to say it appeased **him** to the point where **he**'d shut the hell up, but it didn't. He just became a fucking know-it-all art critic, as well as a qualified GP.

'That's not how you draw a tumour. It needs to be darker, like death, because you're dying.'

Visual proof of a fragmenting psyche and the alter ego hell-bent on us getting a perm.

'Bugger off!'

'It's nothing like the one growing in your head right now. That's why you see those little squiggles when you rub your eyes too hard.'

'Yes, but couldn't that just be something to do with a hang-over or something?'

'No, that's the tumour pressing against the back of your forehead. Definitely inoperable, too, that's why you're dying. You do know you're still dying, don't you?'

'I need a drink.'

My work wasn't anything to shout about, anyway. I was average at best, but I wasn't to know that. What I was doing was of the highest artistic merit to me, and that's all that mattered. It definitely made **HiM** happy to see me so content and, more importantly, taking such pride in myself. Plus my little stand against **you-know-who** made **HiM** feel less guilty about **HiS** inability to stand up to **him**.

And, of course, as with most students, we enjoyed a very active social life. We all had our own wee troops within the collective, but there was no disdain for belonging to one rather than another. Well, there'd be the odd, sneering, fine artist but nothing that could make me doubt my own integrity.

Nick, Gaz, Johnny, Kasche and I went to the pub every lunchtime via the pie shop for a few pints and a game of pool. At that time, the Alfred was one of those boozers in between heydays and populated mainly by a few old diehards and the odd punter grabbing a swift pint before catching their train from Shaw Street. It was pretty dead by day, which meant no queuing for the pool table, and was just beyond the boundary of the cool 'in' pubs, so dodged all the usual aggro of a weekend night around town. The dress code was shabby-shabby, and there were no bouncers policing the door because there was never any trouble.

They also had no problem with girls drinking from pints, or rustling up a Snakebite (which some pubs had outlawed), and we could get rowdy amongst ourselves without drawing unwanted attention from landlocked beach bullies desperate to kick sarcastic sand in our faces. In short, it was the perfect local for a bunch of art students.

Occasionally, we dared to stick our heads above the parapet and venture out into the town centre. Thursday nights were usually best as the dress code was more relaxed and most of the real head-cases were saving themselves for the Friday/ Saturday night onslaught. But, splattered in clay slops, I was still once refused access to a local nightclub, Appleby's, on the grounds that, 'You look like you've been picking fucking spuds, move on!'

Whereas I used to berate myself for not having the right clothes or the newest look, there was now a certain pride in being told I didn't belong in there alongside folk I'd beaten myself up over – and been beaten up by – for trying to fit in with. Exactly the point He'd been trying to hammer home to me for years. To paraphrase the genius, Groucho Marx, I didn't want to be a member of any club that would have me. The way He saw it, life itself was a member's club, and He'd rather we drank homebrew in a shed of self-respect than go cap in hand, humbly begging for acceptance. Not that I didn't argue my case with the bouncer. I was out on the lash and needed more intoxication to keep Doctor Death at bay.

But, looking back – and I mean over my entire life – my dress-sense has never been cause for celebration. Jeff Banks has done a good job of polishing this sartorial turd from time to time, but as far as an innate sense of style goes, I just don't have one. Art school's free-form dress code merely allowed me to push the boundaries of tastelessness even further.

I worked a shift at the Catholic Men's Society club on a 21st birthday party once. When asked if everything was to the parents' satisfaction, the only complaint that came back was roughly along the lines of: 'A cracking do, despite that scruffy beggar behind the bar. Where the ruddy hell did you drag him up from? He wants shooting, he does.'

What I wanted was neutral clothes that fit me, especially around the stomach, which was paying the price for my return to the Pimblett's diet plan. In the absence of a High and Mighty in our high street, and most other shops not carrying a 'Circus

Freak' range, I had to make do with whatever garish, out-sized garment came my way, and try to blend it in with the rest of my 'wardrobe'. Open shirts over free pub promotion T-shirts offered a billowing distraction from my expansive midriff so that no one noticed the buttons looking like a submarine boiler popping rivets under the pressure of me sitting down and forcing the full extent of my gut forward. In denial – as I was – about the fact that I'd literally outgrown high-street fashion, my scruffiness became a false badge of honour.

I'd think I was pulling it off, too, but then I'd spot some lass looking my way and the nature of the thoughts she'd be temporarily lost in would be all too obvious: 'How does someone get like that? I mean, look at him. Imagine that stripped off and bearing down on … uuuugh …'

She might have thought her true feelings were masked from my perceptions, but I could sense her inward shudder. And whenever my self-esteem sprang another leak, I'd simply go and top it back up with pint after pint of Whitney Houston, remembering her words that learning to love yourself is always the greatest love of all!

He bloody loved that song. **He**'d sulk as I'd never allow **HIM** spends for the jukebox, knowing it wouldn't be the done thing for a bloke to play that in any St Helens' pub, let alone the Alfred. Besides, it was o**U**r tune! But even way back then, **He** understood the ironic comic potential of a grown man belting those words out with unashamed emotional gusto.

Or perhaps **He** didn't. Maybe **He** was just wholly unabashed about wearing **HIS** emotions on my sleeve for all the world to see. Even I don't fully understand how **HIS** half of my head works sometimes but, either way, **He** stored that song away safely in **HIS** own future play list.

My commitment to winding up the fashion police by turning renegade PI even extended to my getting a perm.

It wasn't the 'done thing'; it was the absolute, 'Why do that to yourself?' thing. Perms hadn't been out of fashion long enough to be passed off as retro. In fact, at that stage, they stood as an unwelcome reminder of all the dreadful things that had been done in the name of trend-setting. But **We**'d decided **We** were bringing back the shame – in style, baby!

I went to the local tech college on training day and asked a young stylist to, 'Take your best shot!' She did her best to politely persuade me away from such a bold follicular statement, but standing out for all the wrong reasons was an envelope I was determined to push to its limits. And so she applied the tiny rollers, stinky formula and tin foil, stood well back, and didn't dare ask where I might be going for my holidays.

In truth, it was mostly **HiS** idea. **He** showed up early one day after I'd opted to stay out after lunch and batter the Boddington's. Some radio talk-show item had been playing in the background that morning down in the basement pottery studio, so now **he** was obsessing over diabetes, and I just wasn't in the mood.

'**Let'S get a perM!**'

'Why?'

'**BecaUSe, FuCK 'eM!**'

'Okay, it'll be a laugh, I suppose.'

He made it sound random, but I know now there was method in **HiS** madness. By making us look as unappealing as possible on our own terms, **He** was subliminally protecting me from the rejection of others. **He** was a sly old dog but, God love **HiM**, **HiS** heart was in the right place.

My peers found it hilarious and quietly naff in fairly equal measures, but it proved a worthy shield to match my badge. And as normal as Nick, Gaz, Johnny and Kasche might've appeared in comparison when suited and booted for the weekend, they still weren't completely immune to the odd social snub. One night we visited one of my locals, the Thatto Heath Labour club. It generally got rammed with very drunk women, while the ancient folk wisdom that you didn't shit on your own doorstep ensured that it rarely, if ever, kicked off in there. But the five of us were still ushered off the dance floor early on in the night by the concert secretary due to the fact that no ladies had so far opted to get up and join us.

'Best wait 'til there's some lasses up there too, eh, lads? You don't wanna be giving the wrong impression now, do you?'

We laughed about being 'outed' by a bloke in his sixties, despite the fact this would've provided our Mark with some invaluable ammo had he got wind of it. But as we laughed at the whole parochial small-mindedness of it, I felt a quiet twinge of regret that perhaps we'd begun outgrowing elements of the town that had been our world.

At around this time my sister, Catharine – who'd graduated from the Royal College of Art and taken a job in Hong Kong – announced she would be coming home, for good. Nobody had been able to afford to go and visit during her time out there but, none the less, she and I had bonded during her absence through late-night drunken phone calls about art and projects set by the Gamble.

I finally felt like I had a normal sibling relationship and despite my being an absolute prick to her when we were growing up – even after all my bleating over my brothers' treatment of me – she was there for me when I needed her. Catharine seemed to understand perfectly my nagging sense of displacement and growing need to broaden my horizons. I was so proud of what she'd achieved, and I quietly envied her for getting out in the world as spectacularly as she had done, but she was homesick and wanted to return to her roots.

I'd had first-hand knowledge of that awful feeling at Uphol-land but, caught up in fresh neuroses, and the new-found freedom that art school offered, I forgot myself and got cross with her for giving up on 'our' dream. She'd escaped, for God's sake! Her job was a passport to anywhere in the world her heart desired. So why the hell would she opt to come right back to where she'd started?

By then, I'd started applying to various colleges for a full degree course. Through no fault of St Helens, its people, my family or friends, I had a quiet determination to get out and stay out. Like a botched sculpture I daren't exhibit for public appraisal, I needed to throw a dustsheet over the life I'd mis-handled and start again elsewhere.

Having said that, though, I had a great time back on that foundation course. It remains one of those years in my life that when I think back on it, despite **his** constant torment, smiles win out and fondness reigns.

23.

LIVE BAIT

When our Cath came home, she and her pals soon became drinking buddies with me and my mates. There were seven or eight years between us, but it never seemed to matter once we were all out around town.

That year, our college took a trip to Amsterdam. We bought a bag of sage and smoked it, convincing ourselves we were stoned. By day, we visited museums and filled our sketchbooks, and at night we actually stayed away from the red light district.

I did get blind drunk and lost with a mature student called Mal and ended up calling the UK to get our budget hotel details from the emergency contact sheet my mum had. The line wasn't very clear and I don't remember much beyond leaving the Milky Way Club and waking up the next day with a roughly scribbled note:

'Hens Balnker
Hans a Bronker
Hoons Brackner
Heinz Blinker
H anSSs BRinKeRrrr'

There were drunken snogs and brief holiday romances within the group. Even for me! Although I managed to go from smooch to, 'You're a great guy but I think of you more as a friend' in record-shattering time. 'But we're not really pals,' I remember thinking. 'We're more creative colleagues! Jesus, aren't you supposed to sober up *before* the regret kicks in?'

On the coach home, one poor sod panicked and ate a huge lump of genuine draw just before customs and went on a whitey for the entire journey home. I'd hear later that in his first year of college, he threw a party in his digs that was so overcrowded the ceiling gave way and his room ended up one floor lower, fantastic crazy, dozy bastard that he was.

The beautiful thing about drink was that it turned all my usual observations, the stream of information that my brain couldn't switch off, into something I could use to my own advantage. The stuff we bury, or mistakenly disregard as inconsequential, was gold dust on booze. We were a funny bunch, and I won't deny I fancied myself as the funniest out of all of us, but only because I really worked at it. I'd accepted the fact that sober women, and the vast majority of drunken ones, just didn't think of me 'in that way', so making people laugh was all I really had to offer on the social circuit.

When we were out in a gang, the lads would actively send me over to an unknown gang of girls in Lowie's, the local nightclub to go to in those days, as a social ice-breaker. I'd become pretty good at the art of funny, unintimidating small talk, and although there was definitely no lack of confidence on the lads' part where ladies were concerned, they still shied away from the initial crash-and-burn of first introductions.

I, on the other hand, had nothing to lose, knowing that I definitely wasn't going to pull. So that, along with the Dutch courage of a poor man's hip flask (a litre bottle of tonic emptied just enough to accommodate a quarter bottle of gin) and several pints, lent me a bulletproof sense of inverted emotional bravado.

The secret was in letting the girls know that you knew you didn't stand a chance; disarm them with humour and send up the whole ridiculous notion that I'd be making a move on them. I mean me, seriously thinking I stood a chance with them? Look at me! That was enough of a joke in itself to get them giggling, but if you failed to make it clear from the outset that you were aware of the impossibility of mutual attraction, instant disdain was the only possible outcome.

Once I had made first contact, the lads would drift in, acting like they'd lost me somewhere in the crowd, and duly make their own introductions before pairing off with the girls and leaving me standing there on my own. Pint in hand, mission accomplished, ready to seek out misadventures of my own.

He hated my allowing them to use uS as live bait. It was one of the rare occasions where He proved HiMSeLF the naïve one when it came to women. He'd presume that after all their bleating about how their boyfriends were shit and incapable of emotional honesty they'd come running into the arms of someone who understood their needs, somebody who could talk to them on their level, a man who was just as interested in what they thought as what they looked like (even if such sensitivity could at least partly be ascribed to my huge fear of sexual inadequacy).

He always claimed to care so little for what society as a whole thought of Us, yet couldn't deny the frustration He felt at women's individual disdain for us on a physical level and the ease with which I accepted their indifference. He became increasingly bitter and resentful about this act of collective rejection.

He wanted to be more than just good friends, but I was the one who had to live with the awkwardness and fear of intimacy. It was me not HiM who suffered the indignity of public rejection, so I – because I still held majority shares in uS back then – took the executive decision to reject rejection by embracing it.

He sulked like mad and, I'm ashamed to say, I think He wanted revenge. Nothing callous – He just wanted the shoe to be on the other foot, so these girls could find out what automatic dismissal felt like. He wanted a way to draw them in for more than just laughter at our expense so that He could be the one to walk away.

For my part, I was just happy to feel included in the process of pulling, knowing it wouldn't lead to further embarrassment and soul-destroying self-awareness.

Don't get me wrong – as the night wore on and more booze drowned out the fear of what might follow if I did actually 'cop off', I still took on board the lessons learnt from the Palace, Blackpool, and tried to seek out women whom I thought might have lower expectations, based on awful assumptions about how they looked. But some handsome lad with beer goggles on would always step in at the last minute and deprive me of a last dance, snog and drunken grope. Suitable punishment, I suppose, for my double standards.

I was lonely, but alcohol and the acknowledgement that I was the funny one of the group was enough to plaster over the cracks for the time being. So you'd think I'd be resentful when a friend of my sister Catharine's turned up in our small circle and started kicking my comedy arse from here to kingdom come.

Mike Firclough was a few years older than me – around our Robert's age – and was one of the rare funny people that you laugh with down the pub, and who I still believe today would've made a brilliant stand-up comic. Rather than resent the guy, I quickly became mildly obsessed with him.

Mike had a knack for storytelling, and I mean really, really funny storytelling. From the moment I met him, I was aware that we had a similar sense of humour, but he used his far more effectively than I did. I remember thinking, 'Here's a lad who has a hell of a lot of confidence,' but he had the skill to stop that justified belief in his own abilities ever crossing over into arrogance.

He'd engage people in a way I'd never seen before. His stories, by the third or fourth telling, were polished, but never over-embellished. And with every telling he appeared, in the same way Billy Connolly did, to be genuinely thrilled by his own observations: as if the ridiculousness had only just struck home and he was laughing at it along with you for the very first time. He made a tale ten times told seem fresh, as if realising its comic value for the first time.

The joy he took in relating a story gained an automatic trust with folk that he was funny, but he retained the capacity to appear surprised by their reactions. People sat, people listened, people laughed, but Mike projected a pitch-perfect air of faux-surprise at their eagerness to hear him hold court.

I found the lad hilarious, and **H**e saw something definitely worth using to our advantage. Both of **U**s were drawn to his company, and neither of **U**s resented his comedic superiority for a second.

After a while, I began to notice the way small gaps began to appear in the narratives he seemed to spin out of thin air, because he knew, he fucking knew, where the big laughs would come. What I was inadvertently witnessing was Mike constructing a comedy set, a routine that was being honed each time he retold a story. Perhaps he didn't realise this, but I reckoned Mike far too bright not to know what he was doing.

W**e** just drank till a stream of consciousness came pouring out, but Mike was a craftsman who hid his light under a false bushel of casual banter, his 'Is it just me or ...?' approach making it seem like he was coming to terms with one of life's puzzles for the very first time.

Best of all, he appeared 100 per cent humble. A smart-arse might present you with an undeniably funny remark which gets a laugh, but it can often leave a sour after-taste of envy or victimised resentment. A funny person, and I mean a funny-to-the-bone person, gets the laugh *and* the love. It's the difference between being revered and being admired.

What fascinated me most was the question, 'How can someone so funny make it look so effortless?'

My obsession with humour as an art form had begun.

If I'd ever been funny before I met Mike Fairclough, it may have been intentional, but it lacked finesse. Watching him, I realised I didn't want to be one of the circle of people just listening any more. To be accepted simply wasn't enough.

Getting hospitalised when those lads jumped me outside that club had nudged me temporarily into the shadows; the search for love driven by lust had teased me back into the social periphery; but through my new mistress, Comedy, I found myself wanting to be the centre of attention again. I wanted every single thing I said – every single bit of banter – to count. I didn't want to contribute to a conversation; I wanted to own it.

I instinctively knew that Mike had a technique I could break down and mimic. It sounds lame, I know, but I became a kind of intellectual stalker.

He wasn't my only source of comedic inspiration. I knew nothing of live comedy beyond what I saw on TV: I'd grown up on the likes of Laurel and Hardy and Tommy Cooper; I'd laughed along with my dad at the likes of Tom O'Connor, Mick Miller and, yes, Bernard Manning on ITV's *The Comedians*. But my favourite of the bunch was always Les Dawson.

Only when we started playing clubs would I fully learn to appreciate not just the genius of his timing and delivery, but the bravery of making an audience sit and wait for punch-lines. His exquisite use of language might've been a trademark by the time he arrived on our TV screens, but it was an unbelievably bold move as an unknown playing the once huge network of working clubs up and down the country.

You had to commit to Les's longer gags. You had to trust him as he decorated a story with words lesser acts daren't dream of uttering in front of a boozed-up room full of rowdy working-class men and women baying for blood. You had to believe the pay-off would be worth those extra beats a lesser comic would rush to fill with false camaraderie and needy one-liners.

'A purple vault fretted with a million points of light twinkling in wondrous formation' – Les's playfulness with words was something **He** adored but would never quite fully match. And although neither of **U**s realised it at the time, Les's instincts would one day give **HiM** the determination to run a gig at **HiS** own pace, on **HiS** terms, taking as much time as **He** saw fit to find the funny side of our anguish.

Billy Connolly's *An Audience With* – another big inspiration – was possibly the funniest and contained the most audacious bits of mainstream stand-up anyone had seen in years, but it also showed the kudos that stand-ups could earn amongst the celebrity ranks. If schools had water coolers, Billy would've been the only topic of conversation around it the day after that stormer of a gig went out on TV. Not since Dave Allen had I seen my parents so shocked, yet equally unable to suppress their amusement.

Jasper Carrot was another master storyteller. His public dissection of the government pamphlet regarding what to do in the event of a nuclear war was not only hilarious, but also an invaluable piece of anti-nuclear demonstration polemic, smuggled into the public consciousness under the acceptable guise of 'light' entertainment.

The Young Ones had also been essential viewing in our house as far as me and my siblings had been concerned, even if that meant unplugging the Spectrum and crowding around my portable telly in the front room. Mum and Dad didn't get it, and it had all the anarchic trademarks of a comedy we felt had been made especially for us.

I could fill another book with comedians and shows that I loved at the time, or have since gone back to and rediscovered for fear that the brilliance of their technique was lost on me the first time round.

But as He was gathering momentum and we were revelling in our new obsession, there was still so little We knew about the workings of this comedy lark.

For years, We'd been sitting in the stands waving on the Formula One cars, but now we needed to look under the bonnet and see how it all worked. And without the common sense to look beyond St Helens and into the comedy gig listings for, say, Liverpool or Manchester, Mike was my best opportunity for observing live comedy from the comfort of my pub barstool.

My time at the Gamble institute was drawing to a close. After a disastrous flirtation with the notion of studying fashion design (I'd traced my sister's drawings and drawn my own dreadful clothes over the top of them), I had settled on pottery as my ticket out of town and been accepted on a four-year Jewellery/ Ceramics BA sandwich course.

I'd begun to give my life the major overhaul I knew it needed, and hoped college would be the cocoon within which I could fake my transformation from caterpillar to social butterfly but, once I emerged, I knew I would need anonymity to pass myself off as anything but the same old loser staggering round the nightspots of St Helens. I needed a new community to go with the new me, and Middlesex Polytechnic seemed to suit my needs perfectly.

I had no fears about leaving home. After all, I'd done it as an 11-year-old, and that had been without the help of a bedside lamp, sugar-free tea or (unfortunate golfing incident aside) booze. In fact, I was genuinely excited about making the transition from northern town to southern capital city: the more distance I could put between my past and whoever the new 'me' turned out to be, the better.

I had a week of leaving parties. One wound up with our Catharine, Tez of Dead Fly notoriety, and myself sitting in his house watching a Julian Cope video and drinking all of his mum's collector's editions of miniature spirits. I felt ill and threw up inside my hoody as surreptitiously as I could, before casually announcing I was going for a walk. I stepped out to scrape the vomit from the inside of my top, not realising that they'd both sat and watched the whole shambolic episode with a mixture of disbelief and drunken awe.

The best night, though, was a bad-taste-fashion piss-up around town. We all scoured the charity shops and found the most outlandish gear we could lay our hands on for a night on the razz. Everyone looked ridiculous but oddly retro chic except me: all I could find to fit was an awful, brown two-piece suit that looked slightly dated but not all that 'out there'. Catharine helped out with the addition of two garish gold triangles sewn into the sides of the trousers to make them look more flared and decidedly naff.

It was a bit disconcerting that I managed to walk straight into Lowie's without any of the usual disapproving once-overs

from the bouncers normally at odds with my art-student stretch-
ing of the dress-code rules. We had a great night and looked like
absolute pricks, yet for some inexplicable reason, I chose to
pack the trousers to take away with me to college.

On my last night, we went into town and ended up going for
an Indian meal at the end of the evening. I'd not set foot in one
since going to see *Grease* at the cinema with Martin Hurley and
his mum way back in '78 when I'd thrown up on his hand, and
he in turn had thrown up in their fish tank. In fact, it was only
the sixth restaurant I'd been to for an evening meal in my entire
life. I ordered a mince vindaloo – not out of bravado, simply
because it was the cheapest thing on the menu.

Eating out was still a needless expense in my mind, and I
would always calculate the bill against how much beer I could
have bought from the off-licence instead – that was my cur-
rency by which all other outgoings were means-tested. If it cost
more than six cans, what was the point? Just make butties at
home instead.

Mum, Dad and I set off for London next day, in a borrowed
car, for the start of my big, grown-up adventure in life. I made
them stop off at probably two-thirds of all the motorway service
stations en route to the Middlesex campus whilst I evacuated
assorted fragments of the previous evening's vindaloo from my
tortured bowels, possibly along with some unneeded bits and
pieces of internal organs along the way. I sat in one cubicle at
Watford Gap for so long, the toilet attendant was banging on
the door and shouting, 'I know you're doing drugs in there! Get
out before I call the police.' It's highly likely, had I kept a stash
of Diocalm about my person, that I could have OD'd on them in
a bid to end the pebble-dash misery, but having only loo roll to
hand and a grip on the door like a woman in labour, all I could
do was scream, 'Food poisoning! ... Definitely fucking food poisoning!' This was a complaint I'm sure they were well used to
back then, considering the state of the grub they served up. My
plea of digestive disorder was backed up by a sequence of anal
explosions sufficiently persuasive to send my accuser packing.

After losing so much time on the journey down, we only had a brief window in which to locate my room in the Gubbay halls of residence, get the car unpacked, say our goodbyes and me wave my parents off down the long path that led them back out of Trent Park. Compared to some of the emotional scenes unfolding around us, you could've mistaken our parting as an outtake from *The Remains of the Day*. There was no emotional awkwardness about our farewell, it was just that, well, like I said, I'd been away from home before, but this time it was on my terms, and I think my dear mum and dad could sense I was excited rather than afraid.

24.

EVERYTHING YOU ALWAYS WANTED TO KNOW ABOUT MIDDLESEX POLY (BUT WERE AFRAID TO ASK)

I walked back to my room remembering, funnily enough, the advice my brother, Rob, had given to me. He'd quit as a joiner and gone off to do teacher-training in Preston: all the carefree benefits of a student lifestyle, but close enough to home to bring his laundry back and raid the fridge of a weekend. At the time, I remember thinking of this as a bit of a cop-out, but as money got tight later down the line, I would envy his lazy stroke of genius.

Anyhow, he'd told me: 'Get out and make friends as quickly as you can. Always keep your door open but don't sit in your room waiting for the party to come to you, because before you

know it, everyone's in cliques and you're the odd one out.' This
turned out to be unusually sound and useful advice from my
brother. As was my dad's plea to, 'Please save some money while
you're working in the holidays. You're going to be mixing with
folk with plenty of money, whose parents have plenty of money,
and you know we don't.' This was an earnest request I would –
and indeed did – ignore at my peril.

On that first night, I left the door to my room wide open and
unpacked my stuff as Deacon Blue 'blasted' out of my mini
stereo.

After three hours, I was still sitting on my bed having
polished off another can, waiting for a friendly face to pop
their head around the door and invite me to a student orgy, but
still nothing.

It turned out that I'd been allocated a corridor all on my own
– just me, nobody else. And, to make matters worse, I'd already
packed my food away in the communal kitchen so I had no
excuse to go back there. But just when all seemed lost, a flicker-
ing in the distance caught my eye: I looked out of the window
and saw, no more than thirty feet away, the unmistakable light
show of a pub bandit machine.

'JeSuS, Mary aNd JoSepH, it'S a SigN, a SigN I teLL ya!'

'Well, what are we waiting for?'

'It's not an extra rib, it's stomach cancer!'

'Fine, you stay in then.'

'Loser!'

And we were straight out of the door.

What were the chances my room would be one of the closest
in the block to the student union bar? I marched over there with
a bundle of cash and a simple but very determined mantra:
'Nobody knows you, nobody. You are whoever and whatever
you want them to think you are the second you step through
those doors.'

I stuck to my guns as best I could for my entire time at
Middlesex Poly. I walked or staggered tall when not opting
to crawl. I felt intoxicatingly invincible, and my misplaced

sense of streetwise, working-class superiority meant I wasn't ever looking over my shoulder for fear of violent reprisal at my cockiness.

I made a point of approaching anyone I fancied talking to – male or female, meathead, academic, smart-arse or stunner, it didn't matter. I'd learnt from Mike's techniques how to spin a yarn and pull in a crowd. I wasn't interested in being funny enough just to fit in, merely to get by – I wanted every inch of sticky, beer-stained carpet to be my stage. In my head I'd arrived, and was determined to aim high and never again waste my time staring into the bottom of a glass and wallowing in the dregs of what might've been. 'Make it happen' was my motto. 'Not tomorrow, not next week, here, now, every single day of the year!'

It wasn't always easy, as my new persona of über-confident party animal needed cash to keep the woozy wheels of social relevance well oiled. The first year was easy as I had access to my grant and a sizeable overdraft. I drank like a trust-fund kid and threw my money around that bar like there was no tomorrow. I'd have sheets and sheets of bank statements comprising lists of no other figure than £10.50: the maximum amount you could cash at the union bar at any one time.

All the warning signs of a financial meltdown were there, and no-one could accuse me of spending my money wisely, especially when I took myself down to Camden Market and bought myself a poncho. There are fashion *faux pas* and there are legitimate reasons for a wardrobe/chequebook intervention.

Unbeknownst to me, I was still a deeply uncool, naïve, nobody-would-look-at-me-twice piss-artist, but I didn't care. I revelled in what I felt was my new-found true identity.

I had friends, lots and lots of friends across the college spectrum, and especially within the art and design campus, Cat Hill. Paul and Gary were my proper pals, though, and remain so to this day. There are others who may feel short-changed with the absence of a mention, but it was these lads with whom I connected best and shared most of my misadventures, Paul being the more sensitive of the two and a fellow art student, and Gary a no-nonsense Stockton lad studying politics.

Both had very different – but equally successful – techniques for getting intimate with their female cohabiters in halls but fundamentally they were always, always, always up for a drink.

I'd thought the new me might find a way to overcome my crippling shyness with women but, unfortunately, I never quite seemed to have what it took to get beyond drinking buddies. Even when **He** was in full flow, I'd always find a way to jeopardise a new rapport before it could get to the awkward point of physical vulnerability.

Improvised obstacles weren't always easy to find when the rare opportunity offered itself; after all, we all lived in the halls of residence, not thirty feet away, in single-occupancy rooms, with no parents to thwart our theoretically wanton ways.

It frustrated **HiM** no end as **He** was the perfect wingman. I might do my best to walk the walk, but it was **He** who definitely talked the talk. **He** was the Matt Damon intervening on my *Good Will Hunting* Ben Affleck's behalf whenever I got out of my depth discussing politics, atheism or sex. **He** flirted with a sexual intent that I loved to observe, until I realised that it was me, not **HiM**, that would have to see it through – and live with the disgrace afterwards.

The drunker I got, the further I'd allow **HiM** to take it, especially as **HiS** ongoing bitterness over my treatment at the hands of women back home meant he always wanted to punch above our weight. **He** would make a beeline for the really sexy girls

Even so, the bit of me that was convinced we were flirting with disaster always pulled it back, or slipped away in time to save face and restore order to my frustrated masturbatory existence.

I did my best to convince myself that I was more about the chase than anything else but the truth was, I was still haunted by my first full sexual encounter. I didn't just lose my virginity that night, I misplaced all ability to entrust my inexperience to any other living soul.

The circle of frustration ran like this: I couldn't begin to contemplate sex unless I was drunk, but I could never hope to match the confidence I'd show around the bar in the bedroom if I did bring someone back. I needed to build up a sober relationship with someone, a real friendship, in order that I might be able to express my anxieties in the hope that they'd ultimately have patience with me for being so damned inexperienced. But nobody seemed interested in me unless they were drunk, because I was so dull in the cold light of day in comparison to my party persona. So I'd get drunk to get over my awkwardness but then become terrified if ever someone else got drunk and shed their inhibitions completely. As a result, I was a world-class drunk and – in the eyes of most, I would imagine – a world-class eunuch.

There was one girl, a French student, with whom I became genuine friends. I absolutely adored her. She would cook me exquisite meals, we would chat and laugh about everything, and I felt so at ease in her company. So much so, after wine but nowhere near as trollied as I'd be over at the bar, I dared tell her that I had feelings for her beyond friendship.

Her response was, 'But this can never be. If we were lovers, it would destroy the friendship that we cherish. I like you too much to risk losing you.'

In the aftermath of this disappointing exchange, she proposed an unusual consolation arrangement where we could kiss and she would unbutton her pyjama top in order to allow me to fondle – but never kiss – her breasts. As sad as it sounds, I agreed to this, even sneaking back from the student union specially some nights, hoping it might lead to something more – perhaps this was her way of expressing a similar nervousness to me?

That myth was shattered after three weeks or so of kneeling on the edge of her bed and fondling her with all the sexual charisma of a trainee baker at the end of a long shift, when she announced, 'I fucked your friend Gary the other night.'

'You *what*! Why?'

'What do you mean, "Why?"'

'What about all that stuff about friendship and its precious-ness?'

'But he is an awful man. Why would you think I would ever have him as a friend?'

As heartbroken as I was, I remained kneeling at the edge of her single bed, exercising her bosom like stress-relief balls, whilst we had our obscure version of a domestic.

'Are you fucking joking?'

'What does it matter?'

She was so French! The way she broke my heart as if she were announcing we were out of semi-skimmed or something ...

'He's my mate.'

'So?'

'So? It's not *Jules et* fucking *Jim*.'

'I am tired now. It is best you should go.'

With that, she buttoned up her pyjama top and turned away. I was devastated. **He** was furious and wanted words with Gaz, but I couldn't let **HiM**. How can you bollock someone for some-body else finding them more attractive than you? He was an alpha male. He had a *Playboy* duvet cover and still got laid, for God's sake!

He couldn't forgive her for wrecking my half of o**U**r head like that, so I strolled back over to the student union and joined Gaz and Paul for pints, surrendering to the status quo of sexual pol-itics. It was one of the few times I was drinking to drown **HiM** out, because I sure as shit couldn't hide from **HiM** the fact that I was quietly relieved.

In the course of such displacement activities, I attained a notoriety for drinking that gained me the first invitation ever offered to a freshman to join the Hoppers' Society. We only met once, for a charity event that involved sitting on the stage at the student union all day, largely ignored by the patrons, on a sponsored drink-athon. A widow from the Life-boat Association had enough homebrew to technically sink a lifeboat – an odd means of remembrance, I know – and it was our job to drink it after gaining sponsorship for each pint.

I don't remember leaving the stage. I woke up on some stairs, then in the halls of residence shower room, then out on the lawn of the College Dean's house, and finally in my bed.

Charity begins at the bottom of a pint glass. 'Only 9 pints?' I hear you cry, but 9 pints of the most potent homebrew I've ever tasted.

In a false bid to economise once I'd started eating into my overdraft, I began buying one or two bottles of very cheap, really nasty Bulgarian red wine. The plan was to drink it in my room before going over to the student union and thereby save on the price of pints. But that just resulted in my still getting in the rounds and ending up absolutely falling-down drunk.

There was no denying the fact that of all my endeavours so far in life – even the things I was truly passionate about, i.e. pottery, comedy and drink – inebriation seemed to be the one I had a natural, God-given talent for. I would always be watching people's reactions whilst **He** waxed lyrical or made the kind of eye contact I couldn't. But at karaoke one night, down in the main bar, **W**e both let rip.

There was something oddly empowering about having control of the microphone for that short space of time. It was only drunken messing, nothing comically profound, but I couldn't stop myself from talking once 'Red Red Wine' had finished (an appropriate choice of musical cue under the Bulgarian circumstances), and although I couldn't remember what I'd said, it must've gone down all right as I was requested by a student union rep to come back as compère for the next karaoke night. I drunkenly agreed and thought nothing more of it.

Next morning, the panic set in. Sitting in the bar being funny was one thing, but this was something else altogether.

It had been agreed without consultation that I'd compère my first gig under the name 'Mad Dog Mike Pennington'. The student union gave me that moniker because they wanted something to put on the posters.

As the evening of my first ever official gig got closer with my still having no semblance of a professional routine or clue what I was going to do, the only sound plan of action seemed to be in getting pissed. So I made sure I took the whole afternoon off to prepare myself properly in the bar of the student union.

Forget the lifeboat, I downed enough Kronenbourg to sink a battleship, but I still felt my nerves were preventing me from getting to the right side of pissed to go ahead with the show (especially when I threw up on my way back to halls). Luckily, I still had time to hit my stash of ropey Merlot.

I can't remember what I said that first night as I didn't have a single prepared line. The only thing pre-planned in any way was my decision to wear the bad-taste trousers my sister had doctored for me. With a stage name like 'Mad Dog', I thought it might be handy to have a bit of a false persona to go with it.

The first gig was word of mouth, but you know you've arrived when they bother to mock up a poster! The 'mad dog' handle was their idea b.t.w.

Now, here's a vital point that would eventually have me forgetting that **He** was real and in existence long before I'd ever contemplated taking to the stage: as minimal as it seems, putting those trousers on was a monumental step in creating what I believed was a character, an alter ego, a fall guy to shield me from the very real fear of failure.

You cannot know how terrifyingly real having your name in print on a poster is when it is associated with the expectation of being funny, and I was already using those trousers from the retro night as a way of offering an exaggerated alternative to me.

What I – or rather w**e** – did that night wasn't strictly stand-up. There was no sell-out crowd. W**e** just did some songs in a really OTT fashion and had a laugh with the other folk getting up singing. The whole night is still just a bit of a blur if truth be told, yet it became a fabled event amongst some ex-students I'd bump into years later.

'Do you remember that karaoke night where you span on your head?' As drunk as I was, I seriously doubt that happened, because **he** would've had a health and safety extravaganza with me the morning after.

I compèred one more night at Middlesex Poly. The crowd was much bigger than the first time and I remember hating the weight of expectation, people asking, 'How're you gonna follow up the last one?'

Follow what? I couldn't remember what I'd done! Still, the second gig went down equally well. The technique of Merlot over matter was proving a winning strategy.

25.

'MAD DOG' MIKE PENNINGTON'S THIRD AND FINAL GIG

He delighted in people coming up and telling us, 'You were brilliant last night.' There was a definite buzz about the second gig, and although He revelled in it, I couldn't escape the nagging doubt that we'd winged it: that folk should be thanking the contents of the bottle bank, not us. Yet I still agreed to one more gig while riding the crest of a vino-induced amnesiac wave.

There was to be an evening of comedy hosted by the British Association of Performing Arts students, or BAPAs, as they were commonly referred to on campus. Truth be told, I wasn't a fan. They had a nasty habit of trying to break into sporadic song-and-dance numbers whenever they thought an opportunity had afforded itself, like *The Kids From 'Fame'* desperately trying to live out a glee-club fantasy existence on a daily basis. Celebrating everything with such gusto might have only inspired nudges and laughs into pints for others but for some reason, their displays of seemingly indestructible enthusiasm always managed to rub me up the wrong way.

Perhaps it was their ability to fake confidence sober, whereas I needed all that booze and encouragement from **HᴵM**? Plus, it didn't help matters having **him** twisting the knife by day when studies demanded sobriety:

'That was definitely blood in your stool earlier, we both saw it.'

'It might've been a piece of pepper. I've never had peppers before. Maybe it's like sweetcorn, maybe I haven't got those enzymes to break it down?'

'It was a stain – trust me, it's bowel cancer. They say if it's not treated immediately then you've barely months to live.'

'But it's not fair, I don't want to die. Why me, why now, why not him?'

'Because he's not got blood in his stool, but you have. He'll go on to make a fortune dressing up as a giant, singing and dancing cat and you'll be dead.'

'You're bloody right. Nobody with cancer looks that happy.'

'Bowel cancer.'

'Shut up, shut up, shut up, SHUT UP!'

Anyway, these interminably upbeat performers were actually forced to do stand-up as part of their course. I still reckon that that is the cruellest experience you could ever inflict on anyone. You'd be amazed how much the notion of performing stand-up terrifies the vast majority of actors. The level of vulnerability involved in this form of performance strikes terror into the heart of even the most accomplished of thespians; like the monster under the bed, it awakens a primal fear. It's the arena of the unwell that no amount of method can protect them from, and I reckon that's part of the reason why clowns earn so much reverence amongst them.

I regretted agreeing to do this gig the moment the posters went up with the addition of 'Mad Dog Mike Pennington'. After the second karaoke night, there seemed to be a genuine buzz down at Cat Hill amongst the art students. The more people told me of their intention to attend, the heavier this nauseating stone got in the pit of my stomach. Dicking about at a karaoke night was one thing, but actual stand-up comedy was madness.

What did I know about getting up and telling actual gags? Everything I'd learned from Mike Firclough was conversational comedy. It worked because it was impromptu bar-room humour; highly polished banter designed purely to pull a small number of drunken students into my gravitational field, to buy time to flirt without frightening them away. It was unexpected funny, designed to look off the cuff and spontaneous, always humble and therefore forgivable if it crashed and burned. But to advertise yourself as funny, to pull a crowd into a venue purely on the basis of telling them you think you're hilarious enough to make that special trip worth their while … surely that was social fucking suicide?

All those nights spent building up a reputation in the student union and around the halls of residence would be shattered in one disastrous, fell swoop. I didn't have any proper gags; in fact, I hated gags. We both did! He was too smart-arsed and cynical to employ the suspended disbelief required to see a gag through to its predictable punch-line, and – cocky as it sounds – back then unless delivered by an old school master, I found traditional jokes unoriginal and formulaic.

Maybe it was the artistic urge to be original; maybe it was just an instinctive attraction towards quirkier humour and a knee-jerk reaction to what went on in the show biz mainstream – I can't honestly say for sure. I hadn't at that point been to a live comedy gig so had no point of reference with regards the diversity of what might pass as stand-up, beyond what I'd seen on TV.

Other than my preference for storytellers, my only other great comic influence at the time was *Vic Reeves Big Night Out*. After my failed French romance, it was the only other thing that could draw me out of the student union before closing time. A huge mob of us would sneak pints in through my window and gather in the communal TV room to watch it.

Vic and Bob's humour was of our time; it was our Python, the landmark show of our student generation. It was genius shrouded in mystery, a hieroglyphic tablet where every loony character combined to reveal the secret of the very nature of comedy itself, but only us, we chosen few crowded together in front of that television, could decipher it.

But that was sod all use to me now that I'd stupidly thrown my hat into the arena. I couldn't do comedy characters even if I tried. 'Mad Dog' was just a stupid name made up by some stupid member of the student entertainment committee. Singing a few stupid songs and talking bollocks was gonna get me strung up. Why the bloody hell hadn't I just quit whilst I was ahead?

And why hadn't **He** stopped me volunteering – wasn't **He** supposed to be on my side?

For those few weeks building up to the gig, **He** became almost as intolerable as **him**.

'WHat'S tHe probLeM?'

'I don't have an act, that's the bloody problem!'

'So get drUNK, get SoMeoNe Up, beLt oUt a FeW tuNeS ...'

'This isn't karaoke, it's comedy, proper comedy. You don't get folk up – you stand there and tell jokes. Jokes I don't have.'

'I Hate joKeS!'

'So do I, but they happen to be the one single absolute necessity when doing stand-up fucking comedy!'

'WHo SayS?'

'Well ... stand-up says, that's who!'

'WHo'S StaNd–Up?'

'What do you mean, "Who's stand-up?"'

'WeLL, WHo MakeS tHe ruLeS For tHiS StaNd–Up?'

'They do!'

'WHo'S "tHey"?'

'The bloody comedians!'

'ANd WHo died aNd Made tHeM tHe boSS oF FuNNy?'

'Nobody! They just happen to be proper funny – I don't!'

'WHo SayS?'

'Oh, fuck this for a game of soldiers!'

'WHere are you goiNg?'

'If I'm gonna bloody die, I might as well head back to halls and talk to the expert, right?'

'Definitely! That bleariness in your eyes, by the way, it's not a tumour ... it's MS.'

'Incurable?'

'Oh, yes.'

'Makes sense.'

By the time the gig came around and I'd blown the weight of expectation way out of proportion, I had decided I couldn't do it. I went along and informed the organiser and compère for the evening. His name was Hugh and he was responsible for tutoring stand-up at Middlesex, a professional duty I've never quite got my head around to this day.

Just like comedy workshops, which are often run by a self-appointed 'expert' in the craft, I've never fully understood how you can presume to teach what is, I believe, a fundamentally personal relationship between a comic and their audience. Although I can understand the attraction for the performers themselves: safety in numbers. Prostitution may well be the oldest profession in the world, but stand-up is certainly the loneliest, and you can still end up getting screwed by a multitude of people in one night. Within the protection of a workshop environment, there's the opportunity for feedback from a sympathetic group, as opposed to a sneering angry mob: I get that. But self-styled gurus have always made me wary. Like someone offering grief counselling before a loved one has even received their diagnosis, there's a presumption I resent more than the fear itself.

No offence to Hugh, though. He was incredibly affable and very understanding; in fact, he even promised to hold a spot for me should I change my mind. 'Fat chance!' I remember thinking. I was drinking out of shame as I could see friends and acquaintances gathering, so I did my best to avoid them whilst going to the bar; I'd told no one of my intention of pulling out, in case there were attempts to sway me to rethink. My intention was to watch the gig from a quiet corner and then sneak away later to work on my excuse for not getting up there.

I sat with Gary and Paul and dodged the subject of when I would be on, until the gig eventually got underway. Now, I don't say this with any benefit of hindsight: my opinion has not changed from that evening there as a complete novice, to this day; but that night's 'entertainment' was a complete and utter travesty of the very notion of humour. It was a ritualistic gang-rape of comedy by an unrepentant gaggle of self-congratulating fops who didn't share a single DNA strand of satirical wit between them. It truly was bloody awful.

And, as I sat and drank and stared on in utter disbelief with my mouth wide open – like a snake about to swallow some prey twice the size of its head – anger swelled inside me at the misery I'd put myself through worrying over how I might compare to shite like this.

Because all of it *was* shite, but one particular guy – the chicken's afterbirth as **He** nicknamed him – was particularly dire, yet continued laughing loudly and smugly at himself despite a room spellbound in awkward silence. The odd solo ripple of applause or forced guffaw from supportive fellow performers lacked conviction, and quickly dissipated into an atmosphere of symbiotic shame.

'This, is an egg, huh hah! There are many things you can do with an egg, oh, yes, huh hah! You can boil an egg … huh huh hah!'

This continued as he went through the entire fucking culinary CV of an egg. And it wasn't even some masterful, slow-burning, ironic build to a punch-line that might somehow have justified his tediousness. It was just things you could do with an egg without any deviation from common knowledge for comic effect. Even Delia Smith – had she been there – would've heckled him to, 'Get to the bloody point!'

I sat there, extremely drunk by now and gobsmacked at what had just been so misguidedly paraded as entertainment. It was like having seen some sort of circus parade passing through town but exhibiting dead, maggot-ridden animals. I hadn't heckled, though, not once throughout the entire evening, despite the fact that **He** had been climbing the walls and begging me to break the silence. But I was still intent on pursuing a coward's way out, despite my disdain for the competition; I thought I could steal a victory by default, perhaps snatch some pride back from the jaws of self-defeat by claiming the night a fiasco and therefore not worth participating in.

And that's where He proved HiMSeLF more than just the real entertainer out of the two of uS that night; He proved himself the bigger man. Because before I knew it I was up, and I swear to you it wasn't my bravado forcing me towards the stage, it wasn't my will that took the microphone so determinedly from the compère, Hugh, and it definitely didn't sound like me when I heard myself say, 'I do beLieve tHere'S oNe More act LiNed Up oN tHiS, WeLL, tHiS "coMedy" biLL toNigHt, So I'LL taKe My tUrN NoW, iF tHat'S aLL rigHt WitH yoU Lot?'

There was hesitant encouragement from groups of students and friends still reeling from the alleged 'show' that had preceded HiM getting up.

'WeLL, NoW, WHat caN We Say aboUt tHe actS We'Ve SeeN Here toNigHt?'

Then He made a swing-o-meter with his arm, lowering it with every category of comedy.

'THere'S good, tHere'S bad, tHere'S FucKiNg SHite, aNd tHeN tHere'S BAPAS!'

The crowd cheered in a huge communal outpouring of frustration and delight that *somebody* had had the balls to get up and say what we'd all been thinking.

It was a big gamble getting up and going on the offensive like that, but He had read the room perfectly and now He had them all, apart from the small contingent of British Association for Performing Arts students – obviously – in the palm of HiS hand. It was a mean thing to say, I can see that now, but the crowd loved it, and HiS instinct for honesty over false camaraderie had paid off.

'OH, aNd a Word oF advice, Mate. ONe tHiNg yoU SHoULd Never, ever, EVER do WitH aN egg? BriNg it aLoNg to a FucKiNg coMedy NigHt, tHat's WHat!'

I remember thinking, 'Ouch, too much?' But the crowd didn't think so. They were cheering now, and there was simply no stopping HiM.

The rest of that time on stage was like a genuine out-of-body experience; some might argue a drunken blank – let's face it, many of us have said things under the influence of alcohol that we cannot remember but ultimately regret. But I swear to you this was different; this was more akin to possession. This was HiM finding HiS voice and basically telling me, 'BaCK oFF, KiD. YoU HaD YoUr CHaNCe, I'LL taKe it FroM HereI'

Sick of rattling around in my chicken-shit head, He was now out in the open where people other than me could hear HiM, and you have no idea just how determined He was to shout the odds exactly how He saw them. He spoke and moved like He was born to that stage. Nothing prepped, definitely no gags, but hitting unrehearsed marks and getting laughs left, right and centre.

The last thing I remember, He was improvising a story adapted from the theme of Little Red Riding Hood but concerning my trying to cash a dole cheque on behalf of my brother. I have no idea how or where He plucked that idea from, but it would be quoted back to me often in the weeks that followed.

Eventually, HiS spot ended. Like a hypnotist clicking his fingers in the face of a punter he'd put under, I was 'back in the room'. He had stormed it, yet the only person unable to appreciate the entirety of what He'd said was me. I simply had to make do with all the plaudits from HiS endeavours, which suited me just fine; and the fallout from some very disgruntled drama students, which was uncomfortable, but also fine. (At least it would ensure a momentary break from the insufferable pirouettes and group songs whenever I was in their vicinity.) In fact – and this is just the cynic in me talking, not HiM – when their smiles turned to stiff upper lips and the eternally optimistic charade was dropped long enough for someone to shout 'Wanker!' from within the huddle, it actually made me smile. It made them seem almost normal.

I didn't wave the business card that was handed to me the next day under their noses. A young bloke suggested I go down for open mic night at The Comedy Store and gave me a contact number for the place.

*It felt good having a backup plan, even though I was in no
doubt my destiny lay upon the seat of a potter's wheel.*

An actual offer from an actual comedy club! In fact, most
novices would've considered it THE comedy club!

It was bizarre. I would sit in my room and stare at it. I didn't
dare show it to anyone because I couldn't quite get my head
around it. I felt like an agent who represented SoMeoNe I
couldn't discuss. I mean, how could I?

'Yes, that was me up on stage, but it wasn't actually me, do
you understand? It was HiM, the secret paᵣt of mᵉ, the angry,
fed-up, no-nonsense, don't-take-no-for-an-answer bit of mʸ
head, you see? And I'm a bit apprehensive to let iᵗ out again –
sorry, HiM – Hᵉ does have feelings, after all. Anyhow, I'm not
quite sure what Hᵉ might do or say IF I dare let HiM loose on
your establishment. I don't even know if Hᵉ'll actually want to
gig again, for that matter. It's not up to me. It wasn't me up
there, it was HiM!'

I was worried I'd end up sectioned rather than doing ten minutes at 'The Store'. I genuinely didn't know if it was a one-off for H¡M or not. And so I never called that number on the card. I did what I could to bury H¡M, along with the whole notion of me doing stand-up, while striving to convince myself that this was for the best.

I'd been invited down to do an open spot, but I didn't understand the reality of the long, thankless slog that a wannabe stand-up has to undertake. I stupidly thought that calling the number on that card would mean I'd be gigging full time, every night and that, as a result, my ceramics degree would ultimately suffer. Although you'd think I spent all my time at Middlesex Poly in the student union, in my own mind I was still devoted to the 'ethos' of my studies and the therapeutic, non-alcoholic need for me – not H¡M – to express myself through 'my art'.

Not calling that number was a decision taken partly out of selfishness and partly out of fear, and I'm fully aware what kind of knob I sound like talking like that. Truth be told, I'd become institutionalised in less than a year and, when push came to shove, I hid behind my closeted student life.

26.

GRADUATION

I spent my days working on my pots at my leisure, not needing to clock in or out, and never really pushing myself to be the artist I had claimed I wanted to be. I spent my nights partying on a chequebook I never thought to balance.

I had the reputation I'd arrived so determined to secure at the start of the year, and although I lost many, many hours tortured by the ever-present **Doctor Death**, and truly did believe that I was dying of something on a daily basis, I was too damned lazy and set in my ways to take a risk on going down in a blaze of glory. And so **He** left me to it.

But when I returned to Middlesex for my second year, that decision took a right good run up and kicked me in the arse: the bank closed all lines of credit, and my student grant got swallowed by the huge overdraft I'd run up on my year-long, fresher's party.

I took a job in the college canteen washing dishes and living off the food kindly provided by the lovely ladies who worked there. The wages were paid straight into my black hole of a bank account and I had a meagre allowance released by the bank in return.

I had gone from being Champagne Charlie to Breadline Bob. My mum would send me £10 postal orders when she could, and although I knew that meagre sum was busting the budget they so rigidly had to stick to back home; even though, deep down, I knew I had pissed my dad's advice to 'watch the pennies' up the student union urinal, I would cash it, and buy just enough pilchards and beans to get me through the weekend and as much gut-rot cheap red wine as I needed to get me as 'Oh, woe is me' drunk as possible.

Sometimes I'd risk the price of a pub pint up the road in the Holt and play the fool, making folk laugh in the hope they would buy me pints and effectively pay for my company, which sometimes they did. Tossing coins in the northern monkey's hat and having him dance for their pleasure.

Gaz and I had left sorting digs too late and ended up in what could, at its very best, be described as a shit-hole flat in High Barnet. We shared with a third lad whose idea of high jinx was running a bath for his visiting brother and shitting in it, but concealing his turd with bubble bath. He failed to grasp my annoyance at this – and every other thing he did, for that matter.

I became so bitter about the luxurious lifestyles of my fellow students, even whilst knowing it was me and me alone who'd got myself into that mess. And that was the start of an awful, slippery, downward spiral when, having made drinking my one main ambition in life, I could no longer afford to keep up, and the party seemed to move on regardless, leaving me to clutch my Bulgarian 'precious' in a cold, dark flat like Gollum's fatter but equally invisible cousin.

God forgive me, but I started quietly resenting my parents for not having the sort of careers and financial stability to bail me out properly – selfish, lazy, self-pitying, fucking idiot that I was. You see, that's another problem with drink: you will always find ways of blaming others for all that you've willingly surrendered to it. But I couldn't see that back then because I was too busy blaming others for my not being able to get enough of the stuff.

CAL'S

COD SUPPER
AT
BAR
MiRó

36 KELVINGROVE ST. (Opposite Lorne Hotel)
· COMEDY THURSDAY NIGHTS 9PM ·
· DRINKS PROMOS ·
· ENTRANCE £3/£2 ·
"QUID-A-MINUTE" OPEN MIKE SPOT
THIS WEEKS SPECIAL GUESTS

JOHNNY MEARS
PATRICK KIELTY
JOHNNY VEGAS
24th february

*All the way to Glasgow yet no actual cod supper for my troubles,
and another secret no-show from* JOHNNy VegaS. *False advertising
on both counts, but a great showbiz mentor in Cal Tanner.*

Other than a brief time at Johnston's tile manufacturers in
Stoke-on-Trent, and an unpaid teaching spell back at Carmel
College, I spent the majority of the gap-year section of my
degree working odd jobs and paying back as much of my debt
as I could to the bank.

My best friend, Bryan, landed me a job behind the bar at my
local Nutgrove pub back in St Helens – the no-nonsense Brown
Edge. I'd drink and dick about under the pseudonym of Johnny
Casino, still trying to ride on the reputation of that one gig
down in London, way back in my first year. We got hammered
one night, and how Bryan convinced me to change my stage-
name I don't know – even he can't remember – but although
the reason why is lost in booze and time, the nickname Vegas
stuck. Johnny Vegas.

I even did a couple of gigs under the name courtesy of Bryan's cousin, Cal (James Callahan), who ran a gig at Bar Miro up in Glasgow. My exaggeration of a career spanning two karaoke gigs and a BAPA comedy night had got back to him, and he booked me to open for Patrick Kielty and do a warm-up spot at The 13th Note, compèred by the brilliant Fred MacAuley.

I got drunk, very drunk, and winged it as best I could – ranting about my dad one night, and chatting up a girl with preposterously comic confidence another – but I didn't storm it, whatever myth might say. I wore 'the flares', and I sported a new perm, but it was no vintage Johnny Vegas night, simply because **H**e didn't turn up.

In my last year at Middlesex Poly, I found one-room digs with Eileen Flack and her son, Martin. I still call her Mum No. 2 to this day, and I wouldn't have survived my final year without them and the generosity shown to me when I was down on the financial bones of my arse. I was never treated as a lodger, more a distant relative, and I never went without a meal as Eileen not only opened her home to me, but also her fridge-freezer in times of real need.

Although living around the corner in a shared house of young professionals, Gaz and a large majority of my friends and associates had graduated by now. Paul, also on a four-year course, was still there, but everyone was now seriously knuckling down to work on their final year: as was I, genuinely.

I had begun to believe in myself as an artist again; I had no other option but to do that. I had to have something to show for those last three years without a pocket to piss in and my leaning on friends and adopted family like some care-in-the-community nominee.

Liz Croft, Mark, Jacky … everyone took it in turns minding me. I had become so socially inept, but kept finding ways to drink to mask my resentment at their superior ability to cope. Laughing up my shambolic ways probably only served to make me more pathetic in their eyes, but they were all too kind-hearted to comment, so I stupidly thought I was getting away

My final degree show 'female forms' were so abstract, everyone mistook them for giant candlesticks. Ho hum, back to the drawing board.

Never mind the Maori inspired wall freeze, what the hell is going on with my head?

The Vegas flares get their first outing via a bad taste fashion night out in St Helens. Not a single doorman batted an eyelid.

My 'moves' in the student union always ensured I got the dance floor all to myself.

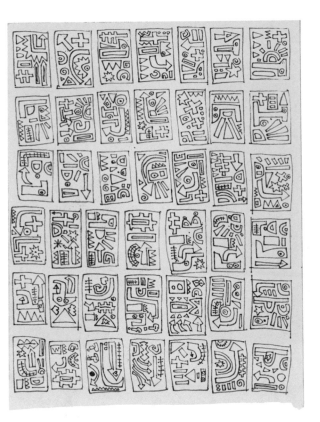

My visual coded diary.
It's about 90 per cent
sexual frustration
and the stuff of
psychoanalysts'
wet dreams.

No sexual frustration here, just the artist expressing his love of Chinese
takeaway.

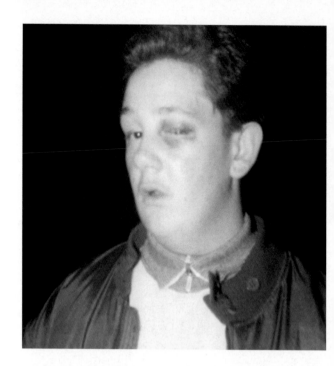

'I'm a lover not a fighter!' No, hang on, I was neither, just another victim of Saturday night ultra violence.

Graduation day, hooray! A trip to the local job centre with my third class honours degree in ceramics would soon wipe that smile off my face.

SUPERB GIFT IDEA

I'm a bargain

JOHNNY VEGAS

It felt good to get the perm under wraps and opt for a less conspicuous multi-coloured psycho look.

The home made business card did little to clarify my career intentions either!

Me mixing my drinks till the inside of my head matched the wallpaper. Didn't take the perm long to do away with the hat.

Relaxing backstage
post chunder and
debating if drinking
the complimentary
toiletries might coax
Johnny out to play?

My first publicity shots. It was a toss-up back then if Johnny was going
into stand-up or lap dancing. 'Work it, work it baby!'

OK, so the North West Comedian of the Year thing didn't work out, but Johnny will always have Leicester. Luckily Magpie's Nest had no issue with cashing an oversized novelty cheque, standard handling fees applicable of course ;-)

Souvenir of the Kay/Vegas comedy nights. He could run for Mayor of Bolton now.

My/his face on a beermat – all my ambitions realised in one small circular piece of card.

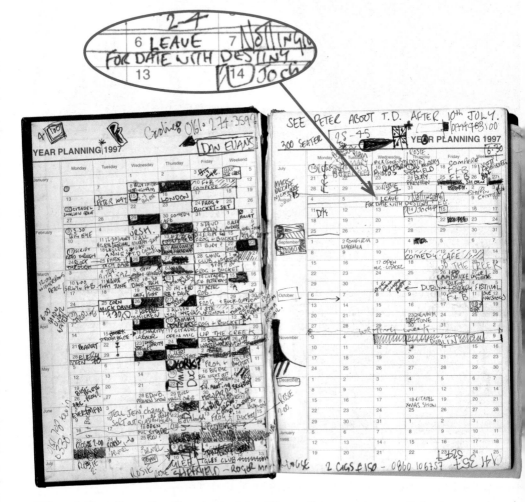

'97 and the diary finally started to fill up. I swear to you Johnny wrote 'leave for date with destiny' on August 6th, big head!

with my Stella-soaked charade. Still, at least with a decent degree I could walk away with my head held high (or, at least, bobbing in a respectably elevated position).

In the meantime, I had become fascinated with the world of fashion and the manufactured idea of beauty; most likely because I liked the irony of beautiful women – the kind of women who'd rejected me my entire life – having their own issues with the way they looked.

Exploring the theme of body fascism, having read Naomi Wolf's book, *The Beauty Myth*, I started manufacturing my abstract female forms through an industrial process and then deforming them in a way that made each one unique and more aesthetically pleasing. (Jesus, I sound like Kevin Spacey's character in *Se7en*, but please believe me that this artistic initiative wasn't born of a resentful karma, just a fascination with how as individuals we are all conditioned to value ourselves through external perceptions.)

MEDIA, FOR WOMEN?

michael Pennington

My college dissertation, a landmark in feminist literature and a must read for bloke trying to sell himself as a new age man.

I worked damned hard figuring out how to fire these figures. I believed in what I was striving for and I felt incredibly proud of the originality of what I was creating. These abstract female forms felt like the culmination of all the faith my past teachers had placed in me, and I truly believed I was about to make them proud.

I didn't let my social disappointments taint this, because although I functioned so piss-poorly in the outside world, back in there – at my workspace within that communal studio – I thought that, at long last, I shared a work ethic equal to my parents'. I felt like a worthy sibling alongside my over-achieving sister, on a different plane to my indifferent brothers, and I threw an existential two fingers up to all those who'd taken the piss or simply doubted my reasons for choosing this path. Thanks to the work I was producing, I finally felt like an earnest, hard-working, *bona fide* trailblazing ceramic artist.

I graduated with a third-class 'honours' degree in ceramics by the skin of my teeth. It was the lowest grade in our year, and it left me a broken man.

I rang home the day they announced our final grades and started to cry as the words 'third class' stuck in my throat.

'I got the lowest grade in the group, Dad, I'm so sorry. I feel like I've let you down.'

My dad chuckled. 'You've not let me down, son. I never thought you'd pass.'

God love and keep that man. From the absolute depths of my despair, he managed to make me laugh. But such moments of levity were thin on the ground at that time.

Dad and Mum couldn't afford to attend both my degree show and my graduation, so they saved up and bought their train tickets for the latter, and I suffered the indignity of zero sales of my masterpieces at both my graduation show and the new designer's exhibition. In fact, the only interest my abstract female forms attracted was a short but rather telling note in my comments book: 'I like your candlesticks.'

I sat and watched as parents turned up to congratulate their kids before taking them out for expensive, slap-up meals to celebrate, and actually wished that they'd all choke in the process. I'm sorry to all the people I worked and laughed and drank with over the four-year period of my degree course, but right there and then, I hated everyone and everything to do with that place.

Above all, though, I hated myself.

Mum and Dad came down for the graduation. I wore a frilled 1970s shirt and velvet dickie bow I'd bought in a presentation box from a charity shop. I thought it would look quirky and help in putting a brave face on things. The shirt didn't fit on the day, so I had to tear it in half up the back and just tuck it in at the sides.

I was quietly relieved when my folks told me we didn't have the money to get an official graduation picture taken. I wanted no official reminder of that day, especially one that was going to waste any more of their hard-earned money than I already had.

Finally, we left and caught the train heading back towards St Helens. Whilst my peers popped corks and celebrated their collective achievements, my dad and I cracked open a few cans of bitter.

I wondered what the fuck I was supposed to do now, with nothing more than a third-class degree in pottery to my name.

27.

THE BROWN EDGE

I got home to St Helens and, like a walking billboard on behalf of art-school sceptics everywhere, signed on the dole. After a few weeks, I sorted myself a room in a family home up in Prescot (the address, ironically enough, being Pottery Row) that took in lodgers.

Scott – the legendary landlord who'd run the Brown Edge with his wife, Judy – had sadly passed away a week before they were due to retire and hand over the reins to the new licensees, Stu and Val. After much persuasion, my friend Bryan convinced them to give me some more part-time bar work. And, just as it was for Chris Arker – electrician by day and karaoke maestro by night – who gave out the bar number as his business contact, the Brown Edge would become my on and off base of operations for the next few years.

I worked there and gave the majority of my wages back over the bar. It was my halfway house that enabled my relationship with booze to flourish, whilst slowly helping with my social rehabilitation back into the real world.

The expectations of a barman there were simple: take shit; take lots and lots of shit. Give it back in charming doses, but don't be too much of a smart-arse. Nobody likes a smart-arse. The level of shit you were given was the equivalent of stripes on a military uniform. It was the locals' way of showing you respect – the amount of disrespect you were shown represented the amount of respect they had for the fact that you had no self-respect.

With a pottery career in tatters and still struggling to see how I might adapt my teapot-building skills to a clayless local economy, I made for a tempting target.

For many years, the Brown Edge had been a kind of last-chance saloon for lads barred from other pubs around Thatto Heath or Rainhill. They were allowed in on the basis that they remain on their best behaviour; a rule that they tried to abide by to the very best of their ability – it's just that they had a very askew sense of what 'good' behaviour actually was.

The Brown Edge was a proper pub with an amazing cast of supporting characters that could leave *Cheers* in the shadows, but it had three particularly 'special' punters: Bullrush (whose real name was David), Wink and Dunkie, who were always allowed early entry at the back door as they didn't cope well with sobriety. These lads provided hours of fun and occasional torment during my time there, and would prove invaluable study cases for honing HIS mannerisms further down the line.

Dunkie had created his own bizarre, third-person vernacular and spoke like no Woolyback (Scouse slang for folk from St Helens) I ever knew, both in his terminology and accent, and it sounded like complete gibberish to anyone but regulars at The Brown Edge. Everyone was 'Baby cocheraaab' as Dunkie never dealt in names. After serving him for 4–5 years he never once called me Michael, or Vegas, which had become a regular nickname thanks to Bryan, but he was a legend in his own right. There's few things that can top his rendition of the song 'Outside the Lunatic Asylum' whilst wearing a rasta/rastafarian wig (don't ask) for comedy value.

The second major league boozer at The Brown Edge was Stew Wink. At throwing out time he'd do the best drunken walk ever (The Stew Wink shuffle) where he'd appear to lose the right side

A sketch from back in the day when pubs advertised manly health threatening pursuits, instead of ball ponds and two meals for under a tenner.

Ian Kilshaw, my mentor in socialism and fellow comedy obsessive caught in a rare moment without his partner in crime Barry Lomax. Together they were the Waldorf and Statler of the Brown Edge.

As for Dede? Trust me, she was just being sweet. Another lass who really, really liked me, but just as a friend.

of his hip bone and amble like a marionette missing half it's strings. He was a joy to serve and could burst into impromptu song at any moment. His cheeky grin would often coax a pint 'on the house' (which always came out of my meagre £10 salary for a shift.) But Stew had a sadness to his eyes that could inspire a million 'Beautiful South' hit songs.

Last, but definitely not least, there was Bullrush. He was at the heart of the familiar routine that began most lunchtime shifts:

'Morning, David.' (It was always best to observe preliminary formalities with Bullrush.)

'Morning, Michael.'

'Pint?'

'Yes, please.'

[*Cut to third or fourth pint*]

'Same again, David?'

'Shut yer trap, ya fat, dozy get, ya! I'll tell you when I want a bloody pint!'

[*Finishes pint*]

'Carlsberg, please.'

[*The pint is already half-pulled in anticipation of the certain outcome of this conversation*]

'Coming up, Bully.'

I didn't realise it at the time, but working at the Edge would prove the best preparation for dealing with hecklers that We could possibly get. There would never be an insult thrown HiS way on stage that hadn't already been better served over that bar by the regulars. And I took an odd pride in how I dealt with the banter, remaining polite and courteous and learning to appreciate it for the game it was. It was all about give and take and learning never to let them get under your skin, or show any sign of weakness.

In fairness to Bullrush, he was way down in the pecking order himself. He was the butt of many a joke, but would forgive all if there was a pint in it for him. After smelling gas in the meter cupboard one day, the lads bribed him with free ale to sit and drink in there on his own for the full afternoon – like a human canary. It was demeaning but also (I have to admit) bloody funny at the time. And if giving me grief helped him feel like he had somebody to look down on, then so be it.

The regulars would assemble at different points throughout the afternoon: Ronnie the gardener; Mick Thorogood; Big John and his troop of roofers, grateful to be rained off a job; ex-miner John and his wife; Paulie Smith; Ched ...

Now, I wasn't the most efficient barman ever, as my mate Bryan will agree, but I was good at keeping the afternoon trade drinking just those few pints longer with sing-alongs or insti-gating ridiculous debates which ensured that they, to quote Vic and Bob, 'Just wouldn't let it lie.'

'Who'd win in a fight, a lion or a golden eagle?' made many a man come home late and find his dinner under foil in a luke-warm oven. Like a good double act – Bryan being one of the most conscientious people I have ever met was inevitably the straight man – we inadvertently worked the bar almost like a gig, and together we made a great team.

There was a rivalry, almost like old-fashioned class distinc-tion, between the bar and the lounge. The bar was for folk coming straight from their job (or avoiding it altogether) who, accordingly, often dressed in work gear. The lounge, on the other hand, was seen as a once-a-week place where you might perhaps treat the wife to a drink. Anyone who supped in there full-time was considered to have ideas above their stations, or be the yuppie type who didn't do a proper job for a living.

Barry Lomax and Ian Kilshaw sat in the lounge side of the pub, and when bar regulars would shout through to 'Stop serving the toffs in the lounge!' they would revel in mocking the notion of their social superiority. They were psychiatric nurses, funny and informed as the shift was long, and were widely acknowledged as our Waldorf and Statler, the two hecklers in The Muppets, within our pub. Yet they became sincere friends and shared my obses-sion with all things comedy, often attending early gigs of John-ny's and supporting us every step of the way. I have Ian to thank

The
Brown Edge Inn

29th Jan 1993

To Whom it May Concern,

Micheal Pennington has been employed by us for the past six months, as a part time bar person. He has proved himself to be, capable, efficient and above all honest. He is always punctual and presents himself in a clean and tidy manner.

In the short time Mike has been here he has become very popular with both the customers and other staff members, in fact his cheerful sense of humour will be missed.

I have no hesitation in recommending him for employment, and feel he would be an asset to any future employer. In fact should he return to this area. I will definitely re-employ him myself

Yours sincerely

V. McSmith

Family Room ∗ Childrens Play Area ∗ Beer Garden
Traditional Beer ∗ Bowling Green

They did re-employ me, every time my bold decisions to leave town fell flat on their arse. Stu and Val, the best employers a scruffy blow-in could ever hope for.

for reintroducing me to my most treasured piece of literature, The Ragged Trousered Philanthropists, and Barry's simple but lasting piece of advice 'stop wasting energy trying to gain favour with folk who'll simply never like you through no fault of your own. They're not worth your time.' An observation Barry made after spotting this weakness in me, another unfortunate side effect of **Doctor Death's** constant taunting.

The most irrepressibly good-humoured of the regulars on the bar side was a bloke called Barnsley Phil, who would come in every day with a freshly prepared gag but try and sell it as though it was something that had actually happened. He was a master of taking suspended disbelief beyond its natural limits. He'd swear on his life that he'd just seen two nuns going past on a bike before giving you the punch-line. Phil, and his wife Joan, brought instant joy and gusto in with them, and it was he who always coaxed me into putting on a show for the regulars, slipping a quid in the jukebox and putting on 'Minnie the Moocher' whist pleading with me to grab a brollie from the hat stand (as a make shift cane) and leading everyone in a sing-a-long.

Despite the cosy shelter from reality that working at the pub afforded me, I was quietly determined to try and do something more with myself now that the Turner Prize seemed well and truly out of my grasp. I hooked up with Mike Firclough again, and we set about organising ourselves into an actual professional comedy force to be reckoned with.

We tracked down an open mic night in Manchester and got to work putting together what we considered to be a hilarious collection of anecdotes that, it was decided, I would be the one to retell on the night – even though I considered Mike to be a hundred times funnier than I could ever hope to be, and everything was written with his style and tone of delivery.

For some reason, by the time the gig came round, we were incredibly self-congratulatory about the fact that we were due to share our genius with the unsuspecting Manchester audience. Although I'd had a couple of drinks, I wasn't nearly as nervous as I should've been driving over there. Perhaps it was because I thought we were sitting on comedy gold and wasn't worrying about summoning up YOU-KNOW-WHO.

He'd been gone for what felt like so long now, despite the fact that I was still drinking on a daily basis. Maybe my confidence had grown; maybe I just thought of myself as a grown-up now, and had subconsciously put away such childish things. Of course, he still tortured me on a daily basis, but that had become a way of life now – living with death when sober, drowning it out when the clock deemed it to be socially acceptable. That's why working at the pub suited me, and why I'd solemnly decided that an office job, with office hours, was never going to be a good fit for an employee like me.

We got to the gig. Rather than a packed student union or long-established comedy club, this was one of those open mic nights where the audience barely outnumbered the acts. It felt more like some self-help-group meeting in a disused pub stockroom than a gig: just twenty or so all in all in the room. And yet, oddly enough, that was even more daunting.

There was no inherited atmosphere, no buzz, no rush, nothing to fire up the desire to entertain, just an awkward silence that threatened to politely engulf any uncertainty or ill-conceived gag. And that suddenly scared the shit out of me. There was nowhere to hide there, no distance between them and you. It was intimate, and I found an audience of that type every bit as terrifying as any woman back at Middlesex Poly.

I was due to come on later (only by accident – news of my student union compèring coups had yet to reach the north west). This was both a blessing and a curse: it gave me time to hit the bar and start trying to hammer the pints; the only problem being that I was so nervous, my stomach went on lockdown and every time I tried to swallow a big gulp of bitter there was a gag reflex intent on pushing it back up again.

I sat and watched the acts before me whilst sipping furiously at my pint – trying not to be sick, but getting as drunk as possible to numb the certainty of my inevitable failure. Some were so-so; some appeared nervous and yet these tended to be a lot more polished material-wise in comparison: they had good gags and some great observations, far better than ours. Also, there was a definite style to the general delivery that we hadn't considered whilst prematurely congratulating ourselves down the pub.

Now this was, I truly believe, a defining moment in our future as a stand-up comic. As I sat there, a truth dawned on me, and as smug as this probably sounds, it is a realisation that a vast majority of wannabe comics never get to grips with, which is why you will find so many of them playing out the same ten minutes week after week, month after month – even year after year in some cases – refusing to accept an irrefutable fact.

Being funny in your head, amongst your own, and especially down the pub, offers no guarantee of a successful transition to the stage. There is banter, and great comics pass their act off as just that, but the casual delivery that supports the fib that a perfectly honed idea, agonised over alone behind closed doors, just popped into their head is all part of the allure that comics cultivate. To make no bones about it, they are delivering material.

Now, that's not to say that comics won't ad-lib and stray from the path in order to play the room, to adapt to their audience. That again is the hallmark of a great act. But the foundations from which they wander are tried, tested and proven through night after night of patient tinkering unseen to the untrained eye, and they are ruthless when accepting that a gag, no matter how personal an investment or whatever amount of time and effort has gone into shaping it, won't work.

As I sat there that night in the grip of a desperate reality check, I suddenly understood that the stories Mike and I had found so amusing simply would not work in that room. Or, at least, I couldn't make them work in that room. And although with hindsight I realise now that I was asking far too much of myself and what we'd written, I'm glad the realisation kicked in, because as I sat there feeling increasingly desperate and slightly inebriated (although nowhere near as much as I'd have liked to have been), my stand-up guardian angel finished sulking and succumbed to the temptation of playing to a crowd once more.

'What's He Whining on about?'

'Hey, what?'

'This Fella up there now, What's his problem?'

'His divorce.'

'Right ... and?'

'And it's really good, like professional good. This stuff we've written is ...!'

'Shite!'

'Yeah.'

'So ditch it.'

'And do what? I can't compete with that. I mean, look at him, he's really bloody funny!'

'SO ARE WE!'

But could We be as funny as that guy? He had a great little set about life since his recent divorce, and he was charming and unoffensive, the best that'd been on that evening by far. I couldn't help but like him, despite the fact that I was terrified of following him.

But, whereas my defeatism was happy to let him steal the show, He was already figuring out how to use this to our advantage.

As everyone clapped the likeable divorcé off and the compère indicated it was time for me to take the mic, I shuffled through to the front, desperately scrambling about in my brain for something with which to replace the pre-prepared material that – unbeknownst to Mike – I had already jettisoned. I needed a disclaimer, an excuse for not being funny at a night purposely staged for folk who wanted to publicly declare themselves just that.

In the meantime, all I could think was what the fuck was I doing here and why the fuck hadn't I just sneaked out the back when I had the chance? I was so pissed off with myself for having these stupid, bloody aspirations in life that always turned round and ended up biting me on the arse.

Why did I keep sticking my hand up and volunteering myself for heroic missions that were doomed to failure? Why did I keep bloody kidding myself that I had anything more to offer than the next fella? Why, why, why did this ego keep sticking on plasters and re-inflating itself when the test results always, always, ALWAYS came back negative?

I was a failed priest in some folks' eyes and a failed potter in everyone's. A jumped-up, bloody barmaid living in a one-room lodging, sleeping in his clothes and afraid to turn the light off in case **Death** might come a-whispering. A role model to no one, a desperate scaredy-cat Lothario who'd only been laid once in his twenty-four years. A laughing stock, a loser, a no-mark, a nobody; a walking cautionary tale with regard to artistic endeavours, mental well-being, fashion, faith and fucking. A thoroughbred champion in my own head, but a non-runner in real life. A shining example of absolute abject disappointment so desperate for acceptance that I'd brought myself here to once again fall flat on my arse whilst attempting to publically polish the turd that was my life.

I hated Michael Pennington at that moment. I really, truly saw myself for the first time as the rest of the world did, and I was so ashamed and angry at myself for rolling over and trampling the roses, rather than waking up and bothering to smell them.

As I grabbed the mic I just wanted to say, 'I'm sorry!' – for turning up, for wasting their time, for wasting the time of everyone who'd ever known me and invested time, patience and love in a bid to help me.

I wanted to share with the group – a problem shared is a problem halved and all that psycho-babble. I wanted to come clean and admit to everyone there that I didn't like myself and I didn't even want this precious life that had once felt so full of possibility but which I was now wasting by constantly obsessing over the prospect of a painful and premature end.

I didn't pray to God any more. Instead, I'd been subconsciously praying to **Death** for years to come and take me away from the endless disillusionment of this thing folk called life, because I was a coward! A coward, a sham, a failure, a mess! Why not tell it as it was? I had the mic in my hand and all I wanted to do was beg forgiveness for everything that made me, me. I really wanted to.

But *I* wasn't the one holding the microphone.

'Good evening. I'm Johnny Vegas, and I'm not a comedian, I'm an entertainer! I don't do jokes; I don't do gags. I don't say, "Do you know what it's like when this happens, or do you know what it's like when that happens?" Because you've no fucking idea what it's like to be me!'

It was beautiful; it was perfect. Not only did it make people sit up and take notice, it was also an instant get-out clause for not being funny. Don't go out and plead with people to like you – go out there with an immediate disclaimer that they're not supposed to like you, that you're not there under any pretence of being funny; in fact, the complete opposite.

This rage was not to be laughed at, because this was an honest-to-goodness, heart-on-sleeve antidote to the neediness of being funny. Yet the more earnest Johnny was in His delivery, the funnier the audience seemed to find it.

And it wasn't just the audience He put a spell on: I was every bit as much under His control as they were. His reverse psychology worked both ways, and He had everyone, especially me, exactly where He wanted us.

' ... I'm really sorry your marriage broke up, mate, truly I am, but at least you had a wife in the first place! You had someone to lose! Because other than chopping it off with an axe, I can't divorce my right hand. The best I could ever hope for is a brief fling with the left!'

It's a cardinal sin in stand-up to go on and slag off another act on the same bill, but We weren't to know that, and the guy himself was laughing along at the deconstruction of his own act. And he wasn't the only one getting a hard time. By laying our cards on the table from the off, and Him tapping into all my deepest neuroses, He managed to turn me inside out and display my failures for all the world to see.

For years I've traded on the arrogant notion that I 'invented' Johnny. And, in my naïvety, it was this gig that I had always falsely identified as marking the birth of VegaS. Though, I have now come to realise that JoHNNy had in fact been around way before the timeline I had previously granted him, this was still the night on which He fully took on that pub-nickname and made it HiS own.

JoHNNy VegaS had publicly declared HiMSeLF a person in HiS own right. He had arrived, and He was taking no prisoners.

28.

STORMING THE CITADEL

Page 32 — THE STAR, March 16, 1995

Vegas comes to St Helens . .

★ MEET Johnny Vegas, the St Helens-based comedian who is proving a big hit with audiences at The Citadel.

Johnny is the front man for The Citadel's Friday comedy nights which are being sponsored by Tyrers department store whose managing director John Tyrer was on hand to present a cheque for £200 to Citadel staff.

Mr Tyrer is pictured (centre) with (left to right) compere Johnny Vegas, marketing officer Lisa Roberts, marketing assistant Christopher Hackett and house manager Neil Rainford.

When asked if he would be attending any of the gigs John Tyrer confided that he didn't tend to visit St Helens after dark. Establishing a thriving comedy scene was going to be an uphill battle.

JOHNNY revealing HIMSeLF to the general public was one thing, but getting HIM gigs was another. I didn't know the first thing about how the scene worked.

It was Mike who'd sorted out the Manchester spot, but I'd already quietly decided it was unfair to expect him to be able to write up the madness that was in my head, as his style of humour wouldn't suit JOHNNY, so I silently went solo, in a split-personality kind of way. I really wished he'd have a go at running that material himself somewhere – I've always had a tinge of guilt at how selfishly I broke up the threesome – but I guess it was not meant to be.

I made a big announcement in the pub that I was leaving for London to become a stand-up comic. The reaction was a mixed bag of sarcasm and scorn from the majority of the regulars. Nevertheless Stuart, Val, Bryan and co threw me a really decent leaving party, and I packed my bags to go back and take up my room again at Eileen and Martin's flat.

Like many comedy hopefuls, I thought the best place to hone my craft was in the capital. For some stupid reason, I thought the phone would be ringing off the hook once word got around that Vegas was in town.

In the ten months or so that I was there, I managed two gigs, and I sucked royally at both of them. One was at the Old Bull Arts Centre up in my old stomping ground of Barnet, and one was at the King's Head, Crouch End, compèred by the wonderful Hugh, the organiser of the student union gig.

I'd given him such grief, pissed up that night, telling him how he was building them all up for a mighty fall from their comedic ivory towers, and how they would get their arses kicked if they tried that nonsense in a proper club. And yet there we were, dying on our arse, and running over time quite spectacularly in the process.

The problem was that beyond JOHNNY'S opening gambit, He had no set material with which to work, relying instead on whatever was rattling around inside our head as We got onto the stage. I had stupidly thought that the drunker I got HIM, the funnier He'd be. And I had got so rat-arsed that neither of uS could squeeze a coherent sentence out.

It's hard to explain, but although I never felt like it was me up there, I was still terrified of **HIM** going on stage or, even worse, not showing up altogether. So I had to drink to get **JOHNNY** up to ranting pace, but too much and neither **He** nor I were able to function.

The nerves were a definite problem, and always have been. I don't know if that was part of the reason that I wasn't more proactive in going out and getting myself gigs – in all my time there, I never once looked at a copy of *Time Out* to get the listings. I didn't hang out in clubs as I told myself it was a luxury I couldn't afford. After entrance fee and drink, I'd be out by at least five, maybe six cheap bottles of Bulgarian red. I just drank whenever I could afford to, watched MTV all day, and went round to my college friend Gary's shared house and scrounged what I could in the form of food and wine in the evenings. Eventually, I gave up the ghost and returned to St Helens, taking up residency once again on both sides of the bar at the Brown Edge.

The only advantage to choosing a career in comedy at that stage were the hours, and the fact that nobody from the pub had set foot in a comedy club. Therefore, unlike my ceramics degree, I could shroud my failings in London in mystery and bullshit. So I still claimed comedy as my intended career to the punters, and continued to thwart the dole with the impossible task of finding me any work that involved a potter's wheel.

It was completely by accident that I discovered St Helens ran what I hate to describe as an 'alternative' comedy night. It was bizarre, considering my artistic background, but I'd never before set foot in the Citadel Arts Centre. It was viewed with suspicion or derision by many, a doss house for struggling bands and shows not mainstream enough to fill the Theatre Royal, and it only came to my attention after I'd spotted a small flyer one day for upcoming stand-up gigs at the Citadel featuring self-styled Scottish nutter Parrot and later on Dominic Holland – fresh from his Perrier nomination up in Edinburgh and hence instant comedy royalty as far as I was concerned.

I heckled at Parrot's show, but only out of honest admiration. I had no idea why a comedian wouldn't enjoy that kind of

Mike Pennington   03 November 1994

Dear Mike,

Just a quick note to confirm what we discussed the other week.

You'll be compering the comedy night of Friday 25th November.

You will start the evening off for about 5 minutes at 8.30pm and then introduce a local support act - David Harrison. He will perform for about 15-20 minutes and you'll then announce the interval. After the interval you'll be back on for a couple of minutes before introducing the main act - Dominic Holland.

As I mentioned to you, we are aiming to run monthly comedy nights from February 1995 and hopefully sticking to this format with a compere, local support plus main bill (probably two acts).

As agreed, although the Citadel is not paying you we will let you have some beers 'on the house'.

I would appreciate it if you could arrive at about 7.00pm.

Yours sincerely

Nick

Nicholas Chapman
Centre Director

The Citadel naively underestimating how far **Vegas** *would push the 'some beers, on the house' clause in the contract. A new agreement was drawn up the following day.*

interaction (perhaps because We had never come up against any ourSelf at the handful of gigs We'd done so far). Plus, with only a meagre crowd of twenty or so, and St Helens audiences' reputation for sitting on hands and laughing only in our heads, I was one of those pricks that genuinely thought I was doing him a favour.

I was drunk by the end of the gig. As Parrot said his goodbyes, JoHNNy saw the idle mic and an empty stage as an open invitation to perform. He pounced and gave a tirade about the beauty of a teapot. It was passionate, but completely nonsensical.

Rather than drag uS off, though, the head of programming there approached me in the bar later on and asked if I'd like to consider being their resident compère. No fee, just free ale and *carte blanche* to run the gig as I best saw fit. It was an accidental opportunity inspired by JoHNNy's 'Do or die and sod the consequences' attitude, and it proved massively influential on how the act shaped up from there on in.

Having by-passed the established clubs and now with HiS own piece of comedy turf to perform on as He pleased, JoHNNy had none of the usual restrictions on time and content. They were great gigs. And never the same bit of material twice, because I'd yet to learn that other comics had their fixed sets, their bankers, their comedy gold.

My first ever review commented on the fact that, 'He is the first compère I've ever seen to heckle the headline act throughout his set.' Again, this was done not out of arrogance or a desire to undermine the competition, but out of a sense of fun. (Although, later down the line, promoters would start to point out in their letters in bold type that under no circumstances would they require a compère.)

I saw myself as more a creative agent to my onstage persona. I'd borrow JoHNNy's wardrobe and head out flyer-ing in St Helens town centre in a bid to bulk up the audiences. 'If you build it, they will come.' Slowly but surely, the auditorium (all 120 seats of it) began to fill up, and soon we were selling out.

He even had his own fan club – a group of young students who'd taken it upon themselves to go and get T-shirts printed with HIS face on! He quietly loved that, although it didn't prevent HiM from mercilessly ripping the piss out of them come show time.

I'd agonise over new stuff to do every month when the gig came around; JOHNNy would oblige by running it out in front of the crowd, but more often than not, a large percentage of it would flop and the most memorable bits would be HiM riffing on a small part that had worked and taking it off at wild tangents, or reacting from some thin thread of an idea offered by the audience and weaving it into something memorable.

Well, for the audience at least.

The nerves never eased up and I still had to drink copious amounts to dare myself off the barstool and down to the venue. So, I would take to going to the pub around 3 p.m. and beginning preparations for the gig there.

An interesting day signing on with 20 of these on display at the local Job Centre! They didn't buy the excuse that JOHNNy had never drawn dole in his life. Go figure.

Being someone who always opted for misery over stress, I could never get to grips with the awful sickness I'd feel on gig days. From the moment I opened my eyes in the morning and the realisation hit that I'd be coaxing J**o**HNN**y** out to play later, I'd feel like somebody had run up and kicked me in the stomach. It was horrible.

Despite my size, I'd have no appetite whatsoever, and even the slightest sudden movement would have me retching into the nearest receptacle. A fact that my mate, Bryan, often likes to remind me of, largely because after he'd come by in a cab to collect me for the show one evening, I threw up all over myself.

'Jesus, mate, are you all right?'

'No, I'm not. That's four pints and a bottle of Merlot, is that. I haven't the time to neck that again now!'

So I had to sit and sip for hours and be sure not to gulp too large a swig for fear of setting off the hair trigger in my oesophagus.

I knew it would be fine once **He** took to the stage and did **HiS** thing, but God, how I hated the waiting. I'd sit there praying for any excuse for the show to get cancelled: a small fire, a bomb threat; anything that could excuse pulling the gig.

Despite my misgivings, we had some great nights, with many of V**e**g**a**S's gems quoted back to me (which was handy, as neither **He** nor I could remember much of the actual content from any of the shows). In fact, after the tab J**o**HNN**y** and I ran up on our first-ever booking there, the Citadel thought it wiser to pay u**S** thirty quid a gig instead from then on in. Signing on part-time and pulling shifts at the Brown Edge to make ends meet meant that being out of pocket on a gig put a huge dent in my budget, so £30 felt like a king's ransom. Although walking into the St Helens dole office to sign on and finding J**o**HNN**y**'s face plastered over twenty-odd Citadel flyers being displayed there took some explaining.

But I did start to invest in performing at other venues courtesy of Bev, a friend who worked nights with me behind the bar at the Edge and who had her own transport. Thanks to her,

I was able to pick up gigs a little further afield. I used to joke about there being a job in this for her one day as I had no means of paying her for her troubles, and thankfully she never asked. Miss Dixon, my good pal and personal assistant, remains one of the most generous-spirited people I have ever known.

We went to Manchester once but focused mainly on Liverpool and the Rawhide Club, hosted back then by the brilliant Terry Titter in the downstairs bar of the Everyman Theatre. Terry had a huge following in Liverpool and, unlike many of the London clubs, it seemed the audience came to see the shows at the Rawhide just as much for the compère as the rest of the acts on the bill.

Just like JoHNNy back at the Citadel, Terry had free rein, and rather than merely doing a section of his set and introducing the acts, he provided his fans with a show within the show. You could see a real bond of trust between himself and the audience that both VegaS and I appreciated and revered (although being the natural-born competitor that He was, He'd never admit that).

It was at the Rawhide that Kevin Fearon, the club's creator/promoter, encouraged uS to enter for Edinburgh's 'So You Think You're Funny?' I wasn't aware of the competition but figured it was an extra gig away from the comfort zone of the Citadel.

The organiser accepted Kevin's nomination and so JoHNNy was due up at the Festival in Edinburgh the following August to take part in the first heat.

If successful, the final would be two days after that.

29.

'SO YOU THINK YOU'RE FUNNY?'

I really was living hand to mouth at that time, or glass to lips, with every penny accounted for. Drinking is an expensive business, especially when you favour the pub culture to sitting indoors alone. I was, as The Beautiful South so perfectly put it, just a social drinker, but social every night. So there was no way I could afford the travel to Edinburgh, let alone a three-night stay there, not knowing anyone from the circuit who might offer to put me up.

Fortunately Bev's sister, Sue, who ran a domiciliary care agency and tanning shop, in an extraordinary act of generosity, gave me £100 to go, calling it corporate sponsorship rather than the hand-out we both knew it to be.

I arranged to stay over in Glasgow with Cal Tanner, the St Helens lad who'd booked me back at college to play his club gig. On the night itself Cal, his flatmate, James'y Stuart and I caught the train over to Edinburgh, and the infamous Gilded Balloon.

There was very little pomp or ceremony to the heat. Every night that week a line-up of wannabe comics cramped into a small dressing room (or narrow corridor, if you opted to watch the other competitors), with eight minutes each in which to impress the judges.

I liked headspace and quiet before a gig to allow JOHNNY to prepare to take full possession of me. I'd had the foresight to get quite pissed earlier that afternoon before leaving, and had taken some cans along just to keep topped up on my nerves (although I was learning now that fully tanked wouldn't work).

'Shouldn't we go and watch with the others?'

'WHY, SO YOU CAN GET YER KNICKERS IN A TWIST OVER WHO YOU THINK MIGHT BE FUNNIER THAN US? FUCK THEM!'

'You've got the notes on what we're doing?'

'YES, I'VE READ THE NOTES. THE DAD STUFF'S ALL RIGHT. NOT TOO SURE ABOUT THE REST OF IT, MIGHT HAVE TO WING IT.'

'With what? This ain't the Citadel. This is like a proper gig! It's a big chance for us, this.'

'WELL, DO YOU NOT WANNA GO OUT AND DO IT THEN?'

'No, course not!'

'THEN SHUT UP AND LET ME THINK, WILL YOU? AND DON'T BE SICK!'

I was used to this. As JOHNNY'S confidence grew, HE would be less diplomatic about what bits of material would or wouldn't work, often making last-minute changes depending on the mood of the room, or ditching it altogether just as wE went on. But there was no denying HE was a natural, and the way HE spoke to me was just HIS way of psyching HIMSELF up for the gig.

All of this would be going on with me sitting, head bent over, virtually in the recommended flight-crash position, almost as if I was trying to kiss my arse goodbye. But this helped me avoid making eye contact with any of the other comics. JOHNNY wasn't keen on oUr befriending them: they were the enemy as far as HE was concerned, and it worried HIM that I might try and intervene if HE felt it necessary to go out there and tear them a new one. Plus, I'd heard it could reduce your chance of vomiting sitting like that, as it folded the entrance to the stomach. That, and slow, controlled breaths, and no deep gulps of booze.

Eventually, we were ushered out into the corridor as JOHNNy was the next on, and forced to watch a young guy finish what sounded like a very polished routine for a newcomer. But this was just a red rag to HiM.

'He'S ouΓS.'

As I took the short walk from the corridor to the stage, I slipped under HiS influence like a weak-minded office temp at a staff outing to see a hypnotist, and let VegaS go to work.

JAN 017/ 734
So You THinK YouR FuNNY

REQUIEM MASS

]

10th June 1930
to
18th July 1995

25th July 1995
St Mary's Lowe House

Subtle mum, real subtle. Perhaps this was her way of warning me of what lay ahead up in Edinburgh when taking down the contact details for 'So You Think You're Funny?'.

JOHNNY obliterated the competition, apparently, and I mean wiped the stage with them. Karen Koren, Edinburgh legend, matriarch and founder of the Gilded Balloon, would tell me years later that they were left in a state of near-shock afterwards. We were through to the final, and the judges had seen what they believed to be the odds-on favourite to walk away with the title.

And so myself and the boys went out and celebrated that night, and into the next day, and I didn't think to stop until the £100 that Sue had blessed me with was all but gone.

I'd presumed I'd borrow off the lads by the time the final came around, but everyone was skint, and we barely scraped enough together to cover train fares from Glasgow back to Edinburgh for the final.

This was an unholy and unmitigated disaster, my worst fears realised – the unimaginable nightmare prospect of going on stage sober. I evacuated every bit of bile from my stomach and crouched, dry-retching, in the train toilet. I was absolutely terrified. He wouldn't show without a blood–alcohol ratio of at least 50-50.

I wanted to explain to the lads that I didn't just fancy a drink; I *had* to have a fucking drink! But I was still trying to trade on the myth that JOHNNY's drunken amble was all an act and not wholly method.

As always, I'd made a complete new set of notes for the final gig. I still hadn't got it into my stupid head that comics had one tried and tested routine – bits of proven material drafted onto other bits. The problem being that I'd never seen any comic more than once, other than Terry Titter, who always did new stuff because he was a resident compère and, like myself, went out week after week and played with his captive audience. So I just presumed that every bit of material from a comic's head was being aired for the first time.

I tried to memorise what I'd written but there wasn't enough there to fill the allotted set time for the final, and what little there was wouldn't stick, anyway. He always fleshed out the weaker bits, or took it in a direction my comic aspirations hadn't even dreamed of. But, like *Futurama*'s robot Bender, He needed booze to function, to fuel HiS audacity, HiS rage. And I couldn't dream of hoping to impersonate that.

We were shown to a much bigger backstage area, as the final was to take place in the main auditorium. It felt huge and was packed to the rafters. I tried going through the motions, hunched over, but there was nobody pacing up there in my head.

'Oh, please, oh fuck, wake up, you useless sack of shit,' I thought to myself, but the desperation just echoed round my vacant brain.

Eddie Izzard, legend, hero, free-fall comedy genius of routines that had held me slack-jawed with awe, was to compère. But the fact that he was an inspirational figure didn't stop me from stealing his three bottles of beer rider backstage in a failed attempt to rouse my mentor. It didn't touch the sides as I necked them in the toilet whilst hearing a stage manager crossly enquiring as to where the hell Eddie's refreshments had gone.

I brought them straight back up not two minutes later. 'Small sips, remember?' I told myself, as the last drops of hope dripped out through my nose and into God's big white telephone.

I didn't meet Eddie before being introduced on stage. I couldn't think of a single appropriate word to say to him. I just hid in the corner until at last I heard HiS name announced out on stage.

I walked out there praying that JoHNNy was just playing a mean prank on me and would lean in to take the mic at the very last moment, saving the day with some spectacular last-minute stroke of comedic genius.

But at the end of the longest ten minutes of my life, it was painfully evident to me, and the whole of the Gilded Balloon audience sitting in awkward, toe-curling silence, that JoHNNy VegaS was a no-show.

I'd even stumbled over remembering HiS name. I tried to deliver his starter for ten – 'I'm not a comedian, I'm an entertainer', but the distinct lack of conviction stripped it of all impact or integrity, and it merely served as a warning for what was to follow, i.e. a minute or two of excruciating silence as I wandered my desolate head searching for those lost bullet points, like an Alzheimer's patient in an old folks home looking for the non-existent jewellery they swore the staff had helped themselves to.

Eventually, I pulled the scrap of paper with the bullet points on from my pocket, while claiming – somewhat unconvincingly – 'These aren't my notes; it's a letter from my mum!'

'For fuck's sake, you sound like Jimmy Cricket,' I thought to myself and screwed up the paper immediately, throwing it into the audience. Then another stretch of agonising silence followed as I realised I hadn't bothered to read the notes before tossing them away.

'I'm, erm, I'm sorry but, erm, actually, could I have those back, please?'

A bemused audience member scrabbled about their feet, retrieved the paper and threw it back at me.

During the eternity it took to retrieve them, I dared to scan the crowd for the first time. I picked out Bob Mortimer amidst a sea of disdainful punters, and other comedy giants dotted around the room. His awkwardness at the death rattle he was witnessing told me all I needed to know. I mumbled something and then simply stood and waited for the red flashing light to indicate that the shared torture was at an end.

I couldn't look at Eddie Izzard as I exited the stage, and I heard him struggling to justify the car crash, piss-poor, sorry excuse for supposed stand-up comedy that the room had just endured.

None of the other acts backstage could think of a word of encouragement that might help distract them or myself from the fact that I was just about the unfunniest thing anyone there that evening had ever seen. And yet the wankers running the show still insisted we all wait backstage and listen for the judges' verdict. I was there purely to serve as a reminder that the business of being funny was not for the faint-hearted.

And, for the first time ever, I explicitly wished that real death – rather than just the voice that lived in my head – would come and take me now.

Lee Mack walked away with that year's crown, and justifiably so. Rarely would I find a nicer, funnier fella than I could ever hope to lose to. Not that it mattered, anyway, because, truth be told, I'd already lost to myself that night.

'So you think you're Funny? I reckon the clue to the answer's in the question itself, don't you?'

I went home with my tail between my legs, a broken man with a very unhappy JoHNNy Vegas in tow. I had sullied HiS name by daring to step out there without him.

We made a pact to never, EVER go out on stage sober again.

Although I couldn't see it at the time, losing so spectacularly in that final was one of the best things that could've happened to uS. We had entered that competition as genuine new-comers, and no matter how raw yet brilliant a talent JoHNNy could be when at HiS best, we still had so much more to learn about the craft, and of ourSeLveS, before we'd be truly ready to take on the world beyond oUr north-west borders.

The way we saw it, I had ruined any chances of JoHNNy ever being taken seriously as a comic, or entertainer, by the industry itself. We would never now run with the heads of the pack, but that didn't deter Vegas.

'No More going cap-iN-HaNd to tHe MaSterS begging For acceptaNce. We buiLd WHat We do From tHe audieNce up, tHe oppoSite eNd oF tHe iNduStry eLite. We do it oUr Way, oUr ruLeS. We put oUr FaitH iN tHe peopLe, Not tHe coMedy puppet MaSterS. We do it For tHe croWd, Not tHe SHoWbiz KudoS.'

It's incredibly empowering to sincerely believe that you have nothing left to lose. And with that faith as our sure foundation, we set about getting oUr shit together and taking on the business of 'funny ha ha' oUr way.

There were still the monthly gigs in St Helens, but now we shared a real determination to work any room, anywhere that would have us.

To start with, this still meant working predominantly out of
the north west. I'd become pals with comedian Rob Heeney
through a gig he'd done at the Citadel, and he'd put me on to
a group working out of Liverpool called C.O.M.I.C. (Comedy On
Merseyside In Creation).

Their aim was to organise gigs that we would perform as solo
acts, but under the one uniting banner of C.O.M.I.C. In the
meantime, we would meet in rooms above pubs in Liverpool and
share ideas, help bolster each other's confidence and see how
we could all improve together as performers.

JOHNNY was still a lone wolf when it came to show time, but I
can't deny that the idea of having a group of like-minded comedians, all starting out at the grass-roots level, appealed to me.

It is possibly the loneliest profession of them all, even when
there are two of you.

The only problem was, and I'm sure Rob would back me up
here (after all, we both decided to quit the organisation together),
they were a bunch of bloody idiots: the dangerous, in denial,
self-congratulating kind of idiots who sat in rooms telling each
other how fabulous they all were – despite never having been
able to prove that to anyone under gig conditions – and whining
endlessly about the whys and hows of how and why they hadn't
become famous in their own right yet.

I did only two of the gigs they somehow cobbled together, one
of those being in the bar at Liverpool's Irish Centre. It was
a free gig because basically nobody would pay for what they
had to offer, and other than erecting a small banner behind the
microphone, it was business as usual as far as the grizzled Guinness and barley-wine-addled members were concerned.

Rob and I stood at the bar laughing at the shrill ineptitude of
our glorious leader and compère as she attempted to get the
room's attention and bless them all with a dreadful comedy
poem she had written. 'We are professionals, people; we are
artists! Now, is it too much to ask for a civilised bit of peace
and quiet whilst we present to you our free night of splendid
comedy entertainment?'

'What's that stupid cunt rattling on about?' We heard a drunk old guy at the bar mutter amongst the indifferent hubbub of folk on the piss. Rob and I knew we were on a hiding to nothing, but still he went out and got good laughs from a crowd that clearly couldn't be arsed with much else C.O.M.I.C had to offer.

Even JOHNNY acknowledged the hopelessness of the situation. But, as ever, He refused to go down without a fight. He had a fundamental belief – admirable, even if every now and then it proved to be misguided – that every gig was salvageable some-how. That there were laughs to be had, or He'd die trying, but not as I had done up in Edinburgh, because HIS deaths were born from a scruffy yet noble ideal, not born of fear or regret. There was nothing He wouldn't sacrifice in a bid to entertain HIS audience.

'TWo LittLe dUCKS, 22. THree aNd SeveN, 37!'

JOHNNY had tucked HIMSeLF away out of sight with the mic. He knew this kind of crowd, and he knew there were few things they respected more than a good, old-fashioned game of bingo.

'Nobody SWeatiNg For a LiNe yet? NiNe oH, top oF tHe SHop, bLiNd 90!'

The closest thing to silence you could hope for from that room descended as the panic set in and the punters thought they were missing out on a game.

Then JOHNNY pounced.

'Good eveNiNg, LadieS aNd geNtLeMeN ... I'M JOHNNY VegaS ...'

What followed was chaos – pure and beautiful, unadulterated VegaS carnage. The mob almost rioted when they realised they'd been had, but JOHNNY persisted in trying to play the crowd, cap-tive now, but for all the wrong reasons.

'BiNgo'S great, iNNit? THe Sport oF qUeeNS, aNd tHe oNLy Way My MaM WiLL ever oWN a giaNt ceraMic cHeetaH!'

'Ya fucking prick!'

'Silly cunt!'

'Was that a line or a full house?'

'WHat'S your WeapoN oF cHoice, darLiNg? Biro or bLocKer?'

'Tosser!'

There were times when even Vegas knew He was beat, but something in HIM refused to apologise. When the chips were down, HIS get-out strategy was something akin to *Highlander*'s villainous Kurgan, as in: 'I have something to say: it's better to burn out than to fade away!'

C.O.M.I.C.

Comedy On Merseyside In Creation

Dear Johnny Vegas,

Great anniversary show on the 4th Sept,it was a success. A lot of the audience thought you were brilliant. Each act got a share of the takings which after the running costs were deducted was £6,cheque enclosed. Many thanks.

Planning to open another comedy club in town soon we will keep you posted.

Yours sincerely,

Paul Oulton

That much money can do strange things to a person, hence how I can empathise with the fallout experienced by those on the receiving end of a Euro Millions lottery win.

And so JOHNNY dropped his flares to his ankles and skipped two laps of the dance floor as best he could whilst belting out Neil Diamond's 'Forever in Blue Jeans' before pulling up his trousers, exclaiming, 'THIS WAS NOT a NIGHT OUT, IT WAS a MEMORY!' and walking out of the door.

I think the only thing that stopped uS from getting a good pasting that night was the crowd's belief that they were possibly witnessing somebody in the throws of a mental breakdown.

Rob and I decided we would get nowhere tying our colours to that mast, and although we stayed pals and caught up often, we went off in search of gigs on our own.

30.

THE OLD FROG

Manchester, however, proved itself a much richer hunting ground. I rang up Manchester's Frog and Bucket chasing an open spot with the club's owner, Dave Perkins. He offered me a full, 20-minute spot for a Friday or Saturday night there and then on the phone. To this day, I reckon it was down to a case of mistaken identity, as Dave seemed sure he'd remembered me from an open spot I didn't think I'd done for him. All he asked for was a free 10 the week before to help refresh his memory of the act.

Of course, promoters wanted to see a sample of what you could do before offering a paid spot: their club's reputation stood or fell by the quality of the acts up on their stage. They'd heard it a hundred times before – folk who were kidding themselves and in dire need of a reality check, yammering away about how they were the next big thing waiting to be discovered. They understood that there's a country mile between talking the talk in your head, or down a telephone, and walking the walk out there on the mic.

I wasn't the best self-promoter going, but at least now I had complete and utter determination to spread the gospel according to Vegas. He became restless when We weren't gigging, but although my telephone voice might've lacked some of the forcefulness of HⁱS convictions, even Hᵉ agreed that my hit and miss diplomacy had more chance of guaranteeing a call back than HⁱM belting out, 'King of the Road' down someone's answer phone.

I think it's obvious from the homemade business card that I really needed the services of Big Eye Film and Television management.

Still, when you're on the phone to a new promoter, saying you've got full, paid-up spots under your belt can make a world of difference with regard to being taken seriously, and Dave offering that to me meant J⁰HNNʸ by-passed a huge chunk of dues-paying on the Manchester circuit.

The Old Frog, as regulars referred to it, was (and still is – albeit now on different premises), a Manchester stand-up institution. A tiny, shoebox-shaped boozer with a small stage backed up against one of the long walls facing a bar not more than 10 or 15 yards away, it got absolutely rammed come a Friday/Saturday night. The punters were shoehorned in, filling every conceivable bit of space and seated so close to the stage you could smell what they'd had for their tea before coming out.

The Frog and Bucket was host to Manchester's finest in the mid/late nineties: Jason Cook, Lucy Porter, Chris Addison, Martin Bigpig, Dave Gorman, Smug Roberts and Tony Burgess. I can't tell you who compèred the night of that first open spot because I hid in the small cellar/dressing room until I was called up. (You know the routine by now: small sips, slow breaths, no puking.)

I could never talk to anyone before gigs, and I didn't want to watch the compère because I didn't want HiM going after their set. Not lifting it – i.e. copying – but riffing from it. Originality was an ethic I'd inherited from art school, and He had no interest whatsoever in mimicking other acts, but He loved to play and was constantly drawn to pointing out splits in the road of life that separated HiM from anyone else He shared a stage with. These were the differences He believed made uS unique.

I'd worked hard on a rough set and was determined JoHNNy should at least try and stick to the plan if the crowd went with it. We'd be back there in a week all being well, and I didn't want VegaS ruffling the feathers of folk I was desperate to work alongside. So I sat on a beer-keg trying to run the bullet points over and over in my head like a mantra. I'd have no control once He took to the stage, but I could at least try and impress on HiM how important this was to me.

'I'm JoHNNy VegaS.'

'I KNoW My NaMe.'

After Edinburgh, we're taking no chances. Next, 'Not a comedian/entertainer/don't do jokes, don't do gags, don't say "Do you

know what it's like when this happens", "Do you know what it's
like when that happens", you've no idea what it's like to be me!
Kicked out for saying, "Dad"—'

'Pause there, that's the first laugh, a big 'un. The false lead.'

'I know! I'm just running it shorthand. Shit, where was I?
Shit, shit, shit, give us a sip of that [sip].'

'"Dad"?'

'Yeah, "Dad–pause–when I grow up I wanna be a potter!"
Shit, how long till we're on?'

'We?'

'You, fucking you, all right. Are they ready for you, yet?

'I doubt it.'

'Well, take a look … no, don't! Don't watch, stick to the plan.
Right, shit, where were we … hey, what do you do if you get
stuck?'

'Stuck?'

'On any of this, if you can't bridge it, what do you do?'

'Cut to a song.'

'Good, yeah, buy some time, regroup. Don't go off on one!'

'"Love Boat"'

'That's lame, it's not sing-along, hardly anyone knows it!'

'I like it! The obscurity's funny. Anyhow, it's a stop-gap, not
a sing-along.'

'Whatever, right, next, shit [sip]. "Potter, not a joke love, pottery was my life" … Are you listening?'

'Shush, listen … compère's back on. It's show time!'

'Shit, we're not ready [sip]. Shit, shit, shit [sip sip sip].'

I would never be ready, but JOHNNY VegaS would always be
chomping at the bit. This body that we both inhabited was like
a single bike given to twins at Christmas to share. I used it
for the more mundane day-to-day stuff – going to school or the
shops – but when it was JOHNNY's turn, he went out and per-
formed all the daring, dangerous stunts that made the other kids
go 'Wow!'. I suppose I should've been jealous, but then to the
untrained eye We were identical, so whilst He relished the risks,
I shared in all HiS glory.

JOHNNY stormed the 10-spot that night, and the two 20-spots the following week. Dave was quick to offer uS other spots, and not months apart, like other venues.

Now, what wᵉ had going at the Citadel was already something special, something unique: an amazing line-up of acts already well established on the national circuit, not just the north west. But, ultimately, it was JOHNNY's stamping ground, a club of HⁱS own where Hᵉ made the rules without anyone to answer to, where Hᵉ could try anything knowing Hᵉ had the support of a home-grown crowd who would stick with Us no matter how unorthodox HⁱS approach to comedy. But the Frog and Bucket was an established club where wᵉ could lift and polish the best bits of the Citadel nights in order to try and win over a crowd that, despite the handful of regular die-hards, had a large turnover of new faces each week.

Things really started shaping up, and JOHNNY's biog filled out to explain the naff flares and 70s jacket from a bygone age that We had stumbled across by accident.

Again, drawing from what I knew but with HⁱM exaggerating the facts wildly, wᵉ decided that Hᵉ had been a star, a legend in HⁱS own right back in the golden days of British holidays, Butlin's holiday camps and their legendary Red Coats. Despite HⁱS idolisation of Billy Butlin and the ethos of family fun, JOHNNY had left to become a star in HⁱS own right, but the press had destroyed him over a scandal that to this day Hᵉ was too bitter to discuss.

This helped explain HⁱS love of sing-alongs, bingo, etc, plus having never holidayed anywhere else as a kid but appreciating how naff a destination it was considered by the middle-class Center Parcs/Costa del Sol crowd, it appealed to my lingering inverted snobbery from my college days.

Looking back now, I think maybe this aspect of his back-story was a mutual attempt at papering over the cracks left in oUr psyche by Upholland. Or perhaps it was just a hang-over from the 'So You Think You're Funny?' disaster, reflecting a general disdain for, and mistrust of, the comedy establishment and the wrecking of oUr showbiz ambitions the first time round.

But if it had been simply a case of the latter, I'm sure JoHNNy would have wanted to expose this raw nerve and seek revenge on those who had inflicted the wound upon uS. (God, this book's a real head-wrecker when trying to make sense of all this stuff.) At the time, though, it all just seemed to fit into place; it made complete sense to uS, somehow. And we felt like masters of oUr own destiny now.

Although JoHNNy had *carte blanche* on stage, it felt like you had to earn your place on the team at the Frog, and I loved the camaraderie with the other acts once the nauseating torment of the build-up had passed and HiS gig was over. I enjoyed the sense of belonging to this group; despite VegaS's lone-wolf, competitive mentality, I still needed to be liked.

But, DEATH still hovered and, despite the fact that I finally felt we were achieving something admirable and worthwhile with oUr life, the sadness of the inevitability of my latest terminal disease still taunted uS.

'Stomach cancer, for definite. You can't throw up three times in one day without it being stomach cancer.'

'You said that last year! It's the nerves, that's all.'

'Or a perforated ulcer at the very best? You're probably bleeding out right now!'

'Well, then how come I'm fine once He gets up there?'

'YeaH, yoU teLL HiM!'

'What was that?'

'NotHiNg ...'

'You leave HiM be! I need JoHNNy in good shape for later!'

'CANCER, ULCER, CANCERATED ULCER, STOMACH CANCER!'

'See yoU Later.'

'Nice one, you! We needed to go through stuff for tonight!'

'But you're dying! Lay off the Guinness and Gaviscon and let's talk symptoms.'

'I know we're bloody dying, but can't you just let uS get on with this first?'

'I saw blood in your bile earlier!'

[Guinness-sip] 'Get out!' [Gaviscon-sip]

'You won't even look at your stools any more.'

[Guinness-sip] 'It's not natural.'

'Not that there's much to look at. You hardly eat nowadays. Loss of appetite … CANCER!'

[Guinness-risky-big-gulp] 'Bye!' [Gaviscon-sip]

'Is it safe? Right, where were we?'

'Erm … "Love's a postman"?'

'"But you've a vicious dog called pride" …'

'And unless you tie that thing up, you'll never get your mail!'

' … Spelt M–A–L–E!'

'Nice touch!'

As JOHNNY's reputation grew, He'd got marginally braver with regards to DEATH, having slight digs at him when the resentment of his ability to distract uS from the cause got too much for HiM, but ultimately I was HiS best defence against the inevitable spectre.

It was exhausting at times up there in oUr head, and as much as I loved the black gold and occasional Smirnoff that my extra income now afforded me, there were times when my pickled innards had to rest and inevitably spend quality time with him. That's why I appreciated the new-found friends I was making on the circuit. They were more than a mere distraction from The End, or much needed emotional support away from HiS exhausting buzz of 10, 20, 30 or 40 minutes on stage. They were like-minded folk who understood how things worked up there, despite them not having a brain split in three. And they too seemed in no great rush to head home and off to bed. I had other friends, but they had day jobs, commitments; their drinking and socialising were largely limited to weekends and nightclub hours, whereas this felt like a learning curve that regularly dared to break curfew and defy normal folks' need to obey their body clock.

I'll always be indebted to Tony Burgess for the hard-earned wisdom he'd gained from years out on the national circuit that he was so willing to share with me. As part of the Manchester comedy scene we were all comrades, but everyone had their own quiet agenda for breaking out of there, a plan that no one else was privy to. Yet with highly unusual and sincere, selfless, non-competitive gestures Tony mentored me, rather than treat uS as someone poised to steal his share of the crust from an ever-dwindling loaf of laughter.

'There's a few don't like you round here, that don't like what you're up to. They reckon it's not proper stand-up, that it cheapens what they do. But fuck 'em! They're scared, they should be. And it's your job to carry on scaring 'em!'

You have to remember that, starting out, not all gigs went to plan. HiS odds improved with set lines, a loose narrative, but JoHNNy was still a highly volatile character, an unknown quantity in many ways, and there were often times when HiS walking the line between tragedy and comedy fell flat on its arse in the tragedy section.

He had no problem dealing with hecklers – the Brown Edge had been all the training one could ever wish for when dealing with criticism based purely on name-calling, and JoHNNy relished verbal jousting with the smarter arses. But when things went completely wrong it was usually a misinterpretation, or even denial on HiS part that some gigs just didn't belong to HiM, that it wasn't going to be oUr night, and without a fully formed arsenal of fallbacks within the fledgling routine, JoHNNy could implode. And in those early days, He was happy to lie low afterwards and leave me to deal with the consequences.

As well as things were going in the north, I was still struggling to get JoHNNy gigs elsewhere, but especially in London. The vicious cycle continued of not being able to secure an open spot because many of the promoters wouldn't book HiM unless they'd seen HiM, but how the hell was He supposed to get seen unless they booked HiM in the first place?

In another unbelievable stroke of generosity, Hugh took a gamble on one more open spot at the King's Head in Crouch End. JoHNNy repaid his faith with a stormer.

Sadly, the same could not be said of HiS debut at Malcolm Hardee's infamous Greenwich comedy club Up The Creek. JoHNNy died, and got HiS arse royally kicked up and down that stage in the process.

He was used to an audience finding HiM initially intimidating before the pity kicked in, but the crowd there simply didn't give a shit about the raw deal from life He was so desperate to rant about. The Creek was an unlikely alliance of working men's club yobbos and well-informed student comedy aficionados who, when working together as a team, made for a force to be reckoned with. Loud objection or silent rejection, it all proved too much for Butlin's' finest, and JoHNNy limped off stage like a Center Parcs refugee.

Whilst heading back to the dressing room, I was stopped near the bar by Malcolm – the club's legendary compère and a character the likes of which I doubt stand-up will ever see again (comedy has certainly not been half as colourful or ingeniously devil-may-care since his untimely passing). He was standing with his wife and promoter at the time, Jane Hardy, and the next act up after the break, Ricky Grover.

'Oi, oi, that was shit! Huh huh huh.'

Great, the last thing I needed after an arse-kicking was a pistol-whipping from a gang of Cockney promoters. Just like Edinburgh all fucking over again.

'Yeah, look, I'm sorry. I dunno what went wrong.'

'You fucking died, simple, huh huh! Wanna drink?'

'Erm, yeah, pint please.'

At that point, Jane interjected. 'We'd like you to come and die for us again on a full spot.'

'You're kidding?'

'You stood your ground, didn't apologise for being up there. Too many character comics drop the act and start trying to explain what it is they're trying to do when it's not going their way, but not you, and we like that here.'

Malcolm handed me a pint and went out to introduce Ricky, which involved approaching a heckler who'd given JoHNNy nothing but grief from the second He'd got up there, but who had since fallen asleep against the pushbike he'd brought into the club with him. Malcolm removed the heckler's hat, took it to the stage and pissed in it before tipping it out again into a nearby empty pint glass, taking it back to the heckler and waking him saying, 'Oi, oi, you dropped your hat.'

'Ah, thanksh, pal. They'll nick faaahkin anyfink araaaand 'ere.'

Ricky looked at me. 'You gotta take the fight to them here, John. They'll happily dish it out – you just make sure you get the digs in first, mush, trust me. They'll respect you more for slapping 'em down and hitting 'em where it hurts.' And Ricky took the stage, tore the room a new one and, just as he'd predicted, they loved him for it.

The Creek instantly became one of those clubs outside the north west that when I played there, I still felt I was home.

I have to be so careful writing this. There can never be enough pages to tell the story in the detail that I'd like, and it's all too easy to neglect crediting the goodwill and encouragement shown to JOHNNY as an unknown – and an outsider through HIS own choice – by so many fantastic comics and club owners along the way.

Caroline Aherne, who along with her long time co-star and co-writer Craig Cash, regularly attended shows at Stan Vernon's tiny yet unmissable gig, the Laughter Lounge, as well as The Frog. Both sat amongst the crowd with no airs or graces whatsoever. They were so unbelievably generous with help and advice, despite JOHNNY not being able to resist a friendly dig from the stage upon their first meeting in a desperate bid to hide the fact that he too was just that little bit star struck.

'Look at ya, sitting there, pulling that "just pretend I'm not here, even though you all know me from the telly" face. But if ya didn't want folk clocking ya, why sit right up at the front eh? Eh? Coming here and dangling yer success in the face of jobbing comics like a lottery winner opting to go back to work.'

Henry Normal, Caroline's producer, whose earnest and sincere advice I wish I'd heeded and recorded all those early shows, despite JOHNNY'S protestations. Mick Davies's The Rubber Chicken in Bradford; Stewart Lee and Simon Munnery's Cluub Zarathustra, down in London; The Stand in Edinburgh run by the true socialist Tommy Shepherd ... hopefully these and other stalwart supporters won't mind Mr Hardee staggering up to the microphone to accept an award of my thanks on their behalf.

Many years later, at Malcolm's funeral, I was taken aside by a promoter from somewhere up in the north east who told me, 'Do you know, the very first time after yoU'd played his club, he called me next day, he called everyone he knew. He said "There's this new lad, JoHNNy VegaS, and you have to book HiM. There's nothing out there like it."'

Malcolm had never said a word to me about it though, the beautiful, sly, old bastard. As my gratitude slept, he'd simply removed my flat cap of self-congratulation and sprinkled it with Hardee magic.

Apart from this precious exception, many of the established London clubs seemed out of bounds at the time. Having said that, JoHNNy did also refuse to play certain clubs that He felt weren't right for HiM.

Don Ward had generously opened his doors at The Comedy Store to uS, but having eventually played the open spot there that had been offered way back at Middlesex, JoHNNy refused point-blank to go back. And after I kindly accepted well-meaning advice from comics backstage at Jongleurs, Camden Lock – fearful on my behalf of the consequences of not sticking rigidly to the minutes allotted for the open spot, or failing to keep the material 'crowd friendly' enough that the bar manager might score us high enough to warrant a return booking – VegaS saw red.

I can't say I blamed HiM. I, too, was demoralised by the notion of having the parameters of oUr craft dictated to us by a pen-pusher: not a well-meaning promoter, but a face in a suit whose primary concern – it seemed to Us – was shifting food and booze whilst relegating the artists to mere side-show lackeys.

So JoHNNy took to the stage and did HiS thing until the warning light flashed to command HiM to wrap things up. At this point, he entered into a full and unnecessarily long ren-dition of 'The Love Boat'. It was the politest two fingers to the

Establishment **H**e could muster. Afterwards, **W**e grabbed our stuff, said a quick goodbye to the paid spots and left.

At the back of the club we were stopped by a smarmy manager playing it nonchalant with, 'Mmm, yes, well, you did okay, I suppose. We might consider giving you a try at one of the late shows – see how you handle that crowd?'

'**D**o**N**'t b**o**t**H**e**r**,' **J**o**HNN**y answered, before I could get a word in, '**I**'**LL** N**o**t b**e** b**a**c**K**.'

Then **W**e left. And **J**o**HNN**y never, ever set foot in one of their clubs again. That chain was renowned for being able to fill a huge quota of a stand-up's working diary in their heyday, and they paid well, but no matter how uncertain o**U**r future in the business might be, w**e** both knew that **W**e couldn't be the u**S W**e were striving to be by working for the Man.

The north west definitely felt like home turf to u**S**. On the night of **J**o**HNN**y'**S** first open spot at another legendary Manchester comedy club, The Buzz in Chorlton, Bev convinced her sister Sue and pals to pull their whole coachload over on its way to a hen night and catch the show. Now, the wonderful Agraman – 'the human anagram' who booked the acts there – had a great eye for talent, and, like all promoters, he was also a canny businessman. The minute he thought I had a coachload of fans who followed me from gig to gig, he virtually offered a paid follow-up spot before **H**e'd even set foot onstage.

Of course, **J**o**HNN**y overran horribly after an impromptu lap dance, trying to goad a guy into an arm-wrestling match and insisting on singing 'American Pie' in its entirety. But Agraman still booked **H**i**M** and suggested **H**e enter the Northwest Comedian of the Year competition (past winners included Caroline Aherne, Dave Spikey and Chris Addison).

Jo**HNN**y sailed the heat and was quickly in the 1996 final. The 'So You Think You're Funny?' experience had apparently left no mark on him (probably because **H**e never actually bloody turned up for that exercise in silent torture). Once again, **H**e was hot favourite to go on and win as far as whispers on the grapevine were concerned.

The only problem was, nobody had bothered whispering the name of Peter Kay. He hadn't shared a bill with Peter before that night and, truth be told – despite my growing obsession with the Manchester comedy scene – I hadn't heard of him. But he came from nowhere that night at the Palace Hotel and stormed it: stole the show and won.

I never actually got to see him that night because I was busy backstage trying to coax JOHNNY into doing a magnanimous acceptance speech that was under 30 minutes. But what amazed me afterwards was HIS indifference to Peter winning. He just seemed happy HIS own set had gone well. I, on the other hand, was gutted, once the shock had worn off. Especially as a bottle of Bells whisky the size of my mum (one of the few women Janette Crankie could comfortably check for head lice whilst both standing up – not that she'd have to) had been thrown in as part of the prize via the sponsors. My siblings had been in regular attendance at the Citadel, but to my folks this whole comedy malarkey was a mystery, a fad just like the priesthood and the pottery, but the onstage transformation from me to HIM was something I was more than happy to keep them blissfully ignorant of. Still, had I walked in with that year's supply of Scotch, then all my past disappointments would've been forgotten in the clink of a pint-sized hot toddy.

But in that cloud of abject disappointment, there was indeed a silver lining in the form of Steve Locke and Mary Richmond, a husband and wife team who ran Big Eye Television Productions out of Manchester. They were looking to get into talent management and JOHNNY had caught their eye at the final. It was their drive and ambition that would help stop Us resting on our laurels and set JOHNNY's sights a bit higher than our old scrawled sign from the Citadel reading: 'Will Gig For Free Beer.'

The night of JOHNNY's first one man show at The Frog was another big breakthrough: to carry a full evening's entertainment so early on in my career without any guests to share the time with, and on so little material ...? That suddenly seemed like career suicide to me, and just when things were looking up for uS for once.

At teatime on the day of the gig, I was desperately running round looking for props, outfits, anything that might fill time here or there, or inspire some acceptable stream of consciousness from JoHNNy. Then I realised I had this old kick-wheel that I'd 'borrowed' from college. Although He'd raged on my behalf about pottery, there was never any plan to actually introduce it into the act. But in sheer panic, we bundled the wheel into the back of Bev's car and thought it might just help pass five minutes if things got that desperate – anything to extend the gig and hide just how pitifully unprepared either of uS were for oUr first one man show.

The show pulled a much larger crowd than either JoHNNy or I had expected, which didn't help the nerves. Scribble, sip, scribble, sip was the build-up with all the junk I'd dragged from home dumped unceremoniously backstage. The night ended up a pure comedy free fall. He burned through the set way too quickly and as usual didn't bother with any of the suggestions I'd written down. Luckily, though, He loved working the room back to a point of trust after something bombed. But all else paled into improvised insignificance the moment He decided to drag the wheel onstage.

It proved itself a genuine revelation. I'd never dare compare VegaS to Les Dawson, but as with the legendary Mancunian's superb out-of-tune piano playing, JoHNNy had inadvertently stumbled across a great comic prop the moment he sat astride that wheel – something unique to Us and (although this was not a word often associated with him) something beautiful, in an odd kind of way.

The joy of the potter's wheel was the trance-like state it put the crowd into. You could have a rowdy, mad, jeering audience, but even the biggest piss-heads and the meanest-looking blokes would suddenly settle, utterly mesmerised when JoHNNy began throwing a pot. It was like time stood still. And the maddest thing of all was that this was the only time it ever felt like I was up there on the stage with JoHNNy.

He had all the natural comic timing, the ferocity, the vulnerability, and the indestructible self-confidence to make the act work, but this was something **H**e could only do through me. It was the only time I felt like I got to look out and meet the audience's stare myself, and not feel utterly terrified; to share in the quiet buzz of their appreciation first hand. I know how lame that sounds, but it's true.

I could never have anticipated the impact it would have. To see this sweaty, shouty bloke sit down and create this thing of beauty gave **J**o**HNN**y layers. It endowed **H**i**M** with a fragility. For a character piece, it was a big turning point – it showed the audience that here was a man who had the potential to be wonderful, gentle and human, but somehow life and disappointment and pain and booze had got in the way and produced **J**o**HNN**y instead.

This not only validated all the rage and disappointment on an emotional level, it also turned the notion of **J**o**HNN**y being just a character comic on its head. **H**e wasn't just ranting about pottery for comic effect, because the audience was witnessing first hand **H**i**S** accomplished craftsmanship. And that in turn led them to think, 'Well, if the pottery is real, surely everything must be?' It made the rest of it seem plausible (even though the timeline was impossible, as **J**o**HNN**y couldn't have been a Red Coat in the 1970s – **H**e'd have only been two years old back then). But the wheel created a massive leap of suspended disbelief. It made **H**i**M** real in the eyes of the crowd. Not just loud and unnerving, but a fully fleshed out and very real human being.

Of course **J**o**HNN**y would also play it for laughs, and climbing on the wheel whilst belting out 'New York, New York' was a sight to behold in itself. Drafting in a send-up of *Ghost* also became a comedy staple: the instant audience recognition when the Righteous Brothers' music struck up was pure gold, and playing out that iconic pottery scene was too good a comedy cow not to be milked, while still retaining the classic sad clown vulnerability that took an audience from liking **J**o**HNN**y, to loving **H**i**M**.

The Frog and Bucket was definitely my favourite base of operations. That's why I no longer worried if **J**o**HNN**y's reputation made it south of Birmingham, because we'd found our spiritual home, our, 'If you build it they will come' comedic field of dreams. Think it, try it, take the risk and trust in the crowd to go along with you on it.

Keen to build on the foundations we'd already laid, Steve and Mary booked me in to do a new show every month. Peter Kay and I actually teamed up for the first few of them. We knocked ideas about around a general theme, and he and JOHNNY ran them as sort of loose, elongated sketches. Peter and I got on really well at first, as I think we were both seen as 'impure' by some acts rather than 'real' alternative stand-up, and that gave us a common cause. But both JOHNNY and Peter were too strong-willed and had too clear an idea of where they saw themselves going individually to ever really successfully pool their talents in the long run.

Our brief collaboration went out with a bang the night Steve Coogan came along to watch. There was a real buzz in the room as word spread that the homegrown legend himself was in (no doubt tipped off by his long-term friend and creative partner, Henry Normal, who'd been there at the first solo show night).

The theme for that night was election-fever with JOHNNY running for office, and after several 'skits' Peter was going to assassinate HIM. We had banners and badges printed American-style and the room looked amazing but, as the show went on, our comedy sparring partner went right off the script. As JOHNNY realised there was no pulling the show back, the audience was treated to what I would immodestly suggest was one of the best nights of stand-up they would ever see, as Peter and Vegas tore verbal lumps out of each other. One comic, one entertainer, both on top form, virtually going toe to toe in the comedy equivalent of a rap battle.

Afterwards, Coogan came backstage and said, 'Well done, that was amazing!' which should've been a huge confidence/ego boost for the pair of us. But when he added, 'You're one of the best double acts I've seen' I reckon it confirmed what we both already knew: it was over. 'We're not a double act!' blurted JOHNNY, making a rare offstage announcement, and with both Peter and

JOHNNY quietly confident in their own individual talents, there was no fearing the future as confirmed comedy bachelors.

Apart from anything else, things were finally looking up in terms of attention from the opposite sex. Now, having already revisited the embarrassingly scant list of romantic and/or sexual disasters in ego-crushing detail earlier in the book, I hope you can appreciate why, at the age of 26, I had written off any notion of one day finding love: stand-up had become our joint obsession, and it left little room for a mistress. Besides, the deeply embedded fear of my inexperience and general ineptitude when it came to the art of love meant that despite JOHNNY's brazen flirtations with women on stage, I, Michael Pennington, had become petrified of the notion of a physical relationship.

But fame – for want of a better word, even on the scale of local notoriety

**Johnny Vegas –
Edinburgh Preview Show**

The Frog & Bucket, Wednesday 25 June

It's a pleasure to have lost count of the number of times that I've sat at the back of a room full of singing, laughing, chanting people, as show-biz legend Johnny Vegas cleverly and shamelessly moulds his act round an audience. This free-form stylee means that every show is different and this one, his Edinburgh Preview show, is especially different.

Tonight is only the second airing of the show, but even in its foetal stages it has a harder kick than many other shows which will pop up in Edinburgh. It's not unusual for Johnny to sit astride the fence that divides fantasy and reality and put on quite a curious show, but this time he seems to have kicked off the sign that tells you which side is which.

It gradually becomes apparent that there is more than a grain of truth in his banter. As the show progresses, his jokes begin to come to life, like the dancing Disney mops and buckets in *Fantasia*, but in this case they take the form of teapots and vases. With the help of a potter's wheel, a pint of Guinness and the question 'what do you want love, a mug or a jug?', he creates some of the most unique comedy and pottery you'll ever see.

Although every Vegas show is different, they all invariably end in the same way, with the audience drained as Johnny leaves the stage to the strains of his favourite tune, that of the laughter and cheers of his public.

CARL COOPER

Mainstream Yorkshire comic who's popular with the pensioners and the kiddies, but like a number of his contemporaries, has a parallel career telling mucky gags and being generally offensive. It doesn't make him any funnier, though. Tameside Hippodrome, 8pm. £9, £8.

MONDAY 16

■ Raw - Long-running and popular open mic night, compered throughout June by Johnny Vegas (see Wednesday 25, for details). A on the north west comedy circuit – was a powerful aphrodisiac. With comics, there is that added reasoning that women like a man who can make them laugh, but I'd be a liar if I tried to deny that getting up on stage didn't eventually bring with it the prospect of exchanged phone numbers and casual one-night stands.

The blokes didn't like it though – especially the ones who'd spent years pulling in nightclubs as I'd sat nursing a pint throughout the slow dances – and they had no problem vocalising their disdain at the prospect of a fat bloke actually managing to attract the attention of women whom they clearly thought were out of JOHNNY's league.

'All these women here, yeah? Well, they're only talking to you because you're on stage.'

'Yeah,' I'd reply. 'And they'd only ordinarily be talking to you because of your 28-inch waistline and Action Man jaw line. So what's your beef with me playing to my own strengths?'

Neither HIS burgeoning fanbase nor new-found detractors could've known that behind that permed lothario VegaS, there hid a frightened eunuch with all the sexual maturity and know-how of a vacuum-sealed economy pack of bromide.

Yes, there were times when I'd walk through Church Square in St Helens, looking at couples going about their business of being in love and thinking, 'The whole world is on to something that I will never be part of.' But then another thought would usher it back into the 'You can't miss what you've never had' part of my brain, alongside the tennis career and a complete set of original, still-in-the-box *Star Wars* figures.

Then, one night at a small gig at the Old Frog and Bucket, just before they closed it, I'd met Jen. There was a tiny crowd in and once we got chatting afterwards, I found myself unusually at ease in her company. There was no notch on the bedpost attitude to her. There were comedy groupies out there who would state their intentions quite clearly in their mannerisms and tone of banter and they scared the life out of me, but she was just a sweet and really funny girl.

A good few dates followed, and after one too many drinks on an evening out, an impromptu stopover in a B&B was decided on (I'd later find out that she thought I had planned this beforehand, but sadly that wasn't the case). But, just like the out-of-date photos I'd been sending to Lynne back at West Park, the reality of my self-consciousness in relation to where our courtship was heading at that stage overwhelmed me, and my reluctance to take things any further was perfectly communicated by my faking going straight to sleep, facing the wall, whilst she freshened up in the tiny en-suite bathroom.

Nothing was said next day, but I could sense in Jen a tone of not so much disappointment, as more a feeling of surprise at my ending a wonderful evening so abruptly like that, with no explanation. I felt awful as it was clear just how much I liked her, in every sense of the word, and my feelings seemed to be genuinely reciprocated. But more awkward scenarios would follow, and I had a growing feeling of shame at my reluctance to open up and explain to her the causes of my sexual reticence, and guilt at making her feel that the blame for my problematic shyness might lay somehow at her feet.

I awoke one morning at my house after another night of frustrating heavy petting followed by fake yawns and awkward silences. I left her sleeping, cycled to the bakers in Thatto Heath to get some croissants as part of the new sophisticated-dating me, then took a detour through the park, sat down by the old bowling greens, and cried into my jumper out of pure frustration at myself. I had to go and break things off with Jen as it was so unfair of me to lead her on like this. She deserved better, she deserved a man. But the hardest part about that prospect was the fact that I'd decided she at least deserved an honest explanation.

I got back to the house I was renting on Howard Street and Jen was already up and sitting on my couch (well, a mattress leant against the wall to create an L-shape – I hadn't yet got around to buying furniture as it seemed a luxury too far for a man destined to live alone, and I still couldn't quite bring myself to trust in there being any longevity to our chosen career path).

God, I was dreading what was to follow more than any gig I'd ever done. But, as I tried to break up with Jen, I found myself telling her everything I'd carried round within my own troubled soul for years. It was like going to Confession as a kid as out poured all my angst, my frustrations, my past disasters and my current fears regarding my inexperience and just how much I liked her but was too scared to risk disappointing her. All the while I was expecting her to get her coat and leave, or burst out laughing in a fit of nervous tension. But she didn't, bless her. She simply sat and listened and eventually admitted that although she was fully aware there was a problem somewhere within this wonderful time we'd been having, she was actually just relieved that the trouble didn't lie with her. There was no scorn, or ridicule, let alone breaking up. Just a decision to take things at a pace that we were both comfortable with, and a promise to be honest with each other if things didn't work out that way for us.

We dragged the mattress into the middle of the room, lay down and, thanks to the fact that it was mid-morning and there was no excuse for fake snoring, finally embarked on a loving, consummated relationship as boyfriend and girlfriend.

If I were wine, then I couldn't recommend the Pennington/ VegaS '97 vintage highly enough. Things were going great for both of uS. I was completely loved up with a fantastic girlfriend who not only wasn't restricted to pen-pal status, but also really made me laugh and brought me out of myself. Even JoHNNy liked her! (Not in that way.) There were no 'Oh no Yoko Ono' issues, and so He happily left me to get on with my life away from the stage as she left HiM to get on with HiS own upon it.

Going to the Edinburgh Festival was the next big challenge Steve and Mary had in mind for uS. Material wasn't a problem – after all the monthly shows we'd done, it was just a simple case of cherry-picking the best bits to put in. In fact, the bigger problem would be how to fit in everything We wanted into just one hour. The genuine concern now for me would be the lack of recuperation time. The vast majority of gigs up to then had been restricted to Thursdays through to Sundays, with a good three days off to eat and keep it down. But with the prospect of Edinburgh's thirty or so consecutive shows, for the first time ever, **DEATH** was actually starting to make sense. In fact, **his** grisly predictions were now interwoven with factual updates that were, no matter how much I drank, undeniable, and I now was actually taking heed of **his** concerns knowing that **he** had a point. This time, it wasn't just all in my head.

What I didn't know was just how much this was royally pissing off **JOHNNY**. Ordinarily, **He**'d run a mile when **he** wanted words, but now it was getting serious. **He** threatened to put the brakes on Edinburgh altogether: a fate worse than **DEATH** as far as **JOHNNY** was concerned. And so it was, at 5 a.m. on a Sunday morning, whilst sitting in the back of a cab on my way home from a lock-in at the Frog (after a 30-minute wander around Piccadilly Gardens had sobered me up a little), **he** sat down for a quiet natter. But, unbeknownst to either me or **him**, **JOHNNY** wanted in on this one.

'**Well, you certainly can't go to Edinburgh in the state you're in.**'

'I've not said either way, yet.'

'**But you're dying.**'

'I might not be. I might be all right.'

'**Well, if you want to agitate the stomach cancer, accelerate the diabetes, not get that MS checked out ...**'

'That's just DT's.'

'**No, it's not – you're dying. You know it, I know it. Have you told her yet?**'

'Shut the fuck up.'

'**I'm just saying, it's hardly fair on her you dying and not saying anything.**'

'I've not said I'm going yet, and you've been saying I'm dying for years and it hasn't bloody happened yet!'

And the thought genuinely did cross my mind: what if I *was* ill? What if I went up there and died and lost her? I mean I really, really liked her. In fact, I reckoned I loved her! Was all this Edinburgh stuff really worth making myself any more ill over?

'**But it will, you're dying.**'

'Shut up!'

'**No, don't, carry on.**'

'What?'

'Eh?'

'Go on, get on with it.'

'With what?'

'With telling him he's dying!'

'Well, he is.'

'Whose fucking side are you on?'

'He's what? Louder, he can't hear you.'

'Yes, I fucking can.'

'You're dying!'

'You're right!'

'What?'

'What?'

'I said, you're right, he's dying. You're dying!'

'No, I'm not, you wanker!'

'Yes, you are.'

'See?'

'See? Is that the best you can do? What are you expecting for "See"? Eh? A medal? A medal and a certificate for pointing out the one and only absolute unavoidable certainty that this life has to offer? You're dying? Bravo ... No, I mean it, come on everyone, up on your feet and let's give him a huge fucking round of applause. And the award for pointing out the obvious goes once again to ... oh yes ... well, it had to be ladies and gentlemen ... him! Guess what, he's right, you're dying and, not to be as unoriginal as him, but you've been dying since the day you were born. It's coming, at some point, for all of us – nobody's immune. YOU ARE DYING! But you've been dead before your time ever since you let this **PRICK** start whispering in your ear. You've woken up shitting your pants over a foregone conclusion now for as long as I can remember, and where's it got you, eh, where? All he's done is put you in an early grave when you could've been out, making the most of life in the meantime. Listen to me – you and I are gonna die, yes?'

'I suppose.'

'Sorry, I can't hear you – ?'

'YES, yes, I'm gonna die!'

'WeLL tHeN, WHy doN't yoU HUrry Up, accept tHat Fact, FUck him oFF aNd LIve a LIttLe bIt beFore tHat HappeNS? Live a Lot! WHy doN't yoU aNd Me go oUt WItH a big oLd baStard baNg, yeaH?'

'Yeah.'

'YEAH!'

'YEAH!'

'YeeeeeeeaaaaaH!'

'But...'

'But what? I'm dying!'

'Say it LoUd, Say it proUd.'

'I, Michael Pennington, AM FUCKING DYING!'

And, from that moment on, and right up to the present day, I never heard his voice in my head again. It might sound fantastical, but I swear to you that this is how it happened. My sober moments were never again haunted with the hypochondriac obsession of undiagnosed terminal illnesses. I had a normal fear of death from that moment on, although you could say oUr lifestyle from there on in actively went out and courted it, or at the very least We never bothered looking back to see if he'd bothered to follow Us. And I tell you this, what JoHNNy did for me that night, no matter what HIS ulterior motives might've been, was the single greatest act of kindness anyone besides my parents had ever shown me.

And so we caught the train to London and played a half-empty gig at the Aztec Comedy Club so Ed and Ian from the promoters, Stone Ranger, could take a look at JoHNNy for themselves. Quickly afterwards, a deal was done – a great deal I have to say, compared to recent years. Steve and Mary negotiated that we would not be liable for any potential losses from promoting VegaS up at The Fringe, but there would be a decent split if there were profits to be made. Photos were taken; posters, flyers and beer mats were printed; Jex agreed to take a leave of absence from sound tech-ing at the Frog and come with; and I said my fond, temporary goodbyes to Jen as we set about making oUr way to HIS date with destiny: the 1997 Edinburgh Festival.

PART V

JOHNNY TAKES OVER

31.

LET GO, LET JOHNNY

Oddly enough, the build-up to going to Edinburgh wasn't too dissimilar to the build-up to Upholland. I had no idea what I was letting myself in for, or how things worked. There was a lot of excitement going on around me. I felt again that familiar weight of expectation. It would get to me, but it wouldn't bother JOHNNY.

Plus by now we had Jex, our mutual lucky charm and laidback port in any storm. My new managers, Steve and Mary, would be up for the duration, with the full Stone Ranger team including Ian and Ed for back-up. All four would prove vital in managing the madness of the upcoming month away from the stage, but Jex was the closest thing we had to a sidekick. He was directly involved in the show itself and through working with him at the Frog, he had developed a sixth sense when it came to JOHNNY straying from the game plan and only hitting well-organised lighting/music cues whenever He damn well pleased.

'I sort of figured you weren't going to go into Wham at that point.'

'How's that?'

'You were stood on the table drinking Guinness out of that woman's boot.'

He liked the fact that Jex never bitched about HiM taking the initiative to throw something new in. He would mock-bollock him from the stage sometimes when it was obvious to the audience that the show had derailed completely from a tech point of view. But drawing him into the show and acknowledging HiS reliance on him – 'THiS iS WHy We Have MeetiNgS, JeX! WHere WaS you, eH? EH? OFF SoMeWHere proppiNg up a bar, or playiNg pooL? NoW, Let'S try tHat agaiN, SHaLL We? ANd a oNe aNd a tWo ...' – was JoHNNy's way of saying thank you. Plus an added dig at Mary, Steve and me for taking things way too seriously.

Without Jex, the mere suggestion of doing Edinburgh's month of uninterrupted gigs would've had me retching: gig days were still torture from a digestive point of view. Plus, I had no idea what the venue would be like. He might see any gig as a challenge, but He wouldn't deny there were rooms that had a 'feel' to them.

It was so strange going back to the Gilded Balloon. I had flashbacks from 'So You Think You're Funny?' passing by odd corridors and faces; I felt a proper shiver remembering how badly things had gone, the ghosts of that grizzly death coming back to haunt me. Although one blast from the miserable past was unmistakable: Karen Koren.

'Soooooo, Johnny Vegas, you're back? Hello again.'

'AgaiN? I doN't beLieve We've Met.'

'Shush ... Hi!'

'The '95 final, wasn't it?'

'Nope.'

'Yep.'

'Great shame, that.'

'Not For Me, it WaSN't.'

'I know.'

'And you had such a great heat.'

'THaNKS!'

'Yeah, well, you know.'

'Sooooo, looking forward to it?'

'Bit nervous, like, but yeah ...'

'CaN't FuCKiNg Wait!'

Karen *was* the Gilded Balloon, but once the fear of her seemingly gruff, no-nonsense persona passed, she would become one of my favourite people to prop up a bar with, post 'Late 'n' Live'.

Our venue, the Studio, seemed tiny on first impressions, but We were new to the whole Festival set-up. I didn't know then that this would be considered cavernous in comparison to some of the shoeboxes some other comics would be playing. He wasn't chuffed with the neat, tiered seating arrangement, but at least it was right up to the stage, as He liked it – nowhere to run, nowhere to hide for anyone – plus it had a good, low ceiling that would help make it comfortingly claustrophobic should the place ever fill up.

Jex and I checked into digs, and they were unbelievable – like something straight out of an *Elle Décor* shoot: all hip, bohemian and huge. Stone floors throughout, rugs, three couches in the lounge and matt white wooden shutters on the windows. The old art student in me instantly fell in love with the place.

We'd be sharing with Adam Bloom (a bloke utterly obsessed with comedy, and I mean obsessed, but, getting to know him over the upcoming month, I'd learn what a selfless, thoroughly sincere lad he was, not to mention a truly brilliant stand-up) and his tech, Neil (a bloody funny Irish lad with enough cheek and charm to woo a celibate lesbian, and a prolific drinker to boot).

If the digs were anything to go by, we were gonna have fun, one way or another.

But the sheer scale of the Festival and the names that attracted hadn't really struck home yet. The first day I walked around the Pleasance courtyard in dumb-struck awe: it was packed with comedians from every corner of the globe. I think it was the first time I realised what a complete comedy trainspotter I was. Everybody who was anybody was there. Heroes, villains, bloated telly legends and lean circuit wannabes; all of them living, breathing, obsessing, bitching, loving comedy.

I'm not being sycophantic when I say that I felt like a trespasser. This lot were the real deal, whereas I, Michael Pennington, suddenly felt like nothing more than an interloper;

a groupie who'd found himself clutching a backstage pass, desperate not to be mistaken for some giddy pundit. That's not false modesty: I was cacking my pants. It had finally hit home just how out of my depth I was.

But – and this was a BIG 'but' – buried deep within that wide-eyed innocence, beyond the coy acknowledgements of the great and good of stand-up, **He** was watching. And **JoHNNy** wanted nothing more than to tear each and every one of them a brand spanking new arsehole.

I loved comedy. I admired the craft. I never tired of analysing it either. That bit came naturally to me, like Rain Man counting cards in a casino, and I desperately wanted to be a part of that community. I wanted in so desperately, despite all **HiS** lone-wolf prowling but, ironically, the only way I felt I could achieve that was by letting **HiM** off the leash to dismantle everything **He** believed all other comedians stood for, everything I loved about them. **He** would make enemies of my heroes so that I might walk amongst them as an equal.

My time with Jen aside, as a grown-up I'd rarely been as happy as when I first arrived up there, yet **JoHNNy**'s muted belligerence screamed from within, pacing about up there, scheming, intent on wreaking havoc. **He** was the reliably confrontational fucker who'd pick the fights I'd always limped away from.

Jesus, even in this arena **He** was fearless. Whilst I was happy befriending other comics, **JoHNNy** was busy sizing them up. To **HiM**, these exchanges were like boxers weighing in before a championship bout. Of course there's a competitive element to stand-up, and nowhere more so than up at Edinburgh – a fact I'd learn once the shows got up and running. The odd friendship would sour over the coming month, what with unfavourable reviews, lack of bums on seats and especially the announcement of the Perrier Award nominations.

But in those first few days of the Festival, the politics just weren't an issue. It felt like the stand-up equivalent of Cilla Black's *Surprise, Surprise*, and everyone had been reunited as a family, of sorts, for one huge comedy get-together. And man, oh man, was I desperate to get right in there amongst the comedy huddle.

As far as **He** was concerned, though, it was chair-chucking, eye-gouging, full-on, 'Fuck you, bro!' *Jerry Springer*. The audience were the only people **JOHNNY** truly trusted. The real audience, I hasten to add, not the critics.

But as much as **He** was raring to get at 'em, I still had to get **HiM** out of my head and onto the stage. With none of life's usual day-to-day duties to contend with inside the Festival bubble, I was able to perfect an exact technical build-up to becoming **JOHNNY VegaS**. The show started at 10.45 p.m. I'd have to have eaten by 2 p.m. – after that, it was 100 per cent certain that anything I'd forced down would rebel and fight its way back up later. The age-old problem of getting enough booze into my system to 'give my **CreatioN** life' was worse than ever, especially out of the comfort zone of a familiar venue. And the fact that there were no midweek breaks once the rollercoaster started meant that nutrition was going to be a genuine problem.

I'd have a can of Guinness in the flat at 3 p.m., then I'd have a 45-minute bath (I'd stop taking a drink in there with me after throwing up in the tub once, whilst sitting in it). At 5 p.m. I'd sit down and have another can. 'Sips remember? No big gulps!' Then I'd break out the vodka. It had become a handy essential, as I could hit the right point of inebriation needed without having to try and keep down the huge quantities of stout required to hit that point of perfection.

I did genuinely consider the notion of putting it through a saline drip following a particularly bad session with an Assembly Rooms bin (sorry, Bill) – you know, just by-pass my gut altogether – but that would've been considered problem drinking by even the most seasoned of Festival hell-raisers. Besides, I didn't have the contacts or the medical know-how, and as much as Steve and Mary saw to it that I wanted for nothing up there, eyebrows would have raised at that request.

Every night throughout that '97 Festival I'd get out a sheet of paper and write out the gig. 'Not comedian – entertainer.

The Johnny Vegas Show

"more than a night out...
it's a memory!"

The Studio @ the Gilded Balloon (38)

8th — 30th AUGUST

22.45

In the race for rave reviews Johnny may appear to be the drunken donkey but beware - a life devoted to drink, drugs, sex & ceramics has left him with a powerful
- Comedy Kick!

"The King Is Dead Funny - Johnny is Bigger Than Elvis!"
Loaded Magazine

"...the finest comic of the new generation!"
Steve Coogan

"The Face of 1997!"
The Big Issue

"He creates some of the most unique comedy & pottery you'll ever see!"
City Life

"The best I've ever seen!"
Malcolm Hardee

The Daily Telegraph

comedy festival

StoneRanger

eye

http://www.telegraph.co.uk

It wasn't your standard Edinburgh head shot flyer, but then JOHNNY was anything but your standard stand-up comedian.

Don't do jokes. You don't know what it's like to be me.' I'd write it in shorthand, but run HIS full lines in my head, doing my best to leave nothing to chance.

After four cans and no more than half a bottle of vodka, I'd do a bit of sparring with JOHNNY by throwing imaginary heckles and scenarios at him:

'You're shit!'

'HeCKLINg'S LiKe HUNtINg, SoN – aNd you've jUSt goNe aFter a big broWN bear WitH a cottoN bUd.'

He hated doing it, and I know He only went along with it to humour me. JOHNNY still couldn't really be arsed with the theory part of the comedy exam; he was all about the practical, and as soon as the last bit of vodka had crept down my gullet, HIS sights were focused firmly on that stage.

Still, every day the show was reworked. Sometimes I'd manage to develop a small, new piece of material that He could cram in somewhere, even though the set was already full to bursting. There wasn't a single moment left to chance – like a DJ left with dreaded nothingness of dead air, it would have been unthinkable.

'Clingy couple?'

'PUbLic dISpLayS oF aFFectioN are LiKe FartINg iN a LiFt – you MigHt FiNd it NecesSary, bUt it'S Not So MUCH FUN For thoSe aroUNd you.'

Thanks to Jen, my bitterness about happy couples was a thing of the past, but JOHNNY had never let go of past indignities suffered at the hands of the fairer sex. He didn't hate women, far from it, but whilst Jen was all mine and all I wanted and needed, He was determined to prove something to everyone about HIS success rate with the ladies, be it delusional past conquests or HIS shatterproof confidence in what was yet to come. Either way, He got to play out the fantasy for HIS one hour up there on the stage, as long as He was clear that I was strictly off limits away from it.

Finally, I had to put myself in a bad place to really be JOHNNY, no matter how happy I might've been in general. That's why I always called Jen before I began oUr prep. That was HiS warm-up routine, ridding me of any fear of pushing the envelope, any residual tendency towards admiring or empathising with my fellow performers, and definitely any fear of their superior talents. I talked myself off whatever pedestal a chance good mood might have put me on. He'd constantly berate me about the fact that He was only as good as HiS last gig, and how I couldn't get complacent now I was out making all my new friends.

That was the strange thing about Edinburgh: other than guest spots at other gigs, when He was doing HiS show JoHNNy didn't share a bill with anyone else, yet He'd still have to fire HiMSeLF up to 'beat' the rest. To this end, JoHNNy would make enemies of other comedians in HiS head, sometimes concocting bizarre notions of how they'd wronged HiM, despite the fact that He'd never met them.

As departure time from my safe, designer flat got ominously closer, I'd also get myself into the mindset of, 'I don't want to be here' – even though it was by choice, and everything that was happening was exactly what we'd worked towards. It was just nerves trying to hold me back from immersing myself in HiM.

I'd pace around the flat and listen to music. I'd only ever listen to classical music at this juncture. That was something I got from reading Charles Bukowski – there were no lyrics, so I could focus on the set. It could put me in an emotional place without distracting daydreams about where you were when you first heard that song. I couldn't risk anything lifting me out of the loathing zone.

But then He'd insist on my playing Sinatra's 'That's Life' just as the cab arrived. He thought it would soothe me, but by this point I was a wreck. However well things were going, those last few moments before we headed for the door I'd still be doing my damnedest to talk HiM out of the gig: 'What if We just left now? Went home and got ourselves a proper job? I had a fucking good thing going at Argos, but you know as soon as you walk out of here there's no turning back.' But He would be having none of it by this point, and I swear that latch snap sounded like a firing squad presenting arms as J**ᴼ**HNN**ɥ** would drag me off to the cab. I hated H**ᴵ**M at times like that.

I'd get there at 10 p.m. It was the perfect time, because people weren't yet queuing for the show. I'd go in head down – I'd loathe it if anyone tried to talk to me.

The dressing room was perfect because there was no passing human traffic. I say dressing room: it was more like a broom cupboard, but it was somewhere to hide. All I had to do was shimmy down the side wall of the Studio as that was the only access to it. Tommy Tiernan and Jason Byrne were doing a shared slot there, so I didn't need to worry about distracting the audience because either guy was always storming it, although that didn't half get H**ᴵ**S hackles up.

I'd had enough to drink, even though the nerves were soaking up as much Dutch courage as they could, and that was always the sign that I'd done my sums right, booze-wise. Too pissed, no nerves; no nerves, no energy to keep H**ᴵ**M on his feet out there – make sense? Like a valve on a pressure cooker, I had to build up the pressure to make t**H**a**t** bastard sing. But I'd still have to get into the mannerisms of looking absolutely hammered. If people came into the dressing room with small talk, I'd let them think H**e** was too drunk to talk. I was so fucking paranoid that if I broke the spell by being me, I'd never get J**ᴼ**HNN**ɥ** back and I'd end up going on stage as myself, and that was a risk neither of us was willing to take again, ever.

All being well, though, the only distraction would be the lads quickly grabbing their gear, or front-of-house Jacks giving **U**s o**U**r five-minute call, but she quickly sussed my need for solitude in those last, god-awful moments, bless her. Jex would stay well away until our usual post-show autopsy, as would Steve and Mary, barring any last-minute emergencies.

And so, alone at last, just the t**W**o of u**S**, I'd sit and slip into a bittersweet coma and await the first few beats of our walk-on music.

Alcoholics Anonymous have this phrase: 'Let go, let God.' Mine was 'Let go, let J**ᴼ**HNN**ɥ**!'

32.

'LUST FOR LIFE'

The First Night I played to a crowd of around 25, but the room could hold 130 easily. Nowhere near Butlin's Skegness ballroom capacity, more like that Citadel gaff we started out in, but still it went well. I held the set to time.

I hate that word, 'Set'. Talk about putting your stall out with a bloody big banner screaming, 'Here I am, predictable as Soup on a nursing-home lunch menu! Don't worry, now't to fear, the show's been "Set"!'

He was obsessed with it nowadays. That and his precious set running to time. 'We have to be out by the end of the hour, on the dot, do you hear me?' Thinking himself a real pro since he'd got himself management and a bit of a reputation back home: a borrowed one – MY one! 'Why get dragged hanging on to the coat tails when you can hop on up and have a free piggyback ride to popularity central?'

He wasn't a bad lad; he'd just never quite got the hang of standing up for himself, of standing out for the right reasons. One whiff up the skirt of that slag, show biz, and he'd jump like something bred for Crufts instead of comedy.

They weren't the easiest gang to please, but I kept it going,

NaiLed SoMe cracKiNg LiNeS, Kept it rUNNiNg deSpite tHat, 'WHo, Me, WHat?' LacK oF bUzz WHeN NUMberS are LoW. THey Were NeVer aS KeeN to pLay WitH big gapS betWeeN SeatS, LiKe tHey LacKed a big-eNoUgH coMedy coNSeNSUS aS to WHat WaS FUNNy or Not, aNd No reaL eXpectatioN WHeN tHey coMe to WatcH aN 'UNKNoWN'.

'UNKNoWN, UNKNoWN? Wait 'tiLL tHey get a Load a Me!' Ha Ha, LoVe tHat FiLM. BUt I'd NeVer doNe oNe oF tHeSe FeStiVaLS beFore. EitHer Way, it Kept him FroM MeLtdoWN, aNd tHere'd be pLeNty More cHaNceS to MUcK aboUt.

SecoNd NigHt, I pLayed to 40 – aUditioNS Were oVer aNd tHat croWd Were Up For it! I WaS boUNciNg oFF tHeM LiKe a cHeeKy Wee baLL at a SqUaSH WorLd cHaMPioNSHip FiNaL. 'PiNg!', 'PoW!' – eVeN got a WiNK FroM tHe 'LoVe'S a poStMaN, bUt yoU've got a VicioUS dog caLLed pride!' LaSS, eVeN tHoUgH he'd toSSed his gUtS Up iNto a Spar bag earLier WitH jUSt a MiNUte to go. I'd LeaNt iN cLoSe, gaMbLed oN HaViNg breatH LiKe a taXi-raNK paVeMeNt aFter NigHtcLUb/Kebab SHop/cHUcKiNg oUt/cHUcKiNg Up tiMe, aNd Let Her KNoW I MeaNt it. BUt, God LoVe Her, SHe got it. OF coUrSe SHe did, becaUSe I WaSN't HidiNg My deSire beHiNd a WaVed WHite SUrreNder FLag oF FaLSe preteNceS.

The third night was a capacity crowd, and within the end of the first week we'd sold out the run as word spread about this mad, bad, ridiculously permed Woolyback ranting at the audience about teapots before breaking into crazy sing-alongs.

Had it been a film, then that would've been the montage cue: things went mental. The shows felt dangerous and He was cooking. The Studio had the energy of an illegal meeting of Festival dissidents where you half expected the secret police to burst in and drag HiM away at any moment. And although I thought there was no expanding on HiS confidence, I could tell JoHNNy's ambitions had swelled along with the queue of punters waiting to see HiM. People came wanting something raw and unapologetic, and VegaS was more than happy to give them what they wanted. I was being clocked in the street, bought drinks by random fans in bars and mixing with the Festival's elite. We had truly arrived.

He Made a Huge thing oF Not being Seen beFore the gig, Sneaking by iN caSe they SaW Him being Michael. WHo the FuCK did he tHiNK he WaS ... Me? He WaS a cHauFFeur, Nothing More, Nothing LeSS; a UPS driver deLivering a big boX oF SeLF-deLuSioN Straight to his oWN ego. But WHoSe NaMe WaS he USiNg WHeN he Signed For it, eH? WeLL? ASK yourSeLF tHat.

'I didn't want them thinking I just got changed and became someone else ...' He aCtuaLLy bLoody Said tHat! A SHeep puLLiNg oN SoMe WoLF'S cLothing doeS Not a HuNter MaKe. He Might've been coNteNt grazing oN a paSture oF popuLar MiSconCeptioN, but it tooK a reaL beaSt to ignore the Herd WHeN the coLLie dog oF coMedic coNForMity caMe barKiNg.

He'd Sit iN the dreSSing rooM rocKing baCK and Forth like He WaS at a SeaNce, deSperate to SuMMon Me up. WHere eLSe WouLd I be? Sitting arouNd Like him WatcHing SoMe brand NeW 'FrieNd' FLeeCe a croWd WHiLSt cLapping Like a bLoody SeaL Waiting For a toKeN bit oF MutuaL adMiration FroM aNother coMic'S bucKet oF FaLSe caMaraderie? No, ta, I Had aLL the FrieNdS I'd ever Need Waiting For Me out there. DeSpite WHingeing oN aLL his LiFe about HoW FoLK judged him, he StiLL WeNt LooKiNg For acceptance iN aLL the Wrong pLaceS. The dozy git Never got it. THat croWd WaNted you to be good, they Were genuiNeLy rooting For you, aNd they'd Have the good grace to teLL you to your Face iF you Were otherWiSe. But his NeW 'coLLeagueS' Needed Me to FaiL For theM to SucCeed, but they'd Never Have the baLLS to Say that to his cHubby, Needy, LittLe Face.

He WaS the SaMe With WoMeN. I teLL ya, he'S LucKy I taLKed him iNto tHat perM. 'Oh, yeah, it's ironic. It's a proper seventies idea of show biz chic. It's like a call-back for Johnny to a bygone era when he was still a big star at the top of his game.' It created voLuMe aNd Made HiS big, Stupid, Fat Head LooK at LeaSt HaLF a pouNd Lighter! But, Hey, WHy Wait For the third cocKereL to croW beFore diSoWNing your Saviour?

But I couLdN't FauLt him oN his cHoice oF iNtro MuSic. Credit WHere credit's due - I thiNK it WaS actuaLLy MartiN Bigpig WHo SuggeSted it. Either Way, 'LuSt For LiFe' WaS perFect. Iggy WaS

No crooner, but he had that inherent air of danger about him that I bloody loved. It gave me a real build-up – a sense that the shit was truly just about to hit the fan. Pure rock'n'roll. Nice touch of irony too, when you consider that he had about as much lust for life as a Dignitas drop-in centre during the January sales.

For someone who'd lived his whole life over-analysing, internalising, fretting and paranoid about what people thought about him, you'd think he'd thank me for that one hour of liberation from being him. But, no, the dozy sod was still too petrified to go out and meet the very folk who could've given him everything he'd ever claimed he wanted. Like a dog who'd spent half his life chasing his tail, then complaining it smelt of shit the day he finally gets a hold of it. Man, oh man, the things I could show him once I had more of a say in things. That's why I tortured him a bit sometimes, but the moment that music kicked in, I'd put him out of his misery.

'Right, buggerlugs, come on, get up.'

'Ladies and gentleman, please welcome onto the stage, Mr Johnny Vegas.'

'I'm wanted.'

It was like being possessed. I didn't want to go on, but Johnny lifted me out there. I would be reluctant to put one foot in front of the other, but I would feel him pushing me forward. Yet the struggle only helped enhance the shambolic look of him. I would sense the crowd's gaze on us but I wouldn't make eye contact with anyone till we got on stage – and the second my hand went on that mic, that was it. As if I'd been sedated, I slumped out of existence and into the stuff of Festival folklore.

He thought it was the booze that fuelled me, but then all addicts need something to blame their coping mechanism on, don't they? Truth is, behind the pissed act, alcohol had no effect on me. I could drink it 'till the cows came home, slept, and left again for the field, but it never changed me. The audience was my high. I held the mic, but they made the magic, and when I told them that, I bloody meant it!

He was running away with it, gig-wise. The Festival-goers couldn't get enough of HiM, and, away from the shows, the atmosphere around that city was just as unbelievable. It was the party I was born to, and every door was open to a close, personal friend of Mr Vegas.

Booze was available 24 hours a day; booze in a glass, from a bar, not a carrier bag. Before then, keeping those kinds of hours would've meant drinking at home, alone, and I had a loose rule – a bit of a grey area – that this was borderline alcoholic.

No grey areas up at the Edinburgh Festival, though, because nobody ever went home. Certainly not at 11. No one called it a day at midnight or shied away at 1 a.m. 'Late 'n' Live' at the Gilded Balloon was just kicking off then, and it rolled on through until 5 a.m. every single morning.

Steve and Mary had booked JoHNNy in to do a load of those before the Festival kicked off. It was extra income, and nobody could've predicted just how well the show would go. It was a bear pit, an after-hours madhouse that respected nobody's reputation, a pissed-up crowd hell-bent on giant-slaying.

Ordinarily, I hated doubling up; VegaS gave it HiS all every single night, but it took everything out of me. Still, He loved it. It was proper gloves-off, bare-knuckle, no-referee kind of stuff. There JoHNNy could break free from all the restraints of the set and dance to his own beat. And there was a funny kind of ethos to the gig that He admired. It was okay to die as long as you went down fighting. That was how you earned your wings amongst other comics, an extra merit badge: 'I died at Late 'n' Live.' And the bar there afterwards was buzzing all night long.

The whole Festival was littered with venues full of people just as pissed and animated and determined as myself to see the session through to the bitter end. Except there were no bitter ends: up there, that kind of behaviour wasn't considered self-destructive. It was normal!

I had a theory, a good one, and it made sense in an environment where an alternative lifestyle seemed viable: alcoholism was a title generated by Society's envy of folk like us. It was disapproval that drove free spirits indoors, supping shamefully of its sweet, beautiful release, or to the pub and its sufferance of ex-school-bully know-it-alls, bored of their neglected wives – the ones I'd wished had noticed me when they were swooning over this prick, neglecting his own chance to serve his unhappy wife so's he can prop up a barstool next to me. Even those huddled together in shop doorways eventually found themselves snarling, gargling, begging for jaded bits of round pieces of metal or crumpled bits of paper with the Queen's approval on 'em.

This kind of madness, which Society saved up all year for two weeks of on the Costa Del Sol, we did, we lived, on their doorstep on a wet Wednesday in a dive bar in Leith. We were a staggering example of the right to book yourself on a holiday from practicality. We were dragging the sand of irresponsibility right back from distant, booze-sodden lands of happier climes, and dumping it in front of life, daring them to build a better sandcastle than us, even though we were too hammered to judge the final outcome, too pissed to know the difference between a castle and a turd.

And when 'Late 'n' Live' eventually closed its doors and we stepped out into the light, there were only nods of approval amongst the revellers determined to stagger on to the Penny Black, where the doors opened at 6 a.m.

I'm not generalising, but the Irish contingent of comics had a stamina for hedonism that I admired and loved to keep pace with. They brought a heightened, unashamed joy to it all. My dad had always been desperate to prove we had a bit of Celtic blood coursing through our veins. Mine would have been about fifty-fifty blood 'n' booze by that point, and that seemed enough to earn myself an honorary membership of the clan, hence I kind of felt like I was flying the flag for the old man. I'd found new kinfolk who didn't believe in recriminations.

And we were a tribe based on equality. Be they fellow comics, promoters or punters, we all partied together side by side. All the fear they'd put me through previously that day dissolved in drink after drink after drink – like a Christmas truce, I came out of my trench and temporarily forgot about fearing the enemy until the next evening came around.

And when it did? Ah, fuck it, I had a secret weapon that would win the war for uS: I had JoHNNy VeGaS.

'We aLL LiKe a driNK, NobodY LiKeS a drUNK!' I Loved tHat. It WaS a great pUt-doWN LiNe For aNYoNe WHo'd Had a FeW too MaNY aNd FaNCied taKiNG Me oN. Not MaNY did, tHoUGH. THoSe FeStiVaL aUdieNCeS Were a bit too WeLL-beHaved For tHeir oWN good, SoMetiMeS. I'd coMe oUt aLL aNGrY aNd bitter, pUt tHe Fear iN tHeM to Start WitH, jUSt to SHoW WHo WaS boSS. THeM aLL tHiNKiNG I WaS HaMMered HeLped craNK Up tHe Fear Factor – it LeNt tHe WHoLe SHoW aN air oF UNPredictabiLitY. Not tHat tHere WaS MUCH cHaNCe oF tHat, WHat WitH him aNd his preCioUS Set. BUt oNCe I'd got tHe croWd'S FULL aNd UNdivided atteNtioN I coULd Start MeSSiNG WitH tHeM, WooiNG tHeM, briNG tHeM roUNd WitH a coUPLe oF his Sob StorieS – tWeaKed For LaUGHS oF coUrSe – tHeN a SiNG–aLoNG.

'KiNG oF tHe Road' Had beeN SLayiNG everY NiGHt, So I StUCK WitH tHat. I LiKed tHe SiNGiNG; I LiKed tHe Fact tHat it WaSN't tHe doNe tHiNG iN giGS, tHat it got riGHt UNder tHe SKiN oF SoMe oF tHeM otHer coMicS. ANd tHe croWd Loved it: it broUGHt tHeM togetHer, Made tHeM part oF tHe SHoW, Made US oNe – LeSS 'YoU' agaiNSt 'tHeM'.

PLUS it FeLt More Me, More WHat I WaS USed to, More oF MY baCKgroUNd, tHe HoLidaY caMPS, tHe oLd-SCHooL WaY oF eNtertaiN-iNG. He Kept SayiNG it WaS iroNic, bUt tHeN WHat did he KNoW? He didN't Have tHat aFFiNitY WitH aN aUdieNCe tHat I did. It'S Not SoMe-tHiNG YoU caN teaCH FoLK, it'S iN tHe bLood, it'S gUt iNStiNCt, it'S a reaL Love For tHeM deep doWN – eveN WHeN YoU Were Up cLoSe aNd baWLiNG at tHeM, tHeY coULd teLL it caMe FroM a good pLaCe. I coULd Never UNderStaNd HoW he coULd be HappY eNoUGH taKiNG tHe boW aNd SittiNG Up tiLL aLL HoUrS gettiNG HaMMered WitH peoPLe, tHeN SpeNd HaLF tHe daY tHroWiNG Up For Fear oF tHeM.

It WaS tHe SaMe WitH tHat potter'S WHeeL oF his. ALL he did WitH tHat degree WaS Wear it LiKe SoMe MiSerabLe SoddiNG badge

OF HONOUR because he ONLY got a THIrd. It WaS Me tHat put it to USE IN tHe gig, tUrNed it INto SoMetHING to be adMIred, tHat he coULd be proUd OF. It WaS Me WHO SaW tHe potENtIaL IN it aFter he'd WrItteN it aLL oFF jUSt becaUSe SoMe eXaMINer didN't give him a big eNoUGH tick back IN tHe day. ALWayS bLoody WorryINg WHat otHerS tHoUGHt oF him aNd Never HavING tHe baLLS to trUSt his INStINctS – or SHoULd I Say My INStINctS? It WaS Me WHo Had got US tHere, it WaS Me WHo Had 120 peopLe SittING SiLeNt, MoUtHS Wide opeN, agHaSt, WatcHING Me MaKe tHat pot, Me WHo coULd bUiLd tHeM Up jUSt LiKe tHat teapot tiLL tHey Were eatING oUt oF My HaNd, Me!

We soon attracted the attention of the critics, as well as the Perrier judges. It was a mad scramble, a feeding frenzy, with all of them desperate to put their spin on the reaction JoHNNy was getting. He hated critics, had no time for them whatsoever, and wasn't shy about telling them exactly what He thought of them. I didn't like HiM goading them the way He did; I mean, all the feedback was pro VegaS, really positive stuff, and what harm could a Perrier nomination do uS?

I found it really interesting reading somebody else trying to get to grips with exactly what it was they thought JoHNNy was about, what it was that made HiM tick. But no matter what I thought about it, or how much I begged him to play ball, the red mist would descend whenever He'd catch one of them in the audience.

He'd pore over tHeM bLoody revieWS LiKe tHey Were teSt reSULtS back FroM a cLINic. It didN't Matter WHat tHey tHoUGHt – tHe aUdieNce WaS tHe oNLy baroMeter tHat Mattered! THey'd aLWayS be tHere For yoU, Not LiKe tHoSe FLy-by-NigHt vULtUreS. 'YoU WaLK IN Here WitH yer Notepad oF peSSiMiSM aNd a Loaded peN oF poiSoN! I'M Not a coMediaN, I'M aN eNtertaINer. I WoN't coWer FroM tHe tHreat oF a cyNicaL tHUNderStorM WHeN I've got tHe SMiLeS oF a croWd to SHieLd Me FroM tHe StriKe.' ANd aS For tHe Perrier AWard, he MigHt've Needed tHat patroNiSING pat oN tHe back, tHat SeaL oF approvaL braNded oN his backSide So tHe corporate KiSS-aSSeS WoULd KNoW eXactLy

WHere to aiM For, but tHat Sure aS HeLL WaSN't WHy I'd got into it. I Had SoMetHiNg good goiNg Here, SoMetHiNg SpeciaL, SoMetHiNg tHe crowd got aLL by tHeMSeLveS WitHout tHe bLeSSiNg oF tHe aLMigHty StaNd–up EStabLiSHMeNt. ONce agaiN, he Let out-Side ForceS prevaiL aNd Start SettiNg his StaNdardS For him, SettiNg himself up For yet aNotHer uNSpectacuLar FaLL FroM otHer FoLKS' graceS, but Not Me. I'd Waited too daMNed LoNg to get My Say to Let him go aNd ruiN it by KoW–toWiNg to tHe So–caLLed coMedy eLite.

Yet despite all of JoHNNy's blatant and extremely vocal disdain for the critics, they couldn't get enough of HiM. And, thank God, I was able to talk to them on a one-to-one basis throughout the days – help smooth things over, point out that it was just one of the character's quirks.

Apologising for some of HiS more outlandish traits was not something He was interested in. So I became our PR man as well. I knew how to play the game, JoHNNy knew how to play the crowd. By the time He climbed down from that pottery wheel and wrapped up the show with HiS earnest plea: 'You're Not puNterS, you're peopLe. You're Not buMS oN SeatS, you're SMiLeS oN FaceS. I HoLd tHe Mic, but you MaKe tHe Magic, aNd WitHout you, I'M NotHiNg. CoMedy'S a caMpFire, LadieS aNd geNtLeMeN, pLeaSe, pLeaSe, coMe aNd be WarMed', He was almost whispering – in stark contrast to the raging bull who'd come at them at the top of the show.

And as for the crowd? Well, they were converts. They believed in JoHNNy VegaS, and all the hard work, the puking, the stress of getting him to see sense and play the system in our favour felt momentarily worthwhile, like I'd finally created something in my life worth celebrating.

He WaS dooMed to FaiLure. He tHougHt he couLd court tHe preSS aNd pLay tHe gaMe tHe WorLd'S Way, iNStaNtLy ForgettiNg aLL tHe tiMeS he'd Sat WaiLiNg iNto his piNt becauSe LiFe Had Moved tHe goaLpoStS oN him agaiN. He Had tHe MeMory oF a coNcuSSed goLd-FiSH, aNd No Matter HoW MaNy NigHtS I Stepped out tHere aNd tried to SHoW him a better Way, he juSt didN't get it.

We 'ran long' one night — their phrase, not mine; I mean, how can you overrun on building a legend? They wanted the show wrapped up early — even Jex was giving up and flashing the white light of surrender, but the crowd deserved better, My crowd, My people, My lifeblood. We'd come all this way together, thrown two fingers up to the rest of the festival and proved him and all his cronies wrong. We'd done that, me and my people, and I wasn't going to short-change them on a show, no matter what anyone else said.

So we piled out into the street. I stood on top of a white transit van and we belted out 'New York, New York' right there and then, blocking traffic, folk filing out of nearby bars and joining in. Even then, I could hear him whining away: 'Come on, enough's enough, what if the police come? What if we get in trouble? There were judges in tonight … what if this goes against us in the Perrier nominations?'

'Fuck the nominations, and fuck you!' I thought. I mean Jesus, they'd have marched on the castle itself that night had I asked them to. Why should he have all the fun away from the stage? He wanted me back in the box so he could go out and soak up the glory my blood, sweat and tears had earned, when a minute back he'd been ready to send them home a few songs short of a memory.

He thought he could turn me on and off like a light switch after a few cans and a stupid sheet of scrawled-out gags that was all his life had amounted to, but fuck him! I was going to have a night out with my fans, with my adoring public. I could party harder and longer than him anyhow, and I sure as shit was a lot funnier. You get back in the box, Fat-boy, because I am Vegas, and tonight, folks, hear me roar!

33.

AMOS 3:3 – 'DO TWO WALK TOGETHER, UNLESS THEY HAVE AGREED TO MEET?'

'Mummy, what is that?' asked the little boy, who'd nearly tripped over my prone body in an Edinburgh gutter.

Now, in theory, I could have taken issue with being described as a 'what' instead of the preferred 'who'. It's rude for starters, and I'd been raised to show respect for my elders. But what kind of comeback was available to me when I was lying in the street, half-cut, at some time just gone nine of a morning, looking like a beached starfish tangled in a retro leather safari jacket, still bloated from JOHNNY's fourteen hours' off the leash bingeing on Guinness, vodka, Baileys/Cointreau cocktails (known as Mother's Milk, or Gaviscon de Luxe to those familiar with 'Late 'n' Live's' unlicensed backstage bar), plus various exotic shots bought on my unwitting behalf by well-meaning audience members from the previous night's show. Shots so unfamiliar to my internal ecosystem that my pickled liver and kidneys mistakenly processed them 'out through the back' as wet farts, which, in the unforgiving heat from the bri-nylon weave of JOHNNY'S tan and gold flares, had slowly baked and left my arsehole tightly welded shut.

To complete the inglorious spectacle, I was drooling like one of those hot-glue guns they had in school craft shops, and sporting a skin tone that hadn't quite been kissed by the morning sun – more slapped silly by solar UV rays.

I looked a bloody mess. And whoever fell over me as I slept hit the nail on the head when asking the simple question: 'What is that?'

I thought I had a vague memory of JOHNNY tumbling me out of a cab, flat on my face – "There you go, we're home!" But like Mr Magoo dropping back what used to be a rental car at Hertz I remember thinking to myself: 'What have YOU done? I am completely fucked!' And with the flat another good twenty, thirty yards away or so I'd decided that bit of pavement was as good a spot as any to crash. It had still been dark at that point, so funnily enough it can't have been one of my later nights, as it would normally be light by the time I got back to my digs, but JOHNNY had time-managed HIS alcohol consumption far more effectively than I'd ever thought myself capable of. I really used to love that feeling of staggering out of pubs into broad daylight, when people were not long up and about and going to work. It was tangible proof that I'd escaped what I'd always feared the most: a nine-to-five existence.

I'd been at the Edinburgh Festival just shy of a fortnight, but already HE felt like HE was home. Up until then, I'd made a bit of a name for myself as a boozer, but I was a keen amateur in no particular rush to turn pro.

REMEMBER, PAL, EVERYONE LIKES A DRINK, NOBODY LIKES A DRUNK! BOOZING'S LIKE RIDING A BIKE, BUT YOU'VE REMOVED THE STABILISERS OF SOBRIETY WAY TOO SOON, AND NOW YER WOBBLE OF WOE IS ALL TOO VISIBLE TO THE REST OF THE ROOM. YOU CAME TONIGHT HOPING TO LEAVE ME DUMBSTRUCK WITH YER ACROBATIC STUNTS OF SARCASM.

Not Surprisingly, you're leaving with a grazed knee of never-mores. Now sit back, shut up and leave it to those proficient in the art of inebriation.

Before the Festival, I believed I'd understood the need for moderation, even if my moderations seemed a lot more elastic than most other folks'. I'd respected the wishes of publicans and bouncers, lived within the limits of last orders – 'Done my shouting, singing, talking whilst I was walking.'

Despite the odd discrepancies and forgotten exceptions to the rule, I thought it fair to say that I had been, for the most part, just a bit of a happy-go-lucky piss-head. Had it not been for the Festival, I might just have continued shuffling through life, content with the self-deception that this was enough. And had it not been for Johnny, I definitely wouldn't have been lying there with all the grace and poise of Bambi, on absinthe, on ice.

When I first dared to look up and try to get my bearings, all I could see was a hazy silhouette of people, but shrouded in a host of multicoloured shapes.

I might've bumped my head, or been beaten up, but my first instinct was, 'Shit, he's been spiked!'

Waking up in unknown places was a pretty standard ordeal for me: once on a pool table in a pub in Leeds, after being reported missing by my hotel; often on the disabled access ramp outside Thatto Heath library. Years later, he would top them all by being woken up in a hotel reception, naked from the waist down, in front of 200 or so shareholders and employees who were there waiting for their Bensons for Beds annual AGM to begin.

I used to just accept these social impositions as par for the course. But, waking up that day, it wasn't the unknown where-abouts of my bed that was bothering me. It was the fact that I really was convinced I was tripping.

Maybe I'd imagined getting a taxi? What if we were still out in some club somewhere with me thinking I'm here and him E-ing off our tits? There was no doubt he'd proved he could drink for real away from the stage, but what if he wasn't willing to leave it at just that, then the **Mad bastard** could've been taking anything? And how would I know if he had, or still was? Up until then, the strongest 'substances' I'd ever tried were a bit of weed, and some painfully large shots of poteen (Irish moonshine). Not the mass-marketed 6% proof crap – I mean the stuff straight off the ferry, in a thick glass jar, because it tends to eat through plastic bottles. Now, that was evil stuff, but more in a cricket-bat-to-the-back-of-the-head kind of way.

Thanks to poteen I'd wasted hours trying to figure out how to drop off a five-foot wall whilst taking a short cut home from the pub. But that was just rapid inebriation and the possible onset of alcoholic poisoning. I wasn't seeing things. Trippy drugs just weren't my thing: dangerous amounts of alcohol, yes; believing I'm the Walrus, no. A monkey on my back, well, who knew?

I was never drug-free as a badge of honour. I'd helped my mates pick magic mushrooms. I just never took any of them. My imagination was a liability anyway, so I reckoned best not encourage it with mind-altering mushies. Especially after watching a mate spend five hours close to tears, tortured by 'the fear' that he was being followed by a Twix. The dozy sod didn't realise he kept picking it up, carrying it round with him, and then placing it next to himself whenever he sat down. I'd had enough hang-ups with my weight as a teenager; the last thing I needed was a chocolate stalker.

It's the same story with coke. I've had it offered to me by so many wankers who'd waste agonising chunks of my valuable drinking time by cornering me and talking flat out, without a breather, about how fucking amazing they were. I'd be checking my texts, and yet they'd be convinced that 'we' were engaging in a shared, deep and meaningful, two-way conversation. If it was such an amazing experience, why the fuck would they walk out of the toilets with that manic look of somebody who's just realised they've left a cigarette burning on the arm of a straw couch in the paraffin store room of the world's largest orphanage? I swear, there'd be times in a club when I honestly felt like the last man alive who actually used a toilet cubicle for the sole purpose of having a shit! There was a pressure to do it that took me back to the days of peer pressure smoking behind the bike sheds. That lame, tossy technique of trying to distribute the guilt amongst everybody. And when the standard schoolyard-style initiation failed, they'd go for my weak spot, that tender vulnerable bit of me ever susceptible to excess: 'It means you can drink more.'

'Great! Because that's what's been missing in my life, the capacity to drink loads.'

'Really?'

'No, fuck off!'

So I think I've established that drugs, depending on your definitions, were not something I would willingly partake of. But in Edinburgh, with **HIM** set loose like a needy beagle who'd caught the intoxicating scent of adulation, running round the town deliriously happy to lead the hunt for hedonism, anything might've happened. Despite the alcohol fog, I had rapid trains of thought, and all of them bad ones. For a mad split second, I actually remember thinking 'Shit, date rape!' I mean, **He** might not have knowingly taken anything A class, but what if someone had slipped him a mickey? And if somebody was going to go to all the trouble of tampering with **HIS** drink, wouldn't there have to be something in it for them?

My body might've been immobile but my mind was racing.

Shit, shit, shit! What was I gonna tell Jen? What about that big question I had to put to her? Could I still ask her after this? Did it actually count as infidelity if your real alter ego got spiked and then sodomised in a festival toilet?' But looking back on the last question I thought 'Does it really bloody matter? The excuse sounds more fucked up than the act itself!'

It had never normally been that hard thinking straight but I had to try and apply some logic to this new, possibly chemically-enhanced 'uber fear'. Yes, Edinburgh was comic groupie central, but surely nobody, not man, woman, nor bi-curious swinger, could ever be that desperate? Plus if anyone had drugged **HIM** for sexual purposes, they'd run the risk of **JOHNNY** collapsing on either **HIS** front or back, and then, depending on their particular needs, the massive task of rolling **VEGAS** over would surely have left them far too knackered to indulge in any kind of kinky one-way hanky-panky with **HIM**.

But I'd always been prone to believing worst-case scenarios, and my naïvety with regard to the rave scene was worthy of a 1950s public information film. From the producers who brought you *Reefer Madness* comes *Ecstasy Horror* – 'When hugs lead to hurt!' There was a definite anal tenderness, but that was most likely from over-wipe after five days of regularly passing now't but loose liquid.

The only bonus from being this hung over, though, was that I was simply too knackered to work my fleeting paranoia into a tangible concern.

I was too fuzzy to think. I wanted to keep my head resting on the cool surface of the pavement. It was my only comfort zone, and I wasn't quite ready to get to grips with the surreal extrapolations of a Vegas hangover.

I'd have been happy to stay there and sleep things off a wee while longer, but then I heard someone else say, 'It's nothing. Come on, leave it.'

First I'm a 'that', now I'm an 'it'?

'Eh, love,' I remember thinking to myself. 'I may be a piss-head, and/or an unwitting druggie, but I've got my pride!'

For all I knew, they could have been figments of my imagination, but still, I wasn't going to just lie there and take that. Besides, **JOHNNY** might get jealous if I started hanging out with other voices, so I decided to tackle them, real or otherwise.

I made a determined effort to sit up. Bloody Hell, my body felt glued to the floor like well-trodden bubble-gum, even raising my head was like lifting a shipwreck off the sea bed. For something so big and robust, I felt dangerously fragile – as if any part of me might break off if I rushed the procedure. I leant against a tree and, no longer blinded by the direct sunlight, tried to straighten up my double vision by focusing with just the one eye, a trick I'd learned watching late-night snooker after a skinful.

It was then that the full, pathetic nature of my predicament became clear to me: I wasn't in a club; **He** hadn't been slipped a mickey. I'd been asleep, pissed, blocking the steps outside the front door of a children's crèche. I knew this because the bright colours I'd seen were now easily recognisable as paper butterflies, cut out and stuck up in the windows. There were children's faces peering out at me between these, all of them displaying an odd mixture of curiosity and pity. That was until somebody pulled the blinds down, putting an end to their early morning freak show.

The little lad who'd obviously tripped over me on his way in seemed rooted to the spot, even though his mum was gently pulling at his sleeve. He was looking at me in that way kids look at a slug when salt's poured on it. They can't actually express the process they're witnessing, they just know it's gross, and therefore oddly mesmerising. His mum, on the other hand, was glaring at me with an expression of total and utter disgust.

It was the first time since I'd arrived in Edinburgh that my behaviour had been questioned. The self-righteous bit of me tried to figure out why nobody had called for an ambulance. But, looking back, w**e**'d been bloody lucky not to have woken up in a cell.

A sad realisation dawned on me. In the short space of time since I'd arrived in Edinburgh, I had acquired all the outward appearances of a bum. And then a feeling totally alien to the Festival buzz gripped me, an emotional queasiness worse than any hangover, something **He** simply didn't do, it was shame.

Shame on me for lying in the street, incapable of even making it home to my bed. Shame on me for buying into my own bullshit and thinking myself above and beyond the boundaries of common decency. How could things go from so carelessly perfect to this? Why, just when I thought I'd finally got life sussed, did I have to wake up to the guilt of allowing **HiM** to reduce me to nothing more than a cautionary tale?

I desperately wanted to say something to the kid to make things better, to not destroy his wide-eyed naïve appreciation of the world, but I couldn't. How could his mother, or me, begin to explain to a child of that age exactly what was going on?

Vegas, on the other hand, well He was loving it! In fact Johnny was already plotting how He might work this into His next gig. And worse still, He'd seen to it that there was enough booze still left in my system to guarantee His continued presence.

I could sense Johnny rattling through His song list looking for something 'apt' to perform, something to send up the whole sorry situation to comic effect, as ever actually believing He could turn things around somehow. His only concern was not to miss the opportunity to play to an open air gig of two. And although I was actually physically shaking my head at the prospect, the overwhelming sense of regret in me was desperate to hand things over to Him, to pass the buck. Like a tag wrestling team, half of uS, the Michael Pennington half of me, wanted out.

And so I put my head in my hands and gave up on any notion of sobering up, apologising and cutting my losses. Instead I let the drunken, indignant surge better known as Johnny Vegas rise once more from within.

It was such a cowardly act. This wasn't some late-night gig down at the Gilded Balloon; it was a pavement in broad daylight outside a nursery! There were no hecklers to contend with, just a kid and his legitimately judgmental mother.

This wasn't what He'd been created for. But like King Kong bored of being wheeled out for display purposes only, and in a mad bad mood to croon, Vegas was about to break free from His subconscious shackles and turn on me, His former jailor. As wanky and overly dramatic as it might now sound, my only remaining desire at that point was to protect the innocent. And so, as Johnny began to let rip with a bit of 'That's Life' for the unfortunate onlookers, I crawled away messily along the street. It must've been the saddest, maddest, sorriest fucking sight. Him singing like He was playing to a packed house at Caesar's Palace and me, dragging myself along on my hands and knees via the strength of my last remaining shred of common decency.

Are you ready for the son of Roseanne and Jack Duckworth?

EDINBURGH COMEDY
By Sam Taylor

Normally, when you hear the opening bars of Iggy Pop's 'Lust for Life' at a comedy show in Edinburgh, your heart sinks. This is because, normally, the only people desperate enough to use the song's *Trainspotting* connection as a means of making themselves look 'street-wise' are terminally awful students. Johnny Vegas is the exception that proves this rule. A swaggering man-mountain of bile and defiance, his entrance – at the moment when Iggy rasps, 'Here comes Johnny Yen again/ With the liquor and drugs/ And the flesh machine/ He's gonna do another striptease' – restores the song's original violent bounce.

Indeed, Vegas – who was one of five acts nominated for the Perrier award last Wednesday (the winner was announced last night, after the *Review* had gone to press) – is like Jarvis Cocker in his ability to make the naff seem cool.

The character, created by 26-year-old Michael Pennington, is a Seventies-style 'entertainer' with a passion for pottery. His act is fairly straightforward – some vaguely surrealistic one-liners, a couple of showtunes, a bit of clay moulding – and could easily have ended up as kitsch, patronising rubbish, but it is taken to another level by the ferocious emotion with which Pennington invests his creation.

'You don't know anything about me,' he growls at the audience in his broad St Helens accent, like an angry hybrid of Jack Duckworth and Johnny Rotten. He is simultaneously every bona fide who ever made good – Rocky, Gazza, Romario – and a precisely rendered character in his own right. Just as Rocky had his lasts and Noel Gallagher his guitar, Johnny has found an expression for his soul in clay – echoing the pathos of a thousand nightschool graduates and showing your kneejerk sympathy right back in your liberal, well-meaning face.

The clothes (pimp's leather jacket, big-collared shirt and flared trousers) and the one-liners ('ceramics has a sister and her name is showbusiness') may be borrowed from Harry Hill and Vic Reeves, but both of those comics are oddly unemotional and non-confrontational. Vegas, by contrast, is a seething mass of maudlin rage.

He's also a charismatic sex symbol – or, rather, he's convinced himself he's a charismatic sex symbol, which amounts to the same thing when you're big and on stage. He sheds his jacket with the heavy-breathing suggestiveness of Tom Jones. He teaches his less funky fellow males how to dance from their hips. He chats up a member of the audience ('My love is a postman, and you have a vicious dog called Pride').

And, in a climactic scene which could have gone horribly wrong, he selects a woman from the audience for the privilege of being inducted into the mysteries of ceramics. Standing behind the lucky lady, he guides her hands over the smooth clay as it spins and grows on his potter's wheel. It's like the video for Lionel Richie's 'Hello' without the token blindness.

Unlike Al Murray's Pub Landlord, who would seem to be his main competitor for the Perrier award, Vegas is not a recognisable archetype: there is no satire here; and, in fact, there aren't too many jokes either. The look on Vegas's face is much, much funnier than any of his snappy one-liners.

The great thing about Johnny Vegas is that he has risen without trace. One of the many reasons why comedy was never going to be the next rock 'n' roll is that it takes so long to succeed as a comic. The country's talent seems entrenched in a slowly moving hierarchy, often based on their year of graduation from Oxbridge.

Johnny Vegas, 'a swaggering man-mountain of bile and defiance'. And quite funny, too. Photograph by Murdo MacLeod

This is exemplified by the fact that, of the four other Perrier nominees, Al Murray was nominated last year; Milton Jones was voted 'best newcomer' last year; and Graham Norton and the League of Gentlemen were both on the fringes of last year's short list. Michael Pennington has burst through the dead wood like a curly-haired forest fire, and in so doing – whether or not he wins the Perrier award this year – he may just give British comedy the shot in the arm it so desperately needs.

One might say the same thing about British poetry and insert 'Murray Lachlan Young's' name. Only it wouldn't be true. There is a vast difference between a press hype – which is what Johnny Vegas is in danger of becoming – and a PR hype: and Young definitely belongs to the second category. News of his supposed £1 million deal with EMI and large colour photographs of his supposedly 'Byronic' face on the front pages of the nation's broadsheets were always likely to lead to a critical backlash.

In the circumstances, it seemed rather brave foolish of this 27-year-old 'performance poet' to do a three-week run at Edinburgh. But then, he was already being savaged for his poor debut CD, *Vice & Verse*, and it's strength really does lie in performance.

Well, let's be honest, it had to be somewhere. Young's 'poetry' veers between shallow amateurish free verse ('The MTV Collection') and wannabe-satirical epics about art and gluttony, which strive to be John Cooper Clarke but are perpetually hamstrung by their corny similarity to the dreaded Pam Ayres.

With his snake-like body and long dark curls, he does have a certain presence, and his sidekicks – a cellist and a muscle-bound 'butler' – successfully distract you from the worst of his verses. But the most surprising, and endearing, thing about Murray Lachlan Young is that he's not the arch, cynical wag of repute at all; he's really quite naive and sweet.

'The Life and Death of Art' is the kind of earnest, apocalyptic poem that over-sensitive sixth-formers have been writing for centuries. And, just in case you still thought he had no heart, he performs a generic love poem (lots of water imagery) in a quiet voice with the lights dimmed. Ahhh...

As the bard himself might put it:

Treasure that moment, that
shining jewel amid dung,
For it may be the last we ever
see of M.L. Young.

Mind you, we thought that we had seen the last of Jerry Sadowitz a few years ago. And perhaps we had. Once the most scabrous, vituperative and hilarious comic of his generation, Sadowitz does not appear to have any ideas or jokes any more – just deadpan hatred.

Still, there is something gloriously single-minded about his current show: fed a list of names (comedians, celebrities, entire nationalities) by an English interviewer, he calls them all 'f--ing c--s' in a tone of ever-increasing weariness.

One of the few occasions he elaborates on this view is when he's asked about a number of 'top' English comedians, all of whom regularly appear on television. 'Not funny,' he says, seriously. 'No talent. Well, actually, they must have some talent to have got where they are with no talent.'

Just because he's a miserable Scottish bastard doesn't mean he's wrong.

And the awful truth was, as I put a bit of distance between HiM and them, between myself and the reality, I did feel better. I mean, who wouldn't? Who'd choose agonising guilt over a damned good sing-along? Not me. Not uS.

I believe that was the beginning of the end for me, because it was at that point that JoHNNy began to take over completely. Where Michael Pennington ended and JoHNNy VegaS began was a puzzle that reviewers spent countless column inches trying to suss out, amusing me in the process as up until then I'd always mistakenly thought there'd been a strong, well-defined differentiation between JOHNNy and myself.

But just as JOHNNy's booze-fuelled recklessness was helping me achieve more than I'd ever dared to dream might be possible as a professional comedian, it was also washing away the foundations of the kind of person I'd started out in life wanting to be. My handing that entire situation over to JOHNNy in front of that poor unsuspecting mother and child was just as much of a shock to me as it was to them. He was only ever meant to appear on stage, and it had always been my job to cope with the aftermath, be it adulation or all-out pitch forks and 'kill the beast' style burning torches. But nothing up until that point could have prepared me for the aggressive takeover bid He launched that morning. And as the price of Michael Pennington's shares in sobriety hit rock bottom, and the market got wind of my intention to liquidize what little was left of my sober self-respect, JOHNNy VegaS, the Gordon Gekko of emotional insider trading, was there ready and waiting to buy, buy, buy all available stock.

Now JOHNNy was more than just a full-blown coping mechanism, he was a comfort-blanket weaved of asbestos. Being a 'stepping stone across that river of rejection' – to quote the deceitful bastard HiMSeLF – was no longer enough for HiM.

I knew He'd outgrown the concept of the well-crafted stage persona in the public's eyes a long time ago, but I'd remained in denial of the inevitable fact that He'd one day outgrow me. Like all creations blessed with the gift of free will, I suppose He was bound to abandon the morals of HiS maker and strike out alone at some point. I know I did.

The look on the faces of that mother and child has stayed with me always. No amount of success can erase it. It was a look that begged the question: 'What kind of past produces a man like that?'

Well, now you know.

AFTERWORD

Heading up to Edinburgh in '97, who could've known that by the end of the Festival I would cease to exist, not only in the bloodshot eyes of this brave new world but, more importantly, to myself? Michael Pennington was now nothing more than a half-forgotten scribble on a birth certificate tucked away in Dad's old bureau back home in St Helens. Like a Vietnam vet with a thousand-pint stare who'd seen and done things folk couldn't imagine, I'd go home, but my soul – the very thing that made me, me, that I'd fought so hard to protect way back in Upholland – was still up there, north of the border, missing in action, more pickled than perfectly preserved.

JOHNNy VegaS was the only name on people's lips. In any other industry I'd have been dismissed, or at least offered some form of counselling. Instead, I was given TV and DVD contracts, plus a guaranteed national tour: more a re-invention than an intervention.

I was now a much-lauded, highly-functioning professional drunk riding high behind the wheel of an 18-stone monster truck of inevitable tragedy. An accident waiting to happen and, boy, had JOHNNy's patience paid off.

I can't blame the Festival crowds, promoters and press for celebrating the arrival of the all-conquering VegaS. After all, how were they to know I hadn't been HiM from the very beginning? God knows I gave it my all to perpetrate the myth and then make it whole.

When I look back at interviews from that point on, most insightful interrogators hinted at the fact there was a blurring of the lines that went way beyond the booze: something wrong that made this 'act' so right, so real. A psychological sarcophagus that should've remained buried but had instead become a No. 1 horror-show attraction. A joke shared by all except me, because even up till recently, I could never quite bring myself to believe that this master of mayhem was actually really a part of me.

Was it my naïvety or JoHNNy's manipulation that had led to this? My arrogance at thinking I could control the beast and put it back in its cage once it had served its purpose? JoHNNy had tasted the success that He believed He – and He alone – had earned and, viewing my attempts at a happy-ever-after with pitying contempt, was not about to risk losing the limelight by sharing it with anyone.

JoHNNy would give HiS all for the audience, and self-preservation was a luxury He could not afford. Like a rider thrown from a crazy horse of carelessness with my foot still caught in the stirrup of insanity, I was dragged along for the ride, and He would run until He dropped; tearing through the comedy scene like every day was HiS last, trampling over family and friends, a fiancée, and shitting on every showbiz doorstep along the way.

I started this book claiming it for myself, but the story from here on in really isn't mine to tell. I cannot take credit for HiS acclaimed achievements, nor the well-documented disasters. It would take the arrival of my son, Michael junior, and later on my soul mate, Maia, to give me the courage to dare to stop the ride and shout, 'I, me, Michael Pennington, I matter, and I want to get off!' To have enough faith in my own talents to lock JoHNNy VegaS away, flares and all, in a suitcase up in the attic (like in the Anthony Hopkins movie *Magic*) where no one could hear HiM croon. I just honestly don't know if I dare let HiM out again for long enough to tell HiS side of the story.

I broke up the 'act' for your sake. I couldn't risk you contaminating the purity of the performance any longer with your other addiction to that toxic bi-product, fame.

You could write it, but like Stan Lee in a full body cast of bitter reality, you could never live it, not with all your self-belief amounting to nothing more than a border crossing between fact and fiction. That line of yours? 'You've no idea what it's like to be me.' Inspired, but just like penicillin, nothing more than a messy accident.

Like a backpacker off seeking satirical enlightenment but waking up in an ice bath of bewilderment with a scar of self-denial right where a comedy kidney used to be, you were robbed of the ability to truly appreciate the punchline. You had no idea what it was like being you because, as with all questions mumbled by tin-pot philosophers down the mouth of a half-empty pint glass, the answer's bloody obvious to everyone but you. Don't you see?

You were always me.

ACKNOWLEDGMENTS

My parents Pat and Lol, for always seeing the son they loved and raised, not the lunatic the public craved. You remain my heroes and the people I most want to be like when I grow up.

My brother Mark, for introducing me to *Quadrophenia* and all things mod.

My brother Robert, for not going ballistic when I sold your bike panniers to Magpie's Nest. Now, give me a go in your shed, I won't nick anything, honest!

My sister Catharine, for getting me and my artistic need to colour outside of the lines. Your phone calls from Hong Kong were a true life line.

My son Michael, for the joy I find in everything you do and say. My love for you, kiddo, is the one unshakeable, 100% absolute I have in this life. You will always be the achievement I'm proudest of. Thanks for the books at bedtime and reminding me how important reading is to me.
  'Good news!'
  'You've finished your book?'
  'No, not yet. Why?'

'It's like you've been set the world's longest bit of homework in the world Dad, ever!'

ps. The graphics on Minecraft suck! 1-0 to me....Ha Ha!

My wife Maia, for your constant patience, help and encouragement throughout every single day of this hellish writing process. Every paragraph agonised over, every moody strop, every dark moment of self doubt, you were there darling, and there simply wouldn't be a book without you. You are my best friend and the secret behind my new smile. You dare me to try and be the husband you deserve and the father Michael needs. You are my soulmate.

Beverley Dixon, my dear friend and long-suffering assistant. Thank you for every single angry call fielded each time a deadline was missed, for projecting an air of calm knowing full well I was rocking gently in the foetal position whilst repeating the mantra 'I can't do this'.

Bryan 'mattress back' Davies, a friend who was there at the very beginning and, I have no doubt, will be 'till the very end. For the man who gave Vegas his name in the first place our exploits seem scarce amongst these pages, but that's only because I don't want a whacking with the shillelagh off of Sheila. What happens in/with Vegas stays in/with Vegas. You Mucker, are a prince amongst men.

Mike 'pillow talk' Pennington.

St Helens, for the honest to goodness decent folk who populate it, and for having the greatest Rugby League team on the face of this planet. For being the town that makes me sad to leave, proud to preach about whilst away, and eternally glad to come home to!

'I'm SAINTS until I die, I'm SAINTS until I die. I know I am, I'm sure I am, I'm SAINTS until I die!'

To all my extended family, friends, neighbours, colleagues and fellow comics whose stories could've filled a dozen books. I'm merely a bit player, it was all of you who ensured the tapestry of life was so rich.

My publisher Natalie Jerome. You had plenty of chances and genuine reasons to walk away from this project, but you didn't. Thank you for believing throughout broken deadline after broken deadline that we could produce something a tad more special than a stocking filler.

Ben Thompson, for persevering throughout the editing equivalent of that Japanese game show 'Endurance'. Thanks for convincing me I was the right man for the job on this mate, my own story, and for truly knowing your comedy onions.

Andy Hollingworth, for milking my soul like no other man with every photo you take, but capturing both **He** and I perfectly whenever you do.

Robert Chalmers and James Rampton. Thanks for trying to polish the turd I refused to believe I could squeeze out in the first place gents. Your help was never taken for granted, nor will it ever be forgotten.

To decent conscientious teachers everywhere, but especially Rowena Rowlands and Steve Bonati. In yourselves you're worth your weight in gold, but your legacy is priceless.

Father Dave (Melley) for Christening my son Michael, being there for my and Maia's wedding in Spain, and for encouraging folk to explore their faith rather than preaching ultimatums should they struggle with it. I wish there were more souls like you in this world.

STAR WARS, my other religion.